PORTFOLIO PENGUIN

THE THREE RULES

Michael E. Raynor is a director at Deloitte Services LP, where he explores corporate strategy, innovation and growth with clients in a variety of industries. He is the co-author, with Clayton Christensen, of *The Innovator's Solution*, and the author of the bestselling and critically acclaimed *The Strategy Paradox* and *The Innovator's Manifesto*.

Mumtaz Ahmed is a principal in Deloitte Consulting LLP and the chief strategy officer of Deloitte LLP, responsible for the US firm's strategy, corporate development, innovation, eminence and brand.

www.thethreerules.com

G000273473

The Three Rules

How Exceptional Companies Think

Michael E. Raynor
and Mumtaz Ahmed

PORTFOLIO
PENGUIN

PORTFOLIO PENGUIN

UK | USA | Canada | Ireland | Australia
India | New Zealand | South Africa

Penguin Books is part of the Penguin Random House group of companies
whose addresses can be found at global.penguinrandomhouse.com.

First published by Penguin Portfolio 2013
Published in this edition 2015
001

Copyright © Deloitte Development LLC, 2013

The moral right of the copyright holder has been asserted

Printed in Great Britain by Clays Ltd, St Ives plc

A CIP catalogue record for this book is available from the British Library

ISBN: 978-0-670-92297-0

www.greenpenguin.co.uk

MIX
Paper from
responsible sources
FSC
www.fsc.org   FSC® C018179

Penguin Random House is committed to a
sustainable future for our business, our readers
and our planet. This book is made from Forest
Stewardship Council® certified paper.

CONTENTS

The Three Rules

CHAPTER 1

More Than a Fortune Cookie

The quest for greatness leads naturally to the study of great companies. Unfortunately, the study of great companies does not lead naturally to great insight. Inquiries into the ebb and flow of top performers yield, as often as not, explanations built on the concatenation of unlikely and impossible-to-repeat events.[1] These often amount to little more than entertaining corporate biography, falling far short of the powerful generalizations we seek.[2]

Getting beyond mere storytelling demands that we isolate the effects of a company's behaviors on its performance from many other significant influences, such as industry structure, the pace and nature of technological change, unpredictable regulatory regimes, globalization, and so on—even dumb luck. These factors constitute the noise of the system in which all companies operate; we must find a way to filter it out if we want to hear the (sometimes faint) signal generated by the actions companies take that affect the outcomes of interest.

With this in mind, our search for the drivers of superior, long-term performance began with a radically different premise: that what constitutes stand-out performance is not obvious. It is not enough simply to set up a performance benchmark, no matter how demanding it might seem, and see who clears it. Neither is it enough to put a sample or even a population of companies in rank order and focus on those at the top of the list. Either approach leaves you highly susceptible to focusing on lucky random walkers. We wanted only those companies that were good enough for long enough that we could be confident something special was going on. We wanted companies that were truly *exceptional*.

To that end, we analyzed forty-five years of Compustat data on more than 25,000 unique companies—nearly 300,000 company-year observations from 1966 to 2010. From that universe we identified a population of 344 exceptional companies in two categories: 174 Miracle Workers, or the best of the best, and 170 Long Runners—still exceptional, but at a lower level and for a longer period of time. (The meaning of these labels will be explained in chapter 2.[3] For now, think of it as the difference between gold and silver medal winners.)

TABLE 1: **The Nine Trios**

Industry	Miracle Worker	Long Runner	Average Joe
Semiconductors	Linear Technology	Micropac Industries	International Rectifier
Medical Devices	Medtronic	Stryker	Invacare
Electrical Wiring	Thomas & Betts	Hubbell	Emrise
Clothing	Abercrombie & Fitch	Finish Line	Syms
Confectionary	Wm. Wrigley Jr. Company	Tootsie Roll Industries	Rocky Mountain Chocolate Factory
Groceries	Weis Markets	Publix Super Markets	Whole Foods Market
Pharmaceuticals	Merck & Co.	Eli Lilly & Co.	KV Pharmaceutical
Trucking	Heartland Express	Werner Enterprises	P.A.M. Transportation Services
Appliances	Maytag	HMI Industries	Whirlpool

Source: Compustat; authors' analysis

Every company's financial performance arises from a combination of skill and luck. We used leading-edge statistical techniques to identify companies that had been good enough for long enough to all but rule out luck as the primary source of their performance. These are the "exceptional" companies.

From this population of exceptional companies we selected a representative sample of trios, three companies from each of nine industries. Each trio consists of a Miracle Worker, a Long Runner, and a third company of average performance that we call an Average Joe. By comparing the very best with the very good, and both with the merely average, we hoped to shed light on two different types of exceptionalism. First, what does it take to pull away from the pack, that is, how do Miracle Workers and Long Runners separate themselves from Average Joes? Second, how do Miracle Workers—the very best—pull away from Long Runners—the very good?

With high hopes born of what we felt was a soundly chosen sample, we began to look for behavioral differences among our case-study companies. We started our investigation with a competitive setting that was as close to a pure footrace as we could find: trucking, a sector that, like air, is essential and invisible. America's trucking companies literally keep the economy moving yet collectively make up what might just be the world's least glamorous industry. There has never been a trucking stock-market bubble, never a global economic crisis precipitated by trucking companies' risk management practices, barely a whiff of glitz or glamour, not a single save-the-world invention, and no Nobel Prize winners.

Better still, the trucking industry's modern era began in 1980 with a dramatic overhaul of the Motor Carrier Act. The previous act, passed in

1935, regulated prices, routes, what could be carried, equipment to be used, employee qualifications—in short, just about every material aspect of supply. In addition, existing or new carriers could not provide services (routes, freight, negotiable terms) to existing or new customers without filing for permission from the regulator.

With deregulation, trucking companies were able to set their own prices, pick their own routes, establish their own labor practices, and so on. This was the equivalent of a starter's pistol firing: new entrants swarmed into the industry and demand exploded.[4] Facing both heightened competition and opportunities to grow, every trucking company, new or old, faced difficult choices with no clear answers. Yet the elemental and uncomplicated structure of the industry would, we hoped, make it relatively easier for us to see more clearly how management, rather than external factors, affected company performance than if we started with a more complex industry.

Our trio of trucking companies consisted of Heartland Express (Heartland), the Miracle Worker; Werner Enterprises (Werner), the Long Runner; and P.A.M. Transportation Services (PAM), the Average Joe. These three were reasonably similar with respect to their size and services offered when the gun went off in 1980, and all three went public in 1986. By 2010, however, their paths had diverged significantly. All we needed to do was sort out what caused what and why.

The effort just about broke us.

Any single pair-wise comparison suggested compelling, or at least reasonable, explanations. For instance, PAM acquired five relatively small trucking companies between 1995 and 2003 as part of its growth strategy, increasing its revenues by about 15 percent as a direct consequence. In contrast, Werner did not do a single noteworthy deal over the entire 1986 to 2010 period, yet was able to grow much faster than PAM, and off a larger revenue base. Finding that our Average Joe was more acquisitive than our

TABLE 2: **Descriptive Statistics for the Trucking Trio**

Company	Category	Year Founded	Observation Period	Revenue Growth	Average Annual ROA	Compounded Annual TSR	Compounded Annual Revenue Growth
Heartland Express	Miracle Worker	1955	1985 to 2010	$19MM to $500MM	14.6%	17.3%	14.0%
Werner Enterprises	Long Runner	1956	1985 to 2010	$74MM to $1.8BN	7.1%	10.6%	13.7%
P.A.M. Transportation Services	Average Joe	1980	1985 to 2010	$20MM to $332MM	2.0%	-1.2%	12.0%

Source: Compustat; company documents; Deloitte analysis.

Long Runner seemed consistent with the oft-repeated conventional wisdom that mergers and acquisitions (M&A) can often destroy value for the acquiring company.[5] Perhaps "organic growth" was a behavior that would prove to be a driver of exceptional performance in other industries as well.

Unfortunately for that idea, Heartland (Miracle Worker) acquired five trucking companies between 1987 and 2002, increasing its revenue by more than 50 percent. This meant that the best-performing company, Heartland, was the most active acquirer while the second-best performer (Werner) did no deals at all, and our Average Joe (PAM) pursued what you might have thought was the most reasonable path, a series of small acquisitions.

The only principle that seemed to emerge on the M&A front was "do the right deals the right way," which is, of course, utterly useless.

What about customer focus? Surely the more customer-focused the better, and when we compared Heartland and Werner, this idea seemed to help. Heartland concentrated on routes in the central Midwest of the United States—the country's "heartland"—and its top five customers routinely accounted for 40 to 60 percent of its total revenue. In contrast, Werner competed across a much larger area—effectively the continental United States. Werner also operated a larger variety of trailer types (e.g., van, flatbed, temperature-controlled) over regional, medium, and long-haul distances. The top 5 percent of its customers (which would have been considerably more than five accounts) rarely generated more than 10 percent of its total revenue.

Since Heartland outperformed Werner, and Werner outperformed PAM, we expected PAM to have a still more diffuse customer base. Instead, PAM concentrated its services in the NAFTA corridor and generated 70 percent or more of its revenue from dedicated fleet services, which entailed taking on the assets and responsibilities of its customers' formerly in-house trucking operations. This was not quite as focused as Heartland, but it was more focused than Werner. Once again, we were left with a meaningless truism: focus on the right customers in the right way.

We then shifted our hypotheses to more conceptual attributes. For example, Heartland was never particularly innovative or a first mover. It typically expanded its routes and customer base via a series of toe-in-the-water moves prior to making a significant commitment. In contrast, Werner was often the first—not only of the three, but also of the entire industry—to adopt in force new technologies such as geographic positioning systems (GPS) in its trucks or paperless logs for its drivers.

PAM was perhaps the biggest risk taker of the three. The company went public in 1986 with an eye to creating a large-scale, national-footprint trucking company and made the investments required to deliver on that vision.[6] PAM's fleet expanded from 172 rigs in 1985 to 724 by 1987, and its capital intensity, at 45 percent of sales, exceeded both the industry average and our two exceptional companies by a significant margin.

Performance fell far short of expectations, however, as through 1991 the company spent more years in the red than in the black. Ironically, it was not a sluggish trucking industry that undermined its plans but a rapidly growing one. A shortage of drivers drove up average wage rates significantly, and as a relatively new player, PAM had to pay a wage premium to draw new drivers into the industry or poach drivers from other companies. Paying higher wages while still turning a profit required raising prices, which required a level of service that PAM was unable to provide. Consequently, much of PAM's new fleet remained idle. The resulting cash crunch meant that the company clamped down on capital expenditures, which aged the company's fleet. This increased maintenance costs and downtime for each truck, which affected service levels, putting further pressure on prices.

The best sense we could make of all this was that if you are going to bet big, be sure to bet right, which is about as useful as suggesting that you pick only winning lottery numbers.

We wandered down any number of other dead ends, blind alleys, and box canyons as we looked at (just about) everything. Nothing seemed to stick. We could easily enough make sense of why Heartland had done better than Werner, or why Werner had bested PAM, but even when dealing with just these three companies we could not find a satisfactory set of objectively measurable behaviors that accounted for both sets of differences. Worse, very little seemed to line up with what the conventional wisdom on many of these issues would have prescribed. All we had to show for our efforts was a two-word sentence of surrender: *it depends*.

In an attempt to find our way out of this muddle, we began looking at the other trios in our sample. If the muddle we found in trucking repeated itself in dramatically different contexts, perhaps we would be on to something after all.

No such luck. Not only were the other trios equally muddled, it was a different muddle each time. In confectionary it was Wm. Wrigley Jr. Company (Wrigley), the Miracle Worker, and the Average Joe, Rocky Mountain Chocolate Factory (RMCF), that grew organically while Tootsie Roll Industries (Tootsie Roll), the Long Runner, was buying its growth—the opposite of what we had seen in trucking.

When we looked at customer focus, the Miracle Worker in semiconductors (Linear Technology) came into its own by branching out into a wide range of industries while the Long Runner (Micropac Industries) saw its performance limited precisely because it remained focused on fewer customers in fewer industries. The Average Joe for that sector (International Rectifier) diversified in precisely the way the Miracle Worker had.

What about innovation and risk taking? In pharmaceuticals, it was the

Miracle Worker, Merck & Co. (Merck) that bet billions, shifting its primary research paradigm from chemistry-based to biology-based in the mid-1970s, which was perhaps as much as a decade before the Long Runner, Eli Lilly & Co. (Eli Lilly), and the rest of the industry made a similar shift. This transformation depressed Merck's performance for the better part of ten years, signaling a willingness to invest for the long term. This early and steadfast commitment to its own reinvention set the stage for nearly two decades of renewed exceptional performance. Merck was also a leader in this trio in adopting aggressively other paradigm shifts such as collaborative and partnership-based R&D models.

In other words, every behavior we looked at was associated with every type of performance. There simply were no meaningful similarities within our performance categories that contrasted in important ways with differences among them. All we could say with any confidence was that exceptional companies did whatever they did "right" while Average Joes did the same things "wrong." This is a prescription for action with the level of insight one might expect from a fortune cookie.

A useful explanatory framework began to emerge only after we shifted our emphasis away from what these companies *did* to a series of hypotheses about how they *thought*. This slowly began to bear fruit. By seeking the decision-making criteria implicit in the many and varied choices our exceptional companies made, we were able to reduce an overwhelming complexity to a much more manageable set of rules that applied regardless of the circumstances. Do a deal or build from within; diversify or stick to the knitting; take a risk or play it safe; and many more besides—the alternatives chosen showed no patterns at all. But we came to see that Miracle Workers made choices that were consistent with three specific rules while the choices of Long Runners and Average Joes systematically violated those rules.

> Attempts to explain differences in performance in terms of patterns in behavioral differences proved fruitless, so we shifted from a search for differences in behavior to differences in how companies appeared to think. We identified a small set of decision rules implicit in the choices exceptional companies made that lower-performing companies did not seem to use.

In the chapters that follow we will present our evidence in full. In particular, we will apply statistical tests to show that the association between the use of these rules and exceptional performance is more than coincidental and adduce evidence that this relationship goes beyond mere correlation. Better still, we will show that these rules are at work in a statistically significant way in our full population of exceptional companies. In other words, we believe that we have gone beyond anecdotal sense making to something approaching empirical proof. Finally, through an examination of differences in how our exceptional and average companies applied the rules, we hope to provide examples you can draw on when using the rules to guide your own decision making.

So here they are: the three rules.

Better Before Cheaper

At the most generic level, whenever we buy anything there are two dimensions to the value we get from our purchase: *price* and *non-price*.[7] Price value is a function of how much we pay for something, and the less we pay, the more price value we get. Non-price value is a function of all the other dimensions of value that are not price: durability, functionality, quality, convenience, ease of use, style, brand, etc. How much of each of price and non-price value a company provides relative to its competitors defines its *position* in competitive space; that is, how a company creates value for its customers.

In the case of trucking, deregulation in 1980 dramatically increased customer choice, which forced trucking companies to define their positions—that combination of price and non-price value that would differentiate them from their competitors in ways that customers would be willing to pay for. Unfortunately, there was no easy way to know which position would be the most profitable. In a newly deregulated industry, there was opportunity to reduce cost and compete on price value, and opportunity to increase service levels and compete on non-price value. The data were sufficiently ambiguous that both alternatives made good sense.

The companies in our trio made systematically different choices across a wide range of issues that collectively served to give each of them a different relative competitive position. Take Heartland's geographic and customer focus. Some customers have complex and unpredictable shipping requirements. This creates opportunities to provide superior non-price value through an on-demand ability to get *this* shipped *there* by *then*. It turned out that an especially effective way to do that was to serve a limited number of customers within a limited geographic area. Heartland's focus was therefore in the service of a distinctive non-price competitive position, which in turn allowed it to maintain a consistent price premium in excess of 10 percent over much of the industry, including Werner and PAM.[8]

In contrast, Werner competed across a much larger area—effectively the continental United States—and provided a much wider range of services. The higher-volume, longer-term, less operationally complex contracts that Werner coveted were also in the sights of many other companies. Consequently, the key to Werner's success seems to have been its ability to claim credibly that it could meet its customers' performance requirements at a competitive price, which it was able to do in a way that earned it Long Runner status. At the same time, a large and diverse customer base is a reasonable hedge against the vagaries of a hotly contested market. Werner's relative lack of focus was not a mistake, but a necessary implication of its price-based competitive position.

For its part, PAM was tightly focused on specific industries (automotive) and customers (General Motors was among its largest accounts). Dedicated fleet services did not entail the kind of complexity Heartland took on for its customers, and when the carmakers' volumes declined, PAM could neither carve out a niche nor cut cost enough to stay profitable. So although PAM was more focused than Werner, it was not focused in ways that created superior price or non-price value.

The relevant difference, then, was not the degree of focus across our three companies, since focus was associated with both exceptional performance and average performance. What mattered was if and how that focus defined a company's position. Heartland had a non-price position while Werner and PAM both had price-based positions—except Werner's proved profitable thanks to superior execution.

This perspective generalized across our trios: Miracle Workers overwhelmingly had non-price positions; Long Runners showed no tendency one way or the other; and Average Joes typically competed on price (see chapter 3).

More compelling still—and a big part of why we feel a non-price position is a material *cause* of exceptional performance—we found that when exceptional companies abandoned a non-price position, their performance subsequently suffered. For example, in the appliance industry, Maytag (see chapter 5) delivered a two-decade run of superior profitability that ended in 1986. Its non-price position was defined and defended by a painstakingly constructed combination of product excellence, effective advertising, and high-touch distribution. Its products consistently won superior ratings from *Consumer Reports*; the Maytag Repairman, who spent his days idled by the legendary quality of Maytag's clothes washers, became an icon of American advertising; and a distinctive network of more than ten thousand independent retailers proved a highly effective sales channel. In contrast, Whirlpool, the trio's Average Joe, spent that same twenty-year period manufacturing appliances for Sears, whose Kenmore brand competed with Maytag largely on price.

Thanks to its non-price position, Maytag enjoyed twenty consecutive years of Miracle Worker performance. Then, beginning in the mid-1980s, consolidation in the retail channel led to the rise of the so-called big box stores. These retailers tended to carry fewer appliance brands and so preferred those manufacturers with a full range of products, ideally across multiple price points. Maytag had only a relatively high-end line of washers and dryers. Fearful of being dropped by the newly powerful channel, it diversified its product line, largely through acquisitions, such as the 1986 purchase of Magic Chef. The gambit failed, however. The company's performance declined steadily and substantially, to the point that Maytag was acquired by Whirlpool in 2004.

So diversification is bad, right? Not at all. When the trucking business consolidated in the mid-1990s, Heartland was similarly under pressure to grow and to offer services over a wider geographic area. It had a choice: do so in ways that compromised its non-price value, or make whatever investments were needed to preserve its competitive position as it coped with industry-level transformation. Heartland chose the latter, expanding its geographic coverage, but investing in distribution centers (DCs) and coping with driver shortages by changing to an employee-driver model.

When Maytag diversified it took on mid- and lower-tier brands. This gave the company heft on a distribution landscape that had shifted from a scattered network of independent businesses to a small number of much larger retailers. However, it cost the company something much more valuable: its non-price position relative to Whirlpool and eventually non-U.S.

competitors such as LG from South Korea and Haier from China. What matters, then, is not diversification per se, but whether diversification serves to protect or extend a successful non-price position.

> There are two dimensions of value along which any company can differentiate itself: price value and non-price value. Our research reveals that exceptional companies typically focus on non-price value, even if that means they have to charge higher prices. It did not have to turn out this way: price-based competition is a legitimate strategy. We have found, however, that competing with *better* rather than *cheaper* is systematically associated with superior, long-term performance.

Better before cheaper is a useful rule because it applies not just to questions of diversification or focus, but to many critical decisions our Miracle Workers faced. The differences in behavior that best explained the differences in performance were consistent with a bias for increasing non-price value, even if it was sometimes at the expense of being price competitive.

Equally important, *better before cheaper* is a rule with some substance because the alternative is entirely reasonable. Advice such as "give customers what they want" is meaningless because "give customers what they don't want" is necessarily a bad idea.[9] In contrast, it could have turned out that price-based competition was systematically more successful than non-price-based competition. *Better before cheaper* is not an aphorism, it is a fact-based description of how the world works.

Of course, no company can afford to ignore its relative price position. That is why the rule is "better *before* cheaper": being price competitive is far from irrelevant, but when it comes to *position* in a market, exceptional performance is caused most often by greater non-price value rather than by lower price.

Revenue Before Cost

A company's position defines how it creates value for customers relative to other companies. A company's *profitability formula* describes how it captures value for itself compared with others. It turns out that just as there is a pattern in how exceptional companies create value (*better before cheaper*), there is a pattern in how they capture value.

We measure profitability using return on assets (ROA), which is defined as income divided by the book value of assets. (For an exploration of why this is a good measure to use, see chapter 2.) Return on assets is the product of return on sales (ROS), or income divided by sales, and total asset turnover (TAT), or sales divided by assets. Consequently, there are only three ways, either individually or in combination, that a company can improve its ROA: increase revenue, decrease cost, or decrease assets.

Our research reveals that exceptional companies are systematically more likely to drive their ROA advantage through higher relative revenue than by lower relative cost or lower relative assets. Going down one more level, a revenue advantage can be driven by higher unit price or higher unit volume, and exceptional companies tend to rely more on price (see chapter 4). And so rule number two is *revenue before cost*.

Heartland enjoyed both an ROS and a TAT advantage over Werner and PAM, thanks to a series of interdependent choices. Its non-price-value position allowed it to charge more than Werner and PAM per ton-mile, creating a relative revenue advantage through higher prices.

Keeping assets relatively lower was accomplished largely in two ways. First, Heartland's point-to-point route structure obviated expensive DCs, whereas Werner needed DCs in order to keep its extensive fleet of trucks and trailers more nearly fully utilized.

Second, Werner and PAM both maintained fleets of trucks operated by employee drivers. Owner/operator (O/O) drivers own their own trucks, and so using O/Os reduces a trucking company's asset burden. Unfortunately, O/Os were typically seen as less reliable. As independent contractors they could turn down last-minute requests or take more lucrative opportunities. In addition, they typically did not maintain their rigs as well as companies maintained corporate assets, which contributed to unexpected delays due to equipment failure. Consistent with industry practice, Werner and PAM used O/Os opportunistically to cope with spikes in demand.

Heartland, however, broke this trade-off by securing the very best O/O drivers, largely through higher wages, by some accounts the highest in the industry. Securing good drivers was only half the battle, however: keeping them mattered, too. Heartland invested in hanging on to its best drivers by, among other initiatives, offering university scholarships to the children of drivers with sufficient service. In addition, Heartland's geographically concentrated customer base allowed it to schedule its drivers to return home weekly, which compared favorably with industry norms of runs of up to six weeks. By making it so much more attractive to work for Heartland, the company was able to skim the cream of the O/O workforce and deploy successfully an asset-light model against a non-price-value position: where Heartland shipped over 50 percent of its freight using O/O drivers, Werner relied on O/Os for just over 15 percent of its freight.

We see evidence of our profitability formula rule in other industries, even ones in which you might think cost leadership would be indispensable. Take, for example, Family Dollar, a discount retailer. For more than thirty years Family Dollar delivered performance that has been hidden in plain sight, besting the legends of discount retailing since the mid-1970s, and doing it in ways few might have guessed.

Family Dollar has consistently focused on serving the needs of customers from lower economic strata. You might think that if ever there were an industry in which lower prices and lower cost were key to superior profitability, discount retailing would be it. Certainly that was our assumption. It did not turn out that way. Family Dollar's success has been a function of *higher* prices, earned through a willingness to incur *higher* cost and tolerate *lower* efficiency than many of its larger, lower-performing (but still successful) discount retail competitors.

How is that possible? How does a discount retailer serving the most cash-strapped customer segments turn in superior profitability for more than three decades with higher prices and higher cost than its most ferocious foes?

Start with Family Dollar's position compared with its competition. To capture the benefits of the low prices of the largest discount retailers, customers must often drive several miles to 100,000-plus-square-foot suburban locations and purchase products in relatively large quantities. In stereotypical, but representative terms, spending $5 on gas to buy a package of 150 diapers at a unit cost of 15 cents adds up to $27.50. That makes more sense than walking three blocks and buying 15 packages of 10 diapers at 20 cents each for a total of $30.

When a customer has $27.50 to spend, the larger discounter wins the business. However, in the days or weeks leading up to the next paycheck when money is especially tight, a customer's calculus is much different. In these circumstances, poorer people can afford only smaller quantities, and typically are shopping only for a smaller range of items that vary on a week-to-week basis. This week one has run out of diapers, last week it was laundry detergent, next week it might be toothpaste. In these circumstances, walking to a 20,000-square-foot Family Dollar located in an urban center for a package of 10 diapers at 20 cents each makes a lot more sense.

Serving customers coping with these constraints has led Family Dollar to build a position defined by convenience, selection, and lower basket size—all non-price dimensions of value. An analysis of the company's financial statements reveals the economic implications of these choices. Family Dollar enjoys a gross margin advantage over its most significant competitors, but suffers a sales, general, and administrative (SG&A) cost disadvantage and inferior asset turns. Of course, a gross margin lead could well be driven by lower cost of goods sold (COGS) and not higher prices, but this is not the case: Family Dollar appears to have consistently higher quality-adjusted prices.[10]

Now, Family Dollar has lower cost, greater growth, lower prices, and better asset turns than high-end retailers such as Bergdorf Goodman. But then, Family Dollar does not compete with Bergdorf Goodman. It is when stacked up against another leading discounter that the nature and significance of Family Dollar's choices become clear: it has incurred the higher cost required to establish a position based on non-price dimensions of value. This has inflicted an efficiency penalty, but the company has been compensated with relatively higher prices. The net result has been more than thirty years of exceptional profitability.[11]

Family Dollar and Heartland both enjoy unit price premiums and are quite a bit smaller than the Long Runners in their trios. However, a revenue advantage driven by unit volume can also support exceptional performance. For example, Merck enjoyed a material profitability advantage over Eli Lilly for much of the period 1966 to 2010 (see chapter 5). But unlike Family Dollar, Merck relied on superior asset turns, a measure of volume-driven efficiency, for fully two thirds of its lead. On this basis, it would appear that Merck is driving profits with lower cost, not higher prices—the exact opposite of Family Dollar, and a seeming violation of our *revenue before cost* rule.

The truth lies deeper. First, note that both Merck and Eli Lilly occupy non-price-value positions in the pharmaceutical industry, competing on the basis of the clinical effectiveness of their patent-protected medications in the therapeutic areas they focus on.

Through the early 1990s, Merck's superior profitability can be attributed largely to the company's decision to globalize earlier, more successfully, and more aggressively than did Eli Lilly: Merck was generating 50 percent or more of its $10 billion in pharmaceutical sales from non-U.S. markets while Eli Lilly was generating barely 30 percent of its $6 billion in sales from non-U.S. markets. Because of differences in market structure, especially government's involvement in paying for prescription drugs, prices in these markets were often lower than in the United States, but Merck never competed on price *relative to the alternatives in those markets*. In other words, Merck drove revenue through higher volume, but it drove volume through higher non-price value, not lower prices.

Selling into markets with lower price ceilings forced Merck to accept higher relative COGS, which explains why Merck's gross margins were not the primary driver of advantage. However, these markets also had structurally lower selling costs while Merck's fixed R&D expenses were spread across a much larger sales base. Economies of scale in drug manufacturing meant that Merck had a lower relative asset base, resulting in higher asset turns than Eli Lilly.

In addition, Merck leveraged its R&D and manufacturing base to diversify its product portfolio more than did Eli Lilly. By some measures, Merck was three times as diversified, but in ways that leveraged a more nearly common asset base, thus increasing volume in a way that created an asset efficiency advantage.

In other words, Merck's superior profitability was not a function of lower cost at a given volume, but of greater efficiencies thanks to higher volume resulting from customer demand generated by non-price value.[12] The result was a decades-long run of revenue growth that made Merck's core pharmaceutical business more than twice the size of Eli Lilly's by 2010, up from barely more than 8 percent larger in 1985.

Once again, although the specific choices made by our exceptional performers in trucking, discount retailing, pharmaceuticals, and the rest are very different, the unifying theme is that driving revenue comes first, and exceptional companies are willing to invest and incur the cost required to generate that revenue.[13]

As with *better before cheaper*, this rule—*revenue before cost*—has the merit of providing meaningful guidance because the opposite could have been true: lower cost might systematically have driven superior profitability. Instead, we found that in eight of our nine trios superior profitability is driven by higher revenue, in many cases earned by incurring *higher* cost. Of the eight Miracle Workers with revenue-driven exceptional performance, six relied primarily on higher prices while two (Merck and Wrigley) relied on volume, either in large part or entirely. Better still, these findings are reflected in our analysis of the full population of exceptional companies (see chapter 4), and so we have grounds for concluding that this pattern is not confined to our sample, but captures a characteristic shared by most exceptional companies.

> A company's competitive position defines how it creates value. A company's profitability formula defines how it captures value. Profitability increases when revenue increases, cost decreases, or assets go down. We find that exceptional companies achieve superior profitability with revenue increases, even if that means higher cost or a higher asset base.

Knowing this, managers facing tough investment decisions can now play the percentages much more consistently. Exceptional companies realize that non-price value must be earned repeatedly and continuously. Regardless of industry, that translates far more often than not into a significant and ongoing investment in assets or other expenditures. Short-run pressure to improve profitability through cost cutting is very often a double-edged sword, and the wrong edge is sharpest. Achieving exceptional results can demand the courage to incur higher cost, even to the point of a cost disadvantage.

You heard that right: a cost *dis*advantage. Whether they are driving revenue through price or volume, exceptional companies tend to have *higher* cost on at least some dimensions—even when, as with Family Dollar, they are competing for seemingly price-sensitive markets. The willingness to incur higher cost allows exceptional performers to create, preserve, and exploit their non-price-value positions by charging higher prices or by generating higher volume.

There Are No Other Rules

The first two rules tell you what you *should* do: *better before cheaper*, and *revenue before cost*. The third rule tells you what you should *not* do; namely, think that anything else matters in a systematic, specifiable way.

Should you focus on your core or leverage your competencies to enter new markets? We found no evidence of a consistent answer to that question. Sometimes Miracle Workers stuck to their knitting, sometimes they ventured far afield. What mattered was whether they had a non-price position and a revenue-driven profitability formula.

Should you focus on talent and developing the abilities of your people, or building processes to extend the capabilities of your organization? Getting this right seemed to turn on whichever answer contributed best to a non-price position and a revenue-driven profitability formula.

What sort of leadership contributes best to corporate success: charismatic, hard-driving, larger-than-life CEOs who move the company forward seemingly by force of will, or humble, deliberate, share-the-glory servant-leaders? As far as we could tell, all that mattered consistently was whether or not leadership was focused on building a non-price position and a revenue-driven profitability formula.

No matter the topic, no matter the conventional wisdom, we could not find a single would-be rule that remained intact, even broadly speaking, across our sample of exceptional companies. Regardless of circumstances, regardless of the constraints, our top performers were doggedly persistent only in their adherence to the first two rules.

Expansionary markets? *Better before cheaper; revenue before cost.*

Recessionary economy? *Better before cheaper; revenue before cost.*

Technological disruption? *Better before cheaper; revenue before cost.*

Plague of locusts? Zombie apocalypse? *Better before cheaper; revenue before cost.*

Perhaps surprisingly, the absence of any rules beyond *better before cheaper* and *revenue before cost* is not permission to shut down your thinking. Hewing to the two rules means that everything else is on the table, and this imposes a heavy burden of active search to determine how best to adhere to the first two rules in the face of sometimes wrenching competitive and environmental change. It turns out that it takes a great deal of flexibility to be persistent.

To illustrate the extent of the change that can be required to maintain a non-price position and a revenue-driven profitability formula, consider once again Heartland's experience. There are two distinct eras in Heartland's performance, which we identified using a statistical method described in chapter 2: 1985 to 1994, and 1995 to 2010. During the first era, Heartland's ROA averaged almost 18 percent while the industry was making do with an average in the mid–single digits, suggesting that Heartland was certainly capturing a good deal of the value it created. However, its ROA steadily declined during this period, from a high of 26 percent in 1986 to the low teens by the mid-1990s.

Then the decline abruptly ended: from 1995 through 2010 Heartland's

ROA averaged just under 13 percent, but in contrast to the previous era it was preternaturally stable, ranging from just over 10 percent to just under 14 percent. Its lead over Werner also declined, from almost 11 percentage points of ROA each year to just over 6 percentage points. Since these differences in performance are statistically significant and economically meaningful, we can confidently look for meaningful differences in Heartland's behavior across these eras.

To help guide our efforts, we exploited an important feature of the accounting identities that define ROA. Using the method described in Appendix A ("Calculating the Elements of Advantage"), we decomposed Heartland's performance advantage into its constituent elements. Table 3 breaks down the Elements of Advantage for Heartland versus Werner. This approach was to become a central analytical tool for our work.

Start at the bottom of table 3: the average ROA difference between Heartland and Werner was 9.6 percentage points (pp)/year for Era 1 (1985–1994) and 6.2 pp for Era 2 (1995–2010). During Era 1, 2.3 pp of the 9.6 pp difference in ROA were accounted for by Heartland's higher gross margin, and 4.1 pp were due to higher fixed asset turnover (FAT), and so on.

Differences in the Elements of Advantage across eras provide additional clues that something has changed; better still, these differences provide some bread crumbs to follow when identifying the behavioral changes that caused these differences. Note that Heartland's TAT advantage in Era 1 has turned into a disadvantage in Era 2 while its absolute and relative reliance on gross margin has increased dramatically. That is strong evidence that Heartland preserved its price premium but had to shift to a much more relatively asset-intense model.

There is strong behavioral evidence that this is precisely what happened. Beginning with its first distribution center in 1993, Heartland had a complement of a dozen by 2004. In order to cope with the demands of customers for more nearly end-to-end solutions, Heartland expanded

TABLE 3: **Heartland's Elements of Advantage Versus Werner**

Elements of ROA	Contribution to ROA Advantage in Percentage Points per Year	
	Era 1: 1985–1994	Era 2: 1995–2010
Gross Margin	2.3	7.4
SG&A	0.0	0.0
R&D	0.0	0.0
Other (incl. taxes)	4.2	0.2
ROS	6.5	7.6
CAT	–1.0	–2.5
FAT	4.1	1.4
Other	0.0	–0.3
TAT	3.1	–1.4
ROA	**9.6**	**6.2**

Source: Compustat; Deloitte analysis
Figures may not total due to rounding.

dramatically, largely via three acquisitions that almost tripled the company's size and expanded its geographic footprint beyond the heartland and into the Northeast and West Coast markets. Its customer focus was diluted as a result: the relative importance of Heartland's top five customers dropped steadily, from around 60 percent of total revenue to just over 30 percent.

> Using ROA decomposition to guide our search for relevant company behaviors forces us to connect our explanation of performance differences to the underlying financial structure of those differences.

Perhaps most significant, Heartland was no longer able to break the trade-off between the use of O/Os and service levels. Operating margins on

O/O freight, which for Heartland had historically run about 10 percentage points higher than for employee drivers, had fallen 15 percentage points to essentially the industry average for O/Os by 2006. Consequently, Heartland's relative emphasis on O/Os peaked at just over 60 percent of total freight in 1996 and then declined dramatically. By 2004, Heartland and Werner both carried less than 15 percent of their freight with O/Os.

All the major changes in Heartland's model that we observed seemed intended to maintain differentiated service, and hence higher prices, rather than cutting cost or keeping the asset base down. For example, its acquisitions—motivated by a need to grow in a consolidating industry—were characterized by an almost contradictory relentless pruning of contracts and routes. In the twelve months following the company's 1994 acquisition of Munson Transportation (Munson), a deal that doubled Heartland's size, management shed 30 percent of Munson's business—not because it was *un*profitable, but because it was not profitable enough. In addition, now that Heartland was much more heavily invested in a fleet of trucks, it chose to carry a large cash balance so that it could buy new assets opportunistically, thereby reducing the cost of maintaining a young fleet—a critically important element of providing superior service.

These changes are all plausible explanations for Heartland's continued superior performance. It is because they line up with the observed Elements of Advantage that we can say with yet greater confidence that they are the differences that made the difference.

Heartland's genius during this transition was realizing that the decline during Era 1 was not a consequence of Heartland's having done anything wrong; it was simply the natural evolution of the trucking industry and the emergence of a much more competitive status quo. Competitors were approaching Heartland's service levels at structurally lower cost thanks to advances, pioneered in some cases by Werner, in the use of GPS and other technologies. It might well have ended in disaster if Heartland had attempted to hang on to such outsized returns. Instead, Heartland seems to have realized that the magnitude of its advantage was necessarily eroding, but that it could still be the best in the business.

If all Heartland had done was adopt the same technologies in the same way as its competitors, it could never have maintained the differentiated service required to sustain its pricing premium. Instead, staying on top turned out to require a complete transformation of the asset-lean model that had been such a big part of the company's advantage for nearly a decade. In other words, the company changed just about everything that had been at the core of its profitability . . . in order to preserve its profitability.

A willingness to change everything in order to hang on to a non-price position and a revenue-driven profitability formula is on display in other trios as well. Take Abercrombie & Fitch (A&F), the clothing retailer (see chapter 4). After being spun off from The Limited as a public company in 1996, A&F increased its number of stores rapidly for four years and enjoyed industry-leading margins and ROA. Its position was defined by a unique combination of leading-edge style, edgy and highly focused advertising, and a highly differentiated in-store experience that made A&F a leader in teen and young adult casual clothing. This often required A&F to incur higher relative cost than its competitors, spending more on, for example, its store locations, store fixtures, and in-store personnel (who were referred to as models and often hired based on physical attractiveness). It generated higher profitability despite its higher cost, thanks to prices that were consistently and materially higher than its competitors'.

Retail, however, has a stereotypical growth and decline cycle. A concept that proves popular can grow quickly and profitably for as long as it remains popular and there are new shopping malls to colonize. Once customers get bored or the real estate runway has been exhausted, a retailer must focus on same-store sales growth and somehow find ways to stay "trendy" and "relevant" to fashion-conscious shoppers for whom there is nothing less cool than what they used to like.

Abercrombie & Fitch tackled this problem head-on, working hard to keep the core A&F brand on the leading edge while also launching new brands that targeted different segments of the clothing market, often defined primarily by age group. A new line, "abercrombie," was launched in 1997, targeting grade schoolers (ages seven to fourteen); Hollister Co. came along in 2000, aimed at the fourteen-to-eighteen age group; Ruehl No.925 in 2004, courting the postcollegiate crowd (twenty-two to thirty-four); and Gilly Hicks in 2008, which focuses on women's lingerie and accessories. They were not all successful—Ruehl was shuttered in 2010—but all shared the same positioning as trendy, "fashion forward" brands with price points that were higher than most of their competitors'. All the while, A&F enjoyed industry-leading ROA results. In short, A&F was willing to create whole new images—perhaps the defining feature of fashion retail—in order to target new segments more effectively. Yet it never wavered in its dedication to a position driven by non-price value and a price-driven profitability formula.

This sort of persistence was not always uncontroversial, even if it has been successful over the years. When the Great Recession hit in 2008 it was not uncommon for many retailers to cut their prices in the interest of preserving volume and market share. Abercrombie & Fitch, by and large, did not follow suit, sometimes provoking outspoken criticism.[14] Although still regaining its footing, there are signs of a rebound at A&F, which appears to be a vindication of the merits of sticking to the first two rules. Its revenues are growing again on relatively modest volume increases thanks to consistently higher prices. Those competitors that coped with the recession with price discounts are finding it difficult to increase their prices, having taught their customers that their T-shirts do not have to cost $30 after all.

Adherence to the three rules does not mean becoming a corporate barnacle, gluing oneself to a spot and then eating one's own brain. As the Heartland case illustrates, in a dynamic economy a company in total stasis is unlikely to even survive, never mind deliver exceptional performance. For exceptional companies, position and profitability formula are the *only* things that are nonnegotiable. Everything *else* is up for grabs.

And everything means *everything*. Human resources model? In trucking we saw a shift from contractors to employees. Research and development? In pharmaceuticals, we will see an evolution from in-house to joint ventures to open innovation. Markets served? In confectionary we will see a shift from domestic to global. Asset intensity? In semiconductors we will see a shift from lower investment to higher. Mergers and acquisitions? In medical devices, deal making goes from irrelevant to a cornerstone of growth and profitability. All more evidence that it takes an awful lot of adaptability to stick with the same position and profitability formula.

> There is no reason for any specific position or profitability formula to be systematically associated with superior performance. There are strong arguments and compelling examples for both sides of each question. Our results reveal that *as a matter of fact* there is a distinct pattern, which we summarize in the three rules: *Better before cheaper, Revenue before cost,* and *There are no other rules.*

This sort of persistence pays off time and again. Higher-performing companies that change what they must to preserve their position and their profitability formula, sometimes in the face of deteriorating performance, overwhelmingly tend to be rewarded with sustained exceptional results. Those that respond to changing circumstances—however rational their strategies might appear—by changing their position or profitability formula overwhelmingly tend to see their exalted status slip away, often never to be recaptured. It is *persistence* in position and profitability formula, coupled with the ability to change anything else, that creates the most enduring exceptional performance.

Stick with *better before cheaper* and *revenue before cost*. After that *there are no other rules*.

Deciding to Be Exceptional

Decision making is the essence of management. Should you expand into new lines of business or focus on existing markets, acquire a large competitor or a small start-up in an adjacent industry, invest in cost cutting or cutting-edge R&D? It is the cumulative impact of these and many other choices, both big and small, that determine an organization's fate.

Unfortunately, only sometimes—perhaps rarely—are the alternatives among which we must choose clearly identified, the trade-offs that come with choosing one alternative over the others quantified, and the consequences of each choice specified. Far more frequently, the data are incomplete, the implications are ambiguous, and limited time and money often leave us forced to choose from among any number of equally plausible but incompatible courses of action.

It is under just such circumstances that the three rules of exceptional performance can be especially useful. When you find yourself having to allocate scarce resources—usually people, time or money—among competing priorities (which you surely will), think about which initiatives contribute most to enhancing the non-price elements of your position, or to earning relatively higher prices or greater volume, and give those the nod.

For example, if your operational effectiveness program is mostly about cutting cost while your innovation efforts are mostly about separating you from the pack, go with innovation. But it could just as easily be the other way around: if pushing the envelope on operations is about delivering levels of customer service your competition can only dream of while innovation seems geared to doing the same for less, then your operations folks deserve the incremental care and feeding.

Is an acquisition being justified in terms of economies of scale, or is it an opportunity to realize the growth potential of a non-price position you have already earned in the markets you currently serve? The former might well be a good idea, perhaps even essential to keeping you in the game, but only the latter is more likely to drive exceptional performance.

Knowing that exceptional results are more strongly associated with superior non-price value and higher revenue makes it more likely that you will strike the right balance between responding to short-term demands and pursuing longer-term goals. Knowing that these objectives are the only nonnegotiables allows you to understand more clearly what can or should not change in the face of environmental or competitive turbulence.

These rules can prove indispensable when you are facing down some of the potentially pathological consequences of many financial ratios. For a measure such as ROA (and all others like it, such as return on net assets, cash flow return on investment, and economic value added), the denominator is some measure of assets while the numerator is some measure of income. These ratios go up if the asset base is reduced and income can be held constant or even just fall by disproportionately less. Discounted cash flow (DCF) methods used to compare the estimated value of different initiatives reward rapid payback over delayed gratification. Worse, the probabilistic methods typically used to account for different likelihoods of success bias our choices in favor of the seemingly more certain.

Consequently, when customers are no longer willing to pay for your latest innovation or lower-cost competitors are snapping at your heels, the too-frequent response is to compete by abandoning challenging markets or dropping prices while trying to preserve profitability by cutting cost and shedding assets. Although we might believe, or at least want to believe, that investing for tomorrow is the right thing to do, the seemingly incontrovertible facts of marginal cost analysis and DCF models compel us to ignore the better angels of our nature.

Most of us know that this is a mistake, a sentiment captured in the adage that no company can shrink its way to greatness. Perhaps our findings can add some empirical heft to what is otherwise little more than a bumper sticker. We have found that exceptional companies have a taste for spending and investment. Companies that fail in their quest for exceptional performance are led astray by the deceptively attractive certainties of short-run cost cutting or disinvestment. Managers can use the three rules to lash themselves to the mast as they sail past these Sirens. We will consider our labors amply rewarded if more managers can persevere in developing the non-price-value positions that earn the higher prices or greater volumes that more typically drive exceptional results.

We are optimistic because the three rules are measurable and hence actionable. Whether you are establishing a position based on greater non-price value than your competition is something that can be measured today. You can know whether the performance of your solution is materially different from the alternatives available to the market segments you are targeting. You can know what your relative price position is, and you can typically determine, to a useful approximation, your relative cost position. Because you can measure the degree to which you are following the three rules, you can adapt your behavior to remain consistent with them, which keeps you moving consistently in a direction that is systematically more likely than the alternatives to result in improved and perhaps even exceptional performance. These features of the rules are crucial, for as our journey has revealed, synthesizing the causes of performance differences into a manageable number of generally applicable principles can too easily devolve into platitudes.

> The three rules constitute useful advice because they define which of many plausible alternatives is systematically associated with exceptional performance. *Better before cheaper* does not mean price competition is irrelevant; it means that when you have a choice to make, and when the data are unclear, go with *better*. *Revenue before cost* does not mean keeping cost under control does not matter; it means increasing revenue is more important. *There are no other rules* does not mean you can blindly follow the rules; it means you must apply all your creativity and insight to follow them in the face of all manner of other changes.

It is a trap that has claimed some of the most famous or well-regarded researchers in the field. For example, we are variously told to confront the brutal facts, find a big enough market insight, have a clear and focused strategy, and be agile, disciplined, and focused.[15] It is difficult to disagree with this advice—but that is precisely the problem. Who would ever want to hide from the truth, look for a market insight that was too small, have a confused and diffuse strategy, or be sclerotic, undisciplined, and unfocused? Consider also the observations that success lies in being specific, methodical, and consistent; in getting the right people on the bus; and in not abandoning your core prematurely.[16] Such prescriptions are helpful only if you thought there might be circumstances where you should be vague, haphazard, and inconsistent; have the wrong people on the bus; or ever do anything prematurely.

In contrast, the three rules are falsifiable but substantiated claims. They are not matters of logical necessity but matters of fact. It could have turned out that exceptional performance was a function of lower prices, lower cost, and adaptability with respect to both. But it did not. For reasons we are about to explain, we believe the path to exceptional performance lies in the persistent pursuit of *better before cheaper* and *revenue before cost* and regardless of the choices you face *there are no other rules*.

The quest for greatness finally has more to sustain it than a fortune cookie.

CHAPTER 2

Finding Signal in the Noise

This book falls into what we call the "success study" genre. You very likely have read, or at least heard of, the more famous and influential exemplars of the field, among which most would include *In Search of Excellence* by Tom Peters and Robert Waterman, and *Good to Great* by Jim Collins. As students of the field we have read quite closely a good many such books (see Appendix B, "Bibliography of Success Studies").[1]

If you have also read some of these books, you fall into one of three categories. You might have found the prescriptions of prior success studies compelling or even just useful food for thought. In this case, we recommend you read this chapter with some care. We will argue here that the findings of previous works have been undermined by deep-seated flaws in method that we have taken great pains to remedy, with important implications for the validity and soundness of our findings.

On the other hand, you might have tended to dismiss the recommendations of previous works due to deep-seated flaws in method. In this case, we recommend that you read this chapter with some care, and for the same reason.

If you fall into neither of those categories (and hence belong to our third category), you can skip this chapter.

Whether you have found previous "success studies" to be compelling or have dismissed them as relatively lightweight, we recommend you read this chapter: our methods for identifying exceptional performers and determining the causes of their exceptional performance are different from what has gone before. Understanding those differences is an important part of being able to take our conclusions seriously.

The bedrock assumption of every success study is that one can infer the causes of differences in performance by comparing the behaviors of companies with higher performance with the behaviors of companies with lower performance. Most success studies set performance benchmarks that are intuitively demanding and then declare that any companies clearing those benchmarks have achieved superior performance.

Here is the problem: our intuitions are terrible judges of what constitutes a meaningful difference in performance. For example, if we told you that the broad market index had an annualized total shareholder return (TSR) of 9.2 percent over a three-month period while over that same time Company A and Company B had annualized TSRs of 9.3 and 9.1 percent, respectively, would you believe it was worth trying to determine what behavioral differences caused those performance differences? If your intuitions are similar to ours in this regard, the answer is no. This difference is simply not material enough over a long enough period of time to warrant deeper investigation.

Now the bad news: if we accept that some performance differences are so small as to have no discernible informational content, we are obligated to specify how large performance differences must be in order to matter. Conceptually, an annualized difference of 0.1 percent over three months is no different from a tenfold difference over ten years. Although the latter certainly *feels* like a significant and material difference, we have no real evidence in support of either intuition. A much better approach is to quantify the likelihood that a given difference really *is* a difference worth exploring.[2] Only then can we hope to hear the signal hidden in the noise.

By way of analogy, imagine that you wanted to determine whether or not someone was good at flipping heads with a fair coin. How would you determine this? You probably would not ask them to flip heads on a single toss and if it came up heads, conclude that they can bias the outcome. What about asking them to do it twice in a row (a 25 percent chance)? Ten times (a 0.098 percent chance)? Any given outcome has a nonzero probability of happening all on its own, but by specifying the desired outcome in advance (all heads) and by calculating the probabilities dictated by chance, you can at least assign a probability to the likelihood that our coin flipper can bias the results based on the likelihood of the observed outcome.

Taking this kind of systemic variability into account when dealing with coin tosses is simple: we know the odds for each individual toss and that each toss's outcome is independent of the others', so we can readily determine the likelihood of specified outcomes given a specified number of trials. But when looking at corporate performance, this is not nearly so straightforward. What are the odds that a company that has beaten the market by tenfold is system-level noise and not company-level signal? Perhaps, like our ten-heads flipper, such an outcome is rare in a single instance, but given enough trials, bound to happen eventually. Since tens of thousands of companies have thrown their hats into the ring over the years and stock markets show high volatility, extreme outcomes are quite likely, and some companies will end up with seemingly remarkable performance because of the system, not because of anything special the company did.[3] We need some way to find the signal—the kind of performance that means something special is probably at work—amid all the noise generated by what we colloquially call luck. As far as we know, no prior success study has tackled this question.[4]

Part of the reason might be that talking about "luck" or "randomness" as a contributing factor to corporate performance can be off-putting. For many, these terms connote some sort of magical, nonrational, or inexplicable animating force, and seem to deny the role of deliberate action in determining corporate performance. After all, most managers pursue specified ends with intent. How can the results be random?

Perhaps it is useful, then, to borrow from the world of statistical process control and think of outcomes as determined by a combination of "common causes" (attributes of the system) and "special causes" (attributes of the company). Outcomes that cannot be distinguished from the background variation of the system should be attributed to common causes.[5] Of course, when we examine a specific case we can almost always come up with something that looks like a special cause, but we are more likely than not deluding ourselves. What we most likely have is merely an explanation built on common causes.

Avoiding the trap of chasing special causes in a common-cause regime requires that we characterize the variability of the system within which individual companies function, and then look for performance that goes beyond the parameters of that system. Only then can we quantify our confidence level in attributing an outcome to characteristics of the individual rather than to the larger system within which that individual functions.

Defining Exceptional Performance

We addressed this challenge in two steps.[6] First, using a statistical technique known as quantile regression, for every company in our database we translated its ROA in each year into a decile rank. Our model strips out the impact of industry, year, survivor bias, and a number of other determinants of performance. This transforms a set of ROA values (for example, 11.3 percent, 9.5 percent, 13.2 percent) into a set of decile ranks (for example, 7, 5, 9), but the deciles incorporate the impact of all our controls. This serves to create a level playing field for the comparison of any company with any other company in any year from 1966 to 2010.

A key feature of this method is that higher absolute ROA values (measured in percentage points) need not yield higher relative performance (measured in decile ranks). Consequently, a 7th-decile performance in software in 1998 might require an ROA of 20 percent while a 7th-decile performance in steel in 1981 might require an ROA of only 5 percent; a financial services company with an ROA of 1.3 percent in 2009 can get a 9th-decile rank while a drug company with an ROA of 18 percent in 1996 could get a 5th-decile rank. In other words, decile ranks capture the *relative* performance of each company as determined by the company-level factors most directly under the control or influence of management.

Decile ranks enable comparisons on a year-by-year basis, but exceptional lifetime performance cannot be identified simply through an inspection of those numbers. How are we to tell whether 7, 6, 8, 9, 7, 9, 8 is better or worse than 6, 3, 9, 9, 9, 9, 6, 8, 7, 9, 5, 2? The second step in our process takes this on. Remember our search for the exceptional coin flipper? This time we are looking for exceptional companies, those that deliver better performance than we expect given the parameters of the system. The difference is that, with a coin, we know what constitutes "fair," and so assessing the likelihood that a given result violates that assumption is straightforward. When it comes to corporate performance, we must observe the parameters of the system and then estimate the likelihood of given outcomes in light of those parameters. Only then can we determine the likelihood that a company's performance constitutes signal rather than noise (see Appendix C, "Identifying Exceptional Performance").[7]

We begin by specifying what outcomes will be treated as significant by defining two categories of exceptional performance: Miracle Worker and Long Runner. Conditional on their life spans, Miracle Workers deliver enough 9th-decile rankings to be sufficiently unlikely that we are willing to conclude there is something other than luck at work, and they are so called because such performance seems to us to be miraculous. Long Runners deliver enough years in the 6th-to-8th-decile band (inclusive) to clear the same threshold of unlikeliness.[8] This label stems from having to spend longer in their focal decile band in order to be equally unlikely because their focal band both consists of a lower level of performance and covers a broader range.[9]

> Exceptional performance is conditional on a company's life span and its focal decile range. For example, to qualify as a Miracle Worker a company with a fifteen-year life span needs ten years in the 9th decile, but only twelve out of twenty. A Long Runner needs fourteen years out of fifteen in the 6th-to-8th-decile range but eighteen out of twenty.

In addition, we define as Average Joes companies with average life spans, average performance levels, and average volatility. These companies are foils for our two categories of exceptional performers. They should not be viewed as "poorly performing" companies—the identification of poor performance would require all the same statistical tests that went into identifying superior performers. Rather, they are companies with performance profiles that are indistinguishable from the background noise, companies with "random walk" performance. That is not to say that their management is not skilled or capable. Rather, it says that this skill cannot be discerned, for reasons we cannot specify, based solely on an examination of the company's performance.

Every method is subject to trade-offs. We have chosen to concentrate on avoiding the false positive problem—that is, calling a company exceptional when it really is not. We pay a price for this: we are subject to a bias toward false negatives—that is, not identifying as exceptional some companies that actually are. This runs the risk that we hurt some people's feelings, since no one likes to hear that their favorite company is perhaps not as great as they thought. However, since the objective of our work is to identify the drivers of exceptional performance, not unfailingly to identify exceptionally performing companies, we feel this is the right trade-off to make.

With this method and these definitions we were able to look at all the companies ever publicly traded in U.S. markets and identify every Miracle Worker and Long Runner that ever existed between 1966 and 2010. It is this population of exceptional companies—174 Miracle Workers and 170 Long Runners—that is the foundation of our research.

Measuring Performance

No measure of corporate performance can capture everything that matters to everyone. We believe that ROA is a useful way to capture company performance as determined by company-specific factors across a wide range of companies. But other measures are important and of material interest, perhaps no two more so than TSR and revenue growth.

We prefer ROA to TSR or growth because we want a measure that captures consistent managerial contributions to company performance. Our view is that revenue growth is not an outcome worth pursuing merely for its own sake. Rather, it is either a leading or lagging indicator of other performance of interest—often profitability or TSR. As for TSR, note that share price responds primarily to unexpected changes in projections of future performance. A company that is doing very poorly as measured by profitability and surprises investors by clawing its way into the black, even if only barely, will likely see a marked improvement in the value of its equity and hence a dramatic rise in share price. In contrast, a company with steady but much higher levels of profitability will likely see its share price move not a whit, delivering risk-adjusted market average returns.

> Total shareholder return (TSR) is a popular measure of performance in success studies. However, shareholder returns are more a function of changes in investor expectations than of consistently superior management. We wanted to understand what makes for a great company, not what makes for a great investment.

To put it on a bumper sticker, there is a deep difference between a great company and a great investment. Profitability is, we believe, better suited to capturing the former and TSR the latter. In any case, our hope is that all that is required for our research to be meaningful is that profitability, as measured by ROA, is seen as at least one of several important measures of financial performance.

In the interests of completeness, we also looked at the performance of our high-performing companies and those companies identified as high performers in the success studies identified in Appendix B as measured by each of ROA, growth, and TSR (see Appendix C). Treating the nineteen studies as a population, in expectation only 12 percent of each sample had exceptional ROA, only 17 percent were in the 9th decile for growth, and only 25 percent were in the 9th decile for TSR. (In all cases, we examine the performance of companies used in other studies only for the time period of relevance in that study.)

A finer-grained analysis does not yield more encouraging results. Four studies that focus on the question of growth—*The Alchemy of Growth, Blueprint to a Billion, The Granularity of Growth,* and *Stall Points*—have

0, 20, 21, and 17 percent of their samples in the 9th decile of growth, respectively. The median decile ranks for the high-growth companies in these studies' samples are 7, 8, 7, and 8, with interquartile ranges of between 1.5 and 3 decile ranks, indicating material variation. By comparison, the Miracle Workers and Long Runners in our study, chosen solely on the basis of exceptional ROA, have median decile growth ranks of 8 and 7, respectively.

In the studies that focus on TSR, such as *Good to Great* and *What Really Works*, 30 percent and 25 percent of the high-performing companies in their samples are in the 9th decile of TSR, and the sample median TSR decile rank is 7. Just over a quarter of our population, and just over a third of our sample, falls in the 9th decile of TSR, and the median decile rank of our population is 7, suggesting that there is not much to choose, with respect to average TSR performance, between companies they chose based on TSR and those we identified based solely on statistically validated exceptional ROA performance.

Note that five of our Long Runners did not meet our stated benchmarks for exceptional performance. This is a compromise forced on us by the need to match companies in a trio according to criteria other than performance, such as years of overlap and comparable revenue at the beginning of a comparison period. Appendix D, "Category, Trajectory, and Era Analysis," provides additional detail.

Based on the analysis summarized in Table 4 we are willing to conclude, first, that many major success studies have not, by and large, been doing what they thought they were doing. On average, the companies they studied do not seem to have delivered performance levels that separate them from the background noise of the population from which they were drawn. And if most of the great, excellent, winning, peak, breakthrough, enduring companies one examines cannot confidently be said to have truly warranted any of those adjectives, the findings drawn from that

TABLE 4: **Comparing Success Studies**

	Companies Categorized*	ROA**			Growth***			TSR		
	# Categorized (% of original sample)	Median Probability of Being Exceptional	IQR (pp)	# (%) Exceptional	Median Lifetime Decile Rank	IQR (pp)	# (%) in 9th Decile	Median Lifetime Decile Rank	IQR (pp)	# (%) in 9th Decile
Alchemy of Growth	17 (59%)	0%	43.5	1 (6%)	6	2.5	0 (0%)	7	1.5	2 (12%)
Beyond Performance	17 (85%)	55%	82.3	4 (24%)	7	2	3 (18%)	7	4.5	5 (29%)
Big Winners / Losers	9 (100%)	0%	61.9	1 (11%)	7	2	0 (0%)	8	3	3 (33%)
Blueprint to a Billion	362 (94%)	0%	18.2	8 (2%)	7	3	73 (20%)	8	2	133 (37%)
Breakthrough Company	6 (67%)	42%	52.7	1 (17%)	7.5	1.8	1 (17%)	9.5	0.4	5 (83%)
Built to Last	16 (89%)	45%	72.6	3 (19%)	5	1.8	1 (6%)	5	1.8	1 (6%)
Creative Destruction	11 (92%)	17%	79.3	2 (18%)	5	3.3	0 (0%)	7	1.3	0 (0%)
Enduring Success	7 (78%)	22%	40.1	1 (14%)	4	0	0 (0%)	7	0	0 (0%)
Essential Advantage	26 (72%)	41%	81.5	6 (23%)	7	2.5	5 (19%)	6	4.1	6 (23%)
Good to Great	10 (91%)	11%	44.7	0 (0%)	6	2	0 (0%)	7	2.5	3 (30%)
Granularity of Growth	39 (76%)	27%	65.3	6 (15%)	7	4	8 (21%)	7	3	9 (23%)
Great by Choice	7 (100%)	88%	29.9	3 (43%)	9	0.5	5 (71%)	9.5	0.4	7 (100%)
How the Mighty Fall	9 (100%)	47%	66.0	1 (11%)	7	1	2 (22%)	7	2	2 (22%)
In Search of Excellence	13 (93%)	29%	55.7	1 (8%)	5	1	0 (0%)	5	3	2 (15%)

Jumping the S-curve	32 (89%)	45%	78.7	8 (25%)	7	2.5	8 (25%)	8	3.5	9 (28%)
Peak Performance	17 (81%)	0%	58.1	1 (6%)	7	5	5 (29%)	7	4.1	5 (29%)
Profit from the Core	27 (73%)	19%	66.0	2 (7%)	7.5	3.8	6 (22%)	7	3.5	7 (26%)
Stall Points	58 (87%)	34%	67.0	7 (12%)	8	4	10 (17%)	8	2.5	13 (22%)
What Really Works	16 (94%)	23%	53.4	1 (6%)	7	2	2 (13%)	7	2.5	4 (25%)
Three Rules—sample	**18 (100%)**	**97%**	**9.2**	**13 (72%)**	**7**	**1**	**0 (0%)**	**6.5**	**3.8**	**6 (33%)**
Miracle Workers	*9 (100%)*	*98%*	*3.9*	*9 (100%)*	*7*	*0*	*0 (0%)*	*6*	*3*	*4 (44%)*
Long Runners	*9 (100%)*	*89%*	*22.5*	*4 (44%)*	*6*	*2*	*0 (0%)*	*7*	*3*	*2 (22%)*
Three Rules—population	**344 (100%)**	**97%**	**5.6**	**344 (100%)**	**5**	**3**	**17 (5%)**	**7**	**3**	**90 (26%)**
Miracle Workers	*174 (100%)*	*98%*	*4.2*	*174 (100%)*	*6*	*3*	*11 (6%)*	*8*	*3*	*63 (36%)*
Long Runners	*170 (100%)*	*96%*	*5.9*	*170 (100%)*	*5*	*3*	*6 (4%)*	*7*	*2*	*27 (16%)*
TOTAL****	699	–	–	57 (8%)	–	–	129 (18%)	–	–	216 (31%)
MINIMUM	6	0%	18.2	0 (0%)	4	0	0 (0%)	5	0	0 (0%)
MAXIMUM	362	88%	82.3	8 (43%)	9	5	73 (71%)	9.5	4.5	133 (100%)
MEDIAN	16	27%	61.9	2 (12%)	7	2	2 (17%)	7	2.5	5 (25%)
IQR	17	30 pp	21.1	4 (12 pp)	1	1.4	6 (22 pp)	1	1.6	5 (11 pp)

Source: Studies cited; Compustat; Deloitte analysis

*Due to data availability we cannot include every company in every study. We examine only the time periods examined in each study.

**For each company identified in each study, we calculate the probability that it has exceptional ROA using the method described in this chapter. We report the median probability of exceptional ROA in each study for those companies in each study for which we do have sufficient data.

***Using the "cumulative residual" method described in Appendix C, we calculate the lifetime TSR and growth decile rank for each company in a given study and report here the median and interquartile ranges for the companies in a study on which we have data.

****These summary statistics for the population of studies exclude our research.

examination must be viewed with extreme caution. It is not for us to say that those studies' prescriptions are wrong. However, our statistical analysis suggests rather strongly that the evidence that they are right is rather weaker than we might have appreciated.

Second, this analysis leads us to believe that our sample is different in important ways, but also the same in ways that are perhaps just as critical to the credibility of our findings. We have focused on ROA where other studies have not, and therefore, predictably, our companies have systematically higher relative ROA than those featured in other works. Consequently, we can conclude with some confidence that on this measure of performance, at least, we have identified a fundamentally different set of companies.

> The companies identified as superior performers in other studies have actually delivered relatively unexceptional results. In contrast, our sample is demonstrably exceptional as measured by ROA and not noticeably worse than others' superior performers when measured by growth or TSR.

Yet our population and our sample do not appear to suffer much, if at all, when performance is measured by growth or TSR. Our companies perform the same as those featured in prior work, insofar as they do about as well on growth and TSR as companies *chosen* on the basis of growth or TSR. We do not believe this would have been the case had prior researchers sought to develop statistical tests for exceptional performance. It is because their benchmarks were chosen on the basis of face validity that they proved to have set too low a bar.

Since our exceptional companies happen to have growth and TSR performance that is largely similar to those of companies featured in prior work, our prescriptions for action, at a minimum, would not appear to impose a TSR or growth penalty. In other words, there is no evidence that following our three rules in the pursuit of superior profitability comes at the expense of shareholder value or revenue growth. Better still, our three rules might even contribute to growth and TSR that are on a par with those of companies chosen for their performance on these measures.[10]

Profiling Performance

In assessing company performance, we used the entire observable lifetime of each company. Few success studies do this, choosing instead to focus on specific periods of time, say, ten or fifteen or even thirty years.

This is a mistake. It creates a very real possibility of falling victim to what is known as the "Texas sharpshooter" problem, in which the target is defined only after the shots have been fired. When you get to draw the target after you've shot, you can easily create the illusion of accuracy by placing the bull's-eye over whatever random cluster of bullet holes you can find.

So, for example, *What Really Works* takes a microscope to the decade 1986 to 1996 while *Big Winners and Big Losers* focuses on 1992 to 2002. The periods under examination in the two studies overlap by five years (from the beginning of 1992 to the end of 1996), and both books identify Campbell Soup as a company worthy of study. Yet *What Really Works* holds up Campbell Soup as a "winner" while *Big Winners and Big Losers* sees the company as a "big loser." Who's right?

It turns out that Campbell Soup had a great run from 1986 to 1998: the stock went from $4.17 to $54.61, outpacing the market more than threefold. Then from 1998 to 2002 it declined to $23.47, such that for the full sixteen-year period covered by the two studies it was about even with the Dow Jones Industrial Average. The moral is that if you want to say anything about the performance of any company you have to look at all the data available for it. The fundamental unit of analysis is the company life-time, or a sufficiently reasonable approximation, subject to data availability: anything less creates the risk of seeing greatness or incompetence when in fact there is little reason to impute either.[11] It would appear that it is a lot easier to decide whether Campbell soups are mmm-mmm good than it is to determine whether Campbell Soup is mmm-mmm great.

But could there be meaningful patterns in performance, periods of higher and lower outcomes that signal important changes in behavior within a company across time? We tackle this challenge with respect to both relative performance (ROA decile ranks) and absolute performance (ROA values) and use different statistical methods for each in order to account for their fundamentally different natures.[12] A company is a Miracle Worker by virtue of how many 9th-decile years it delivers over its observed lifetime. It has a Kept It *trajectory* if those 9s are distributed randomly across all observed years; it has a Lost It trajectory if those 9s occur in a streak at the beginning of the period with a notable lack of 9s at the end; and it has a Found It trajectory if the 9s come in a streak at the end of the observation period. An Other trajectory captures everything else, but consists largely of companies with an in-out-in profile. The same trajectories (Kept It, Found It, Lost It, Other) apply to Long Runners. Average Joes have no discernible trajectory.

Absolute performance can show evidence of patterns, what we call eras, quite independent of any streaks in relative performance that define a trajectory. For example, a company on a steady and unchanging upward trend in absolute ROA can find itself leaving behind relative mediocrity and ultimately turning in enough 9s to earn Miracle Worker status. Such a company would have a single era but two streaks and a Found It trajectory. Conversely, a Miracle Worker might find itself in an era of declining ROA for a time, but reverse this trend before its relative performance suffers. In this case, we would see two eras but one streak and a Kept It trajectory.

This analysis of patterns in both relative and absolute performance provides us with more nearly objective and potentially significant time periods over which to look for patterns or differences in behavior. We tend to look at ROA on an annual basis, and we have a salience bias to treat relatively short runs of, say, the most recent three to five years as significant because that is a relevant time horizon for many managers. It is worth noting, however, that there is no necessary reason for either the periodicity of the Earth's orbit about the Sun or the tenure and trajectory of managerial careers to have a meaningful impact on the processes that generate profits in complex organizations. Success studies are most credible when they analyze performance—both its magnitude and its patterns—entirely independently of possible causal explanations: if we let our prior beliefs about what might matter color our characterization of performance, we are assuming the answer we seek.

Our sample of nine trios has three Miracle Workers with Found It, three with Lost It, two with Kept It, and one with Other trajectories (see Appendix D for more detail). By comparing Miracle Workers and Long Runners during their streaks of higher relative performance to each other and to Average Joes, we hope to understand what drives superior performance. By comparing behavior during streaks of higher and lower performance within individual companies we are able to gain some purchase on what sorts of changes in behavior drive changes in performance. This proved to be enormously valuable, for it turned out to be another test of our primary findings. Not only have we concluded that our three rules account for differences between individual companies and categories of companies, but also that changes in the degree to which a company's behavior adheres to these same rules account for that company's trajectory.

Appendix E, "Performance Profile Charts," provides Performance Profile charts for all twenty-seven companies in our study that capture all these dimensions of performance graphically. Heartland (see page 301) has a Kept It trajectory—that is, consistent 9th-decile performance across the full observation period, despite a few years below the 9th decile. The company also has two eras, as described in chapter 1, each characterized by different average, trends, and variation in ROA.[13]

> We identify companies with lifetime performance that can be heard above the noise. We then find the signal in the noise of the performance of each exceptional company by looking for patterns in that company's performance over time. Streaks in relative performance and eras in absolute performance are powerful indicators of meaningful changes in corporate behavior.

Consequently, when looking for behavioral differences that explain relative performance, we should treat the entire period from 1986 to 2010 as a single period. However, when looking for changes over time within Heartland, we should compare 1986 to 1994 with 1995 to 2010. The year-to-year fluctuations in ROA can be safely ignored: they are simply noise. It is the parameters of the company's Performance Profile that reveal the signals: Heartland is a lifetime Miracle Worker, it has been consistently a Miracle Worker, and its performance suggests two distinct eras characterized by different Elements of Advantage.

The Causes of Performance

Finding companies with performance that can be heard above the noise and defining its contours allows us to identify meaningful comparisons. The performance differences among Miracle Workers, Long Runners, and Average Joes are our *dependent variable*, or what it is we hope to explain. We turn now to how we have gone about identifying our *independent variables*. These are the behavioral differences that make Miracle Workers *Miracle Workers*, that explain how Long Runners made it to Long Runner status but failed to break through to the top echelon of performance, and why Average Joes remained relegated to no better than mediocrity.

The Halo Effect

There are two especially deep pits one might fall into when attempting to explain corporate performance. The first of them is known as the "halo effect," which is manifest when superior performance leads commentators to attribute all manner of positive attributes to anything and perhaps everything a company does.[14] When the stock is up, leadership is decisive and bold; when the stock is down, the same people magically become narrow-minded and arrogant.[15] This would not be a problem except that many success studies rely on the journalistic record as a major source of data. Consequently, in the words of one commentator, many of the most famous success studies are not studies of what causes great behavior but studies of how great behavior is described.[16]

We address this challenge by focusing as much as possible on independent variables that can be quantified entirely independently of a company's performance. So, for example, in our discussion of the causes of Heartland's superior performance we talked about customer focus in terms of geographic coverage and the percentage of sales generated by their largest accounts; we explained relative asset intensity in terms of the percentage of freight hauled by O/O drivers; and we documented the company's price premium.

A side effect of this approach is that discussions of people and personalities might appear notable by their absence from our case studies. We do not talk about culture or values, the character traits of the—often very colorful—people at the helms of our exceptional companies. That is not because we feel these factors do not matter; they certainly do. But because we are often looking at decades of performance, the sort of evidence one would require in order to say something substantive and substantiated is simply unavailable.

It is tempting, perhaps, to accuse us of conducting a "drunkard's search": looking for our keys under the lamppost because the light is brightest there, rather than in the dark alley where we dropped them. We prefer another metaphor: we are corporate paleontologists, forced by circumstance to deal only with the fossil record. We might like to know what color dinosaurs were, or what their mating calls sounded like. We can hazard a guess based on the application of principles such as camouflage and sexual selection, or make inferences based on the shape and size of nasal cavities as revealed in the shapes of their skulls, but skin color and lustful bellows do not fossilize, and so we can never know—never *really* know—the answers to those questions. Similarly, organizational culture and the motivations of individual actors, among other corporate "soft tissues," are not preserved unless they were studied in real time and in the right ways, which is only too rare. We might like to know more about the personal struggles of particular executives as they reinvented their organizations to preserve their exceptional performance decades ago, but we cannot.

This lack of data is not all bad, in our view. The three rules are inferred by identifying those decision-making criteria that, if applied to the circumstances faced by our sample companies, would have led them to make their choices in the ways observed. We do not know if they *actually* applied these criteria, but we can hope to demonstrate that they behaved as if they did. Consequently, you are no longer required to be like them, but only to be sufficiently creative in finding ways to apply the rules to your situation.

We hope this comes as a relief. What if you had found that you needed to be a level five leader, for example, yet you conclude that you simply do not have the chops for that role?[17] Instead, you can now look for ways to apply your own leadership style, whatever it is, to following the three rules, thereby putting exceptional performance within your reach.

Post Hoc Ergo Propter Hoc

The second of our two pits one might fall into when attempting to uncover the "true" causes of any given outcome is filled with variations of *post hoc ergo propter hoc* (after this, therefore because of this), or more mathematically, "correlation is not causation."[18] Just because there is a given behavioral difference between two companies does not mean that the behavioral difference caused the performance difference in which we are interested. What is typically missing is a more nearly objective and ideally quantifiable connection between differences in behavior and differences in performance.

This can be extraordinarily difficult, if not impossible, with measures of performance such as TSR. With a variable as noisy and overdetermined as equity market valuation, it can be an insurmountable task to identify the truth amid all the competing Kiplingesque *Just So Stories*.

In chapter 1, we alluded to the power of decomposing ROA into its constituent elements—what we called the Elements of Advantage—and the guidance this provides when seeking behavioral explanations for performance differences. For example, Medtronic, a Miracle Worker in the medical devices industry, enjoyed a 2.1 pp/year ROA advantage over Stryker, its Long Runner comparison in the industry. Both have Found It trajectories. Medtronic's advantage is made up of 5.2 pp/year of ROS advantage and 3.1 pp/year of TAT disadvantage. That is, Medtronic has *higher* return on sales but *lower* asset turnover.

> Explaining performance differences in terms of behavioral differences demands that we stick to the "fossil record" and appeal only to behaviors that can be described independently of performance. Possible explanations must be tested against their consonance with the underlying financial structure of advantage and their materiality.

The financial structure of the performance difference between these two companies is a form of *independent variable* because the structure of an ROA advantage is independent of the ROA advantage itself. As a result, the Elements of Advantage for Medtronic over Stryker impose important constraints on the behaviors (additional independent variables) we can credibly claim caused the relevant difference in ROA. Was Medtronic's TAT lower than Stryker's because of inefficiencies, or was there something about how Medtronic generated higher ROS that imposed a trade-off that led to lower TAT? As we will see in the next chapter, Medtronic's success can be attributed in large part to its adoption of a common product development platform, its improved manufacturing capabilities, and a series of well-executed acquisitions. These actions served to establish a position built around non-price value and a profitability formula driven by higher prices. Its lower TAT was a function of the need to invest more heavily in specialized assets in order to remain at the leading edge of a rapidly and dramatically changing medical devices market.

In contrast, Stryker competed less on the differentiation of its products than did Medtronic and more on price. It had a narrower product line that it was able to manufacture consistently and efficiently on a relatively smaller asset base. The company grew, on a percentage basis, about as fast as Medtronic—and actually performed much better than Medtronic when measured by TSR. But its growth and asset efficiency were not enough to compensate for Medtronic's particular combination of position and profitability formula.[19]

Once behaviors that have the desired qualitative impact have been identified, we can assess, to at least some degree, the materiality of their impact. The more water a given behavioral difference must carry, the greater the burden of proof. In some instances, we were able to create crude financial models that allowed us to assess the plausibility of a given explanation.

For example, our Elements of Advantage analysis showed that Heartland relied on higher ROS for most of its performance advantage, and most of that turned on higher gross margin. We found that Heartland had a 10 percent or more price premium. This is a behavioral trait that is consistent with the financial structure of Heartland's advantage. Constructing a very simple and transparent model—simply lopping 10 percent of Heartland's revenue off its net income—allows us to assess, in a rough and qualitative but still instructive way, the degree to which the observed price premium has a legitimate claim on being part of the right explanation. In this case, the price premium proved material in a way that, say, a 2 percent price premium would not have. We did the same for many of the behaviors we felt mattered in the explanation of performance advantages: we created "sniff tests" or "sanity checks" to establish, to a first order approximation, that the behaviors that appeared to matter were credible explanations.

Note also that the Elements of Advantage are presented in average percentage points per year over periods of time that can be a decade or more. It is worth confirming that these averages are in fact representative of patterns over time; after all, differences in ROA and the components of that difference can be subject to extreme variation: an ROA advantage might be driven by nonoperating income one year thanks to a gain on the disposal of assets and by an asset turnover advantage the next because the comparison company paid a large premium on an acquisition. If we are looking for consistent behavioral differences when the underlying phenomenon is fluctuating wildly, but invisibly, we are likely to be led seriously astray. Appendix F shows the consistency of the elements within ROS and TAT as well as absolute measures of consistency for the sample and for each pair-wise comparison across each relevant period. Our conclusion is that the Elements of Advantage are consistent enough, both within pair-wise comparisons and across the sample, to require general behavioral explanations.

Generalizing the Findings

Let us say you believe us to this point: we have identified a believable sample of exceptional companies and identified the behaviors that cause performance differences. Those behaviors imply a pattern of choices consistent with the application of the three rules: *better before cheaper, revenue before cost*, and *there are no other rules*. For all this, the usefulness of our research depends in large part on how confidently we can apply what has been learned to companies other than those that have been studied with such care. It is a study's generalizability that establishes the credibility of its prescriptions for action.[20]

In many success studies, claims of generalizability most often turn on the diversity of the companies in the sample—the range of industries, the time periods examined, and so on. We have adopted this approach as well: our nine trios are drawn from a diverse set of industries, including pharmaceuticals, electrical wiring, confectionary, trucking, and fashion retail.

A diverse sample is certainly more likely to be generalizable than a homogenous one, but diversity per se is far from sufficient, especially given what is at stake. The problem is that we cannot know what characteristics of similarity and difference are relevant. Should the industries studied be different with respect to asset intensity or growth rates? Regulatory constraints or technological change? Competitive pressures or exogenous shocks? There are simply too many ways to be different for any sample to be different in every possibly relevant way. Diversity helps, but it will not suffice.

In our case, we identified the population of exceptional companies and then chose a sample essentially at random from that population. We can confidently claim that our case studies at least potentially matter because they shed light on a much larger number of companies. Our explanations have a hope of saying something about companies other than the ones we happened to study.[21]

Such considerations might matter less, however, than your own intuitive sense of whether our findings apply to you. Seeking our own betterment through the study of greatness of any kind can become strangely discouraging. Should a physics student model him- or herself after Newton, Einstein, and Hawking? Should an aspiring writer try to emulate Shakespeare or Tolstoy or Twain? Should a rising business leader adopt the practices of Sloan or Welch or Jobs? Those people were . . . exceptional. Can *we* really learn something from *them*? Maybe what worked for them worked for them because they were who they were. What if the most important ingredient of being great is not what you do but just the brute fact of being great in the first place?

Similarly, the study of great companies can leave us wondering if we have set our sights too high. Google is *Google*, for heaven's sake. The company certainly captures our imagination, but perhaps we are kidding ourselves if we think that the drivers of its exceptional performance are relevant to the rest of us. Within the ranks of exceptional companies are not only the search giant but also many other marquee companies, among them General Electric, ExxonMobil, and Johnson & Johnson. Perhaps we simply cannot relate at a visceral level to these companies. Whether their exceptionalism arises from the seemingly unique features of their industries or from their individual idiosyncrasies, there is often a gap between "them" and "us." If we cannot connect in an almost personal way with the experiences of exceptional performers, our quest is ultimately quixotic, for we cannot internalize and act upon the lessons we learn.

The good news is that alongside the iconic, magazine-cover material of Microsoft and Oracle in software or Amgen and Genzyme in biotech, we find many companies and industries that exist on a much more human scale. 3M, with its legendary innovation and thousands of products in commercial and industrial markets, is on the list, but so is WD-40, a company built on a single, nonpatented product originally designed to prevent corrosion on nuclear missiles—and which, unchanged, has been the bane of squeaky hinges ever since. The globally ubiquitous McDonald's proves to be exceptional, but so does Luby's Cafeteria, a chain with forty-three locations, and only three outside of Texas. IBM makes the list, and so does Syntel, a company 0.5 percent of IBM's size.[22] Precisely because our method isolates the effect of managerial decision making on performance, we find exceptional performers of all shapes and sizes.

> Our belief is that our findings are useful because they are substantive claims, not truisms. That is important but not sufficient. For our claims to be taken seriously when making important decisions they must be true— or at least true enough. That is a determination that can only be made on the strength of the methods we used to find the evidence supporting them.

Similarly, our research sample includes companies and industries that are quite likely familiar to you: Maytag in appliances, Wrigley in confectionary, Abercrombie & Fitch in clothing retail, and Merck in pharmaceuticals are, if not household names, certainly readily recognizable. These companies owe their greatness in part to iconic brands that have endured over generations, to aggressive globalization, to cutting-edge advertising that became a cultural phenomenon, and to superstar CEOs. These are aspirational tales, for they give us a sense of what is possible.

But we also include much smaller and lesser-known companies competing in less attention-grabbing industries. Heartland, a small family-run trucking company, shows how focus can lead to superior profitability. Thomas & Betts reveals that innovation can be a significant driver of success in the lowest-tech segments of electrical wiring. Weis Markets demonstrates the enduring power of bold strategic moves in the grocery business of rural Pennsylvania. These are perhaps more inspirational examples in a very different way, for many of us can more readily see our own experiences reflected in their stories.

We have devoted this early chapter to a description of our methods and, to the extent propriety admits, a comparison of our methods with others'. Our methods are not perfect; no method is. But we believe that we have developed and employed material improvements in the identification of truly exceptional performance, isolating periods of higher and lower performance and connecting behavioral differences to performance differences in ways that justify a higher level of confidence in our conclusions.

In the chapters that follow, we will illustrate our methods and present our evidence in support of the three rules—*better before cheaper*, *revenue before cost*, and *there are no other rules*. By the time you reach chapter 6, you will be able to adjudicate for yourself the legitimacy of our claims.

CHAPTER 3

Better Before Cheaper

Better before cheaper distills to its essence what our research reveals about the relationship between competitive position and exceptional performance. Of course, competitive position has been the subject of research and discussion for decades. For all the seeming differences among the various approaches, competitive space has typically been defined in terms of the non-price value the customer receives and the relative cost of production of competing suppliers.[1]

For us, competitive position defines how a company creates value for customers, and thus the more useful of these two traditional dimensions is non-price value. For example, when buying a car, customers typically consider a variety of attributes, including safety features, reliability of operation, carbon emissions, styling, acceleration, top speed, handling, comfort, customizable features (for example, color or interior upholstery), the sales experience, ease and accessibility of servicing, and so on.

Most elements of non-price value can be measured, albeit with different degrees of precision: a car's acceleration is highly quantifiable, safety ratings less so, and "stylishness" can be given at best perhaps the appearance of specificity. Tools such as conjoint analysis can use these measurements to estimate the relative importance of each dimension, allowing companies to assess on which aspects, alone or in combination, they should seek to surpass the competition in order to win the business of specific customers or customer segments.[2]

The second dimension of traditional approaches to positioning analysis, relative cost of production, is not directly relevant to *better before cheaper* because it does not describe how companies create value for customers. Companies can choose to exploit a lower-cost position to enjoy superior profitability at prices similar to their competitors'. In that situation, although lower production cost is good for the company, it is irrelevant to the customer. Since *better before cheaper* is about creating customer value, our second dimension of position is relative price value, where price value (as perceived by customers) typically goes up as price goes down.[3] Price—what a customer pays for something in money—is readily quantifiable, so one can usually determine fairly easily which of two sufficiently substitutable offerings is less expensive (has superior price value).

A car that was better than all other cars on all dimensions of value in the eyes of all customers would have 100 percent market share. No car has 100 percent market share, however, because different customer segments want combinations of dimensions of value that are necessarily negatively correlated. Some customers want a larger car (say, for seating capacity) and some want a smaller car (say, to fit in small parking spaces). In any pair-wise comparison, no car can be both larger and smaller. Similarly, speed and energy consumption are negatively correlated (all else equal) because it takes more power to move a given mass faster. Still other limitations are entirely contingent: creating a minivan that has more sex appeal than a sports car requires only that people's tastes change.

In other words, constraints impose trade-offs. No product or service can be all things to all people, and everything we know about the power of market segmentation and focus is based on this inescapable fact. Companies that refuse to accept trade-offs among different dimensions of performance very often end up "splitting the difference" in ways that make few people happy.[4]

In summary, the dimensions of position are price value and non-price value. Products or services occupy different locations in competitive space to the extent that they differ along these dimensions. Thanks to the existence of trade-offs among at least some dimensions of value, differentiated competitive positions can be profitable while positions based on being better along all dimensions of performance simultaneously are rare.[5]

The Relativity of Position

Competitive position, like physical position, is entirely relative. There is no absolute frame of reference to which one can appeal. We cannot answer the question "What is company X's position?" without also specifying to which company or companies we are comparing company X.

Take the hotel business. What would you say is the competitive position of Four Seasons? You would be a rare bird if you said it competes on price. The company's hotels are renowned for their luxury and service, the quality of which is reflected in their prices, which are typically higher than most of the hotels with which most people are familiar. Similarly, if asked to put Motel 6 somewhere in the price/non-price space, we expect that most people would say it is a price-based competitor because its prices are lower than those of many other hotels.

These qualitative, commonsense judgments are based on implicit comparisons with some unspecified "average" hotel or motel that we conjure up in our minds. Such comparisons, however, are of little practical use, for customers do not make choices between a specific option (Four Seasons or Motel 6) and a hypothetical average. They make choices among specific alternatives. It is simply not good enough to say that Four Seasons competes on non-price value; we must first specify *against what* it competes on non-price value.

If we compare Four Seasons with Motel 6, few people would disagree that Four Seasons is the non-price competitor while Motel 6 competes on price. However, the validity of that assessment turns on how closely substitutable are the services being provided by each company. We have a sense that both companies are in the hospitality business, and so we can say with a straight face that they are, broadly speaking, substitutes for each other: should you need a room for hire, they each offer a viable solution.

But they are not especially close substitutes. How many people who seriously consider booking a room at the Four Seasons for a specific trip sometimes choose Motel 6 instead for that same trip because it is less expensive? How many people looking for a Motel 6 happen to drive by a Four Seasons and impulsively decide to splurge a little? It is a big world, so both of these scenarios have almost certainly played out, but it hardly seems typical.

Perhaps a better competitive set for Four Seasons consists of the Ritz-Carlton, Le Méridien, and Conrad chains. Faced with these choices, we might give Four Seasons a different position based on the relative price and non-price attributes of each of these alternatives than it got when compared with Motel 6. Similarly, if Motel 6 was compared with La Quinta, Red Roof Inn, and Best Western we might not be quite so quick to conclude that it is a price-based competitor.

There is no right or wrong comparison upon which to base an assessment of a company's competitive position any more than there is a right or wrong frame of reference when determining physical position. Instead, there is a broad range of applicable choices bounded by extremes of limited utility. A comparison between two companies that are too different is all but useless. What is the relative positioning of Toyota automobiles compared with Procter & Gamble shampoos? A car and a hair product are such weak substitutes that comparing them seems pointless. If anything, they serve such different needs that each competes with the other for discretionary spending based entirely on non-price dimensions of value: you choose a Prius to drive somewhere and Pantene to wash your hair.

Comparisons that are too close are also unlikely to yield much insight. If we insist on *perfect* substitutability along non-price dimensions, then by definition, there is no basis of competition left save price, and so there is no latitude to learn anything about non-price differentiation.

Despite their differences, then, comparing Four Seasons and Motel 6 can reveal much about the almost certainly very different operational choices they make in their efforts to provide superior levels of non-price and price value, respectively. We can learn something else quite useful by understanding how Four Seasons and Ritz-Carlton compete with each other. Their much closer positions in price/non-price space reveal the finer-grained trade-offs that each makes among those dimensions of value that allow differentiation within a more narrowly defined segment. In each case, we must be careful to interpret what we learn entirely within the context of the comparison we are making.

Position and Performance

There is no logically necessary relationship between any particular competitive position and exceptional performance. There are compelling arguments in favor of both price-based and non-price-based competition, and academic research on this question has yielded mixed results.[6] In our attempt to understand the relationship between position and performance we assessed the position of each company in our trios compared with each of the other two. Our assessments are based, insofar as possible, on objective data. When we claim that one company competes on price compared with another, we typically have evidence of lower prices for products or services that constitute the bulk of that company's sales. Claims of a non-price position are supported by evidence of superior non-price value on dimensions relevant to the appropriate product markets and customer segments.

Keep in mind that position can be assessed only relative to a specific alternative. If we had examined duos in each industry we would have had no choice but to have named one company the non-price competitor and the other the price-based competitor.[7] With three companies, one of them can be "in the middle."[8] Also, with three companies, not every company need occupy a different position: two companies can be different from a third company in the same way, and hence occupy the same competitive position even if they are not, strictly speaking, identical. For example, a Long Runner

TABLE 5: **Competitive Positions Within Trios**

Industry	Non-Price	In the Middle	Price
Semiconductors	Linear[MW-F]	Micropac[LR-K]	International Rectifier[AJ]
Medical Devices	Medtronic[MW-F]	Stryker[LR-K]	Invacare[AJ]
Electrical Wiring	Thomas & Betts[MW-L]	Hubbell[LR-L]	Emrise[AJ]
Clothing	Abercrombie & Fitch[MW-K]	Finish Line[LR-K]	Syms[AJ]
Confectionary	RMCF[AJ]	Wrigley[MW-F]	Tootsie Roll[LR-K]
Groceries	Whole Foods Markets[AJ]	Publix Super Markets[LR-F]	Weis Markets[MW-L]
Pharmaceuticals	Merck[MW-OTH] Eli Lilly[LR-K]		KV Pharmaceutical[AJ]
Trucking	Heartland[MW-K]		Werner[LR-L] PAM[AJ]
Appliances	Maytag[MW-L] HMI Industries[LR-L]		Whirlpool[AJ]

Source: Authors' analysis

Performance category: MW = Miracle Worker; LR = Long Runner; AJ = Average Joe.
Performance trajectory: K = Kept It; F = Found It; L = Lost It; OTH = Other.

and an Average Joe could both be price-based competitors compared with the non-price-positioned Miracle Worker, with the remaining differences between them deemed immaterial.

Finally, measuring competitive position is not like measuring height or weight, and so the position we give to any particular company is not beyond dispute. In the course of this and the next two chapters we will explain at length why we believe table 5 captures accurately the competitive positions of the companies in our trios. For now, we ask that you take these claims at face value, knowing that you will have a chance to assess them as our argument unfolds.

Based on these categorizations, differences in performance appear to be strongly related to differences in position: we can be more than 90 percent sure that companies from different performance categories will have different competitive positions (see Appendix G, "The Statistical Analysis of Small Samples"). Furthermore, and far more important, we found that companies with non-price positions tended to be Miracle Workers, that companies with in-the-middle positions tended to be Long Runners, and companies with price-based positions tended to be Average Joes.

The significance of the rows captures the likelihood of a relationship between category and position; that is, there is a 97.5 percent chance that the Miracle Workers in our sample are not randomly distributed across the three position types and instead tend to have non-price positions.

The significance of the columns captures the likelihood of a relationship between position and category; that is, there is a 94.1 percent chance that the companies with price-based positions in our sample are not randomly distributed across the three performance categories and instead tend to be Average Joes.

Recall that we have four possible trajectories (Kept It, Lost It, Found It, Other) for each of our two categories of exceptional performance (Miracle Worker, Long Runner). This allows us to characterize each company's

TABLE 6: **Which Positions Tend to Perform Better?**

Category	Price	In the Middle	Non-Price	Likelihood of a Relationship Between Category and Position
Miracle Worker	Weis Markets	Wrigley	Abercrombie & Fitch Heartland Linear Technology Maytag Medtronic Merck Thomas & Betts	97.5%
Long Runner	Tootsie Roll Werner	Hubbell Finish Line Micropac Publix Super Markets Stryker	Eli Lilly HMI Industries	56.5%
Average Joe	Emrise KV Pharmaceuticals International Rectifier Invacare PAM Syms Whirlpool	Rocky Mountain Chocolate Factory Whole Foods Markets		97.5%
Likelihood of a Relationship Between Position and Category	94.1%	94.7%	88.4%	

position during its periods of higher and lower relative performance. For example, Maytag is a Lost It Miracle Worker. Its period of higher relative performance was from 1966 to 1989, during which time it had a non-price position. During this period, its absolute ROA fell steadily. It began to shift its position toward the price-value end of the spectrum in the early 1980s, and by the time its period of higher relative performance ended it had become largely a price-based competitor, a position it held throughout its period of lower relative performance from 1990 to 2005. This is a pattern among Lost It exceptional companies: shifting away from a non-price position appears to be a key cause of a fall in relative performance. In contrast, Found It exceptional companies, especially Miracle Workers, typically break through into a period of higher relative performance as a consequence of shifting toward a non-price position.

The figure below summarizes the regression analysis detailed in Appendix H, "Changes in Position and Changes in Performance." The vertical axis captures any change in a company's position over time: does it shift either toward a more price-based position, toward a more non-price-based position, or is there no change relative to the other companies in its trio? From chapter 1, recall that Heartland did not change its position over time while Maytag did, shifting toward price-based competition. The horizontal axis is our dependent variable, relative performance, and captures a company's trajectory: Lost It companies suffer a decrease in performance, Kept It companies have no material change, and Found It companies enjoy an increase in performance.

	Lost It	Kept It	Found It
Toward non-price based differentiation			Linear Technology (MW) Stryker (LR)* Publix Super Markets (LR)*
No change	Weis Markets (MW) Hubbell (LR) Werner Enterprises (LR)	Abercrombie & Fitch (MW) Merck & Co. (MW)** Heartland Express (MW) Micropac Industries (LR) Finish Line (LR) Tootsie Roll Industries (LR) Eli Lilly & Co. (LR)	Wrigley (MW) Medtronic (MW)
Toward price based differentiation	Thomas & Betts (MW) Maytag (MW) HMI (LR)		

Change in Position (vertical axis)

Performance Trajectory (horizontal axis)

KEY:
MW = Miracle Worker, LR = Long Runner; K = Kept It, F= Found It, L=Lost It, OTH=Other

*Publix and Stryker just miss our formal thresholds for upward shifts in performance, but their qualitative results suggest strongly that they might be Found It Miracle Workers. Stryker is discussed in this chapter, Publix in chapter 4. Appendix H provides regression results with Publix Super Markets and Stryker as Found It and Kept It.

**Although Merck's trajectory is Other it is treated here as Kept It. See chapter 5 for details.
Source: Authors' analysis

FIGURE 1: **Changes in Position and Changes in Performance**

What this means is that:

1. Position matters.

    a. Differences in position are associated with differences in performance.

2. Non-price positions tend to be more profitable.

    a. Companies with non-price positions are the likeliest to be Miracle Workers.

    b. Companies with in-the-middle positions are the likeliest to be Long Runners.

    c. Companies with price positions are the likeliest to be Average Joes.

3. The most profitable companies tend to have non-price positions.

    a. Miracle Workers are the likeliest to have non-price positions.

    b. Long Runners are no more likely to have one type of position than another.

    c. Average Joes are the likeliest to have price positions.

4. Changes in position are associated with changes in performance.

    a. Shifting toward a price-based position is associated with a decline in performance.

    b. Shifting toward a non-price position is associated with an increase in performance.

We find the connection between position and performance in our data highly suggestive, especially since there is good reason to think that position contributes in a material way to performance. But we need still more evidence before we can conclude that it is position that causes performance and not vice versa. That means digging deep into the specifics of each case. If there is a consistent, plausible, and compelling narrative connecting position and performance in ways that explain performance outcomes, then causal claims have a whole new level of credibility.[9] In the course of this book we will recount all of our relevant case evidence. For now, we will double-click on three trios that illustrate the position-performance relationship especially clearly: semiconductors, medical devices, and electrical wiring.

If your position is:		Then you are most likely to be a:
Non-price	$\Longrightarrow$	Miracle Worker
In the middle	$\Longrightarrow$	Long Runner
Price	$\Longrightarrow$	Average Joe

The Bottom Line: Better Before Cheaper

As we attempted to sort out how position contributed to performance, we were forced to tackle what has long seemed an intractable question in the science and practice of management; namely, how do position, execution, and industry interact to determine company performance? We found that the connections among the three can be captured using the metaphor of a roller coaster.

On a roller coaster, the goal is to go fast, and how fast you go is a function largely of two factors: how high you climb and how efficiently you ride down the other side. The higher you climb the more potential energy you are storing up. You turn that potential energy into kinetic energy by screaming (actually and metaphorically) down the other side. Not all the potential energy created by the climb is converted to kinetic energy on the way down, however. Some of that energy is necessarily lost to friction, and if your ride is poorly designed, this can materially detract from the thrill of the plunge.

Competitive position is the height of the climb. Execution is what allows you to turn potential energy into kinetic energy by riding down the other side. Both the height of the climb and the efficiency of the ride down are indispensable to the overall experience. A big climb with no descent is essentially worthless, and a train that stutters down the other side is arguably not much better. The smoothest car in the world cannot make up for a puny drop. Similarly, you cannot compensate for a poor position with great execution while poor execution can compromise even the most promising position.

In short, position determines how fast you *can* go; execution determines how fast you *actually* go.

But wait: whenever you talk about motion, you must specify your frame of reference. When you crest in the roller coaster do you then rush toward the ground or does the ground rush toward you? Changing the frame of reference can turn a rapid descent into complete motionlessness.

Industry is the frame of reference for the potential and kinetic energy. As an industry's structure changes—new technologies, new regulations, new entrants, and so on—exceptional companies understand that all performance (or motion, in the roller-coaster metaphor) is relative, and so they adapt in ways that preserve their ability to store potential and release kinetic energy.

Average companies, and exceptional companies that lose their way, seem to forget that the key is relative position within an industry and instead begin matching their behavior to industry-level forces. If an industry is consolidating, they go on an acquisitions binge; if an industry is suffering a downturn, they begin cutting cost and price; if an industry is expanding, they invest and grow. That all seems reasonable, but it amounts to moving in the same direction and with the same velocity as the frame of reference itself—in other words, it amounts to standing still. Exceptional performance is built on being different, and making choices dominated by industry-level considerations makes you average.

Position: Potential Energy

For perhaps a decade—from the mid-1990s to the mid-2000s, when the personal computer was making the crossover from fancy new gadget to mainstream consumer electronics device—the semiconductor was a topic of everyday conversation. Thanks to Intel's success, prominence, and marketing savvy, many of us had at least a cocktail-party level of familiarity with terms such as "clock speed" and "x86 architecture."

There is much more to the chip business, however, than Intel and the personal computer. Semiconductors come in a wide variety of flavors and are an integral part of countless devices of all kinds. The chips in our personal computers and smart phones are digital logic integrated circuits, similar to the products made by Micropac Industries (Micropac), the Long Runner (Kept It) in our semiconductor trio. International Rectifier (IR), the Average Joe, focused on discrete semiconductors while Linear Technology (Linear), our Miracle Worker (Found It), concentrated on high-performance analog integrated circuits.[10] Competition in the industry is keenest within each segment, but technological advances have increased substitutability across these boundaries.

As of 2010, Linear and IR were both billion-dollar companies with thousands of employees. Micropac generated less than $50 million in annual revenue with fewer than two hundred employees. From their respective initial public offerings (IPOs) until 2010, Linear multiplied its equity value sixty-two-fold, IR sixteen-fold, and Micropac tenfold. Our belief is these differences in size, shareholder returns, and of course profitability are the consequences of a relatively small number of critical choices that defined each company's competitive position.

Micropac was founded in 1963 and entered our database in 1974. Based in Garland, Texas, the company has an enviable thirty-five-year history of gradually increasing ROA and steady relative performance. This track record is all the more impressive in light of the company's small size. The companies that dominate the digital logic semiconductor segment are the titans of the industry: Intel, AMD, Cyrix, and others— companies with tens of billions in revenue, and capital expenditure (capex) and research and development (R&D) budgets to match.

TABLE 7: **Descriptive Statistics for the Semiconductor Trio**

Company	Category (Trajectory)	Year Founded	Observation Period	Revenue Growth	Average Annual ROA	Compounded Annual TSR	Compounded Annual Revenue Growth
Linear Technology	Miracle Worker (Found It)	1981	1985 to 2010	$17MM to $1.2BN	16.9%	20.0%	18.4%
Micropac Industries	Long Runner (Kept It)	1963	1974 to 2010	$4MM to $23MM	6.8%	10.2%	5.2%
International Rectifier	Average Joe (N/A)	1947	1966 to 2010	$29MM to $895MM	1.5%	5.6%	8.1%

Source: Company documents; Compustat; Deloitte analysis

Carving out a niche in this segment seems to have been a key to Micropac's success. Specifically, the company focused on relatively low-volume, fixed-price contracts with the U.S. Department of Defense (DoD). Many of these contracts required military certifications, which restricted the uses to which equipment and design expertise could be put. Consequently, taking on government contracts was not only technically challenging, it also imposed a very real growth trade-off: the volumes were low, and the investments made to secure those limited volumes had limited applicability beyond the government business that justified them.

It was by embracing the implications of these trade-offs, however, that Micropac was able to translate constraints into a source of superior profitability. By focusing its investments on only those technologies required by its chosen customer segment, Micropac was able to keep its capex at 5 to 8 percent of revenue, below the industry average of 6 to 12 percent, and its R&D spend at 5 to 10 percentage points of sales below the industry average of 10 to 14 percent, without sacrificing the performance of its products. These joint R&D projects with customers coupled with the careful husbandry of its facilities combined to give Micropac a level of asset turnover that was materially better than that of both Linear and IR.

In short, Micropac appears to have been a well-run and highly focused company.[11] It managed to walk a tightrope strung between the need to deliver cutting-edge technology and the discipline required to remain consistently profitable on fixed-price contracts. The company's ability to execute consistently well over decades warrants not merely respect but also admiration.

What makes these choices genuine trade-offs, however, is that Micropac was unable to escape the downside. Focusing on the U.S. military made it difficult for the company to grow internationally due to security issues associated with technology transfer: barely 10 percent of the company's revenue came from customers located outside the United States. In addition, because so much of the company's profitability turned on focusing its investment and product development on its primary customers, there was very little slack that might have served as the foundation for diversifying into other markets or product segments of the industry. Consequently, Micropac's success with fixed-price contracts led to increased reliance on fixed-price contracts, which accounted for upwards of two thirds of the company's revenue.

Contrast Micropac's gilded cage with the growth and steadily increasing profitability of Linear, our Miracle Worker. Founded in 1981 and going public in 1985, Linear got its start as a second-source supplier of analog semiconductors focusing on the more standardized products, such as voltage regulators. With half its sales coming from the U.S. government and another third from the industrial and automotive sector, Linear in many ways looked very much like Micropac: a well-run and profitable niche player. These similarities were reflected in their similar relative performance, as both companies landed in the 5th to 8th deciles in the latter half of the 1980s.

By the early 1990s, however, it was clear that the two companies were on radically different growth and profitability trajectories. Linear's ROA was routinely in the double digits, and for several years was over 20 percent while Micropac continued to deliver steady, if relatively pedestrian performance in the high single digits. Relative rankings reveal the significance of these shifts: from 1991 through 2010 Linear delivered an effectively unbroken string of 9th-decile ranks while Micropac was still churning out annual ranks of 6 through 8. Linear had "found it"—namely, its particular recipe for exceptional performance.

So what changed? First, note that Linear did not pull away from Micropac because of any failings on Micropac's part: it is one of the few Kept It Long Runners in our sample. Rather, Linear materially improved its performance by fundamentally changing its position and competing more on non-price dimensions of value. In contrast, Micropac remained both victim and beneficiary of the constraints that defined its position closer to the price-value end of the continuum.

Specifically, Linear reinvested its profits from early success as a second-source supplier into capex and R&D, deliberately diversifying its customer base and product portfolio. The shift was gradual, but steady and unrelenting: by 2006 over 70 percent of revenues came from outside the United States, and government sales were less than 3 percent of total revenue. Although no single customer accounted for more than 10 percent of sales, Linear was focused on high-performance, mission-critical integrated circuits that typically were not a high proportion of its customers' total cost. This combination of attributes allowed Linear to charge relatively higher prices and so capture much of the value it created.

For example, a representative Linear customer sold high-performance mobile data scanners for thousands of dollars. Linear's chips improved battery life, a key differentiator for this product, yet one that accounted for less than 5 percent of the total materials cost for each scanner. Consequently, this customer typically looked elsewhere to ensure the cost competitiveness of its products, which allowed Linear significant pricing power. In addition, with a highly diversified customer base, if this or pretty much any other customer became especially price sensitive, Linear was less compelled to accede to pricing pressures than, say, Micropac, which had a much more concentrated customer base. Generalized across its portfolio of more than fifteen thousand customers, Linear was consistently in a position to capture a greater proportion of the value it created through higher prices than most other competitors in the industry.

We can see the financial impact of these choices in the structure of Linear's performance advantage over Micropac across the two streaks of relative performance. Linear's streak of lower relative performance ran from 1986 to 1991. Linear averaged 5.8 pp per year ahead of Micropac on ROA, an advantage that is driven entirely by its return on sales (ROS) advantage. This in turn is driven by a gross margin lead of more than 18 pp per year, which is eroded by an SG&A disadvantage, higher relative taxes (a consequence of being more profitable), and current and fixed asset turnover disadvantages.

Linear's subsequent streak of higher performance, from 1992 to 2010, has a similar complexion but generates much larger performance differences and earns the company its Miracle Worker status. The company generated a gross margin advantage over Micropac of more than 25 pp per year, offset by disadvantages in R&D, depreciation, taxes, and current and fixed asset turnover. This shift in performance is entirely coincident with Linear's having established its non-price position.

TABLE 8: **Linear's Elements of Advantage Versus Micropac**

Elements of ROA	Contribution to ROA Advantage in Percentage Points per Year	
	Period of Lower Performance: 1986–1991	Period of Higher Performance: 1992–2010
Gross Margin	20.2	25.7
SG&A	–9.0	2.8
R&D	0.0	–5.2
Other (incl. taxes)	–2.5	–7.1
ROS	8.7	16.2
CAT	–2.3	–4.2
FAT	–0.5	–0.9
Other	–0.0	–0.2
TAT	–2.9	–5.3
ROA	5.8	11.0

Source: Compustat; Deloitte analysis
Figures may not total due to rounding.

It is worth underlining that by 2010 Linear had more than fifty times Micropac's revenue yet suffered from a fixed asset turnover disadvantage—the opposite of what one might expect, since thanks to economies of scale, asset turnover often increases with revenue growth. That Linear's R&D expenses were a relative drag on profitability compared with Micropac is perhaps also surprising, since economies of scale could have had an impact there, too: at more than $1 billion in revenue, why would Linear need to spend a higher percentage of revenue on R&D when its absolute spend would be so much higher even at lower relative levels?

The answer seems to be that Linear and Micropac were making precisely the trade-offs required by their very different competitive positions. With its lean asset base and highly focused R&D, Micropac kept its costs low and asset turnover high despite its relatively low revenue. Linear spent aggressively on intellectual and real assets because that was how it created products with the non-price value required to command the price premiums that translated into superior and sustained profitability.

The lesson we take away from this analysis is that there are limits to how far great execution can take you. Micropac rarely set a foot wrong, coping with the ups and downs of defense and space program budgets, the challenges of fixed-price contracts, and the exigencies of the quality and security demands of a small number of customers on whom it was highly dependent. Its success is a testament to its ability to perform a complex set of activities consistently and well.

But however effective Micropac might have been in rising to the challenges it faced, the company's performance was limited by its competitive position. Forced to compete on price to a larger extent than Linear, Micropac had little choice but to drive profitability through smart cost containment and judicious investment. That its performance fell short of Miracle Worker status is no indictment of Micropac as a company, but instead is an inherent limitation of its position.

To return to our roller-coaster metaphor, Micropac delivered among the smoothest of rides, making the most out of its climb. But Linear found a way to climb higher still. In its early days as a second-source supplier, Linear was dependent on a small number of customers, and so it had to rely on execution to drive profitability. Over time, Linear crafted a non-price position that held much more potential energy, and when it crested that climb, it was able to translate that potential into kinetic energy through consistently strong execution. The result was seventeen of nineteen years in the 9th decile and a twenty-six-year history of exceptional performance.

International Rectifier, the Average Joe of the trio, sheds additional light on the relationship between position and execution and reveals the dangers of responding to industry forces at the expense of both.

Founded in 1947 and public since 1958, IR is the longest-lived of the trio, and that longevity warrants its own form of respect. The semiconductor industry can change rapidly and dramatically, and simply staying alive for more than sixty years is a noteworthy achievement.[12] Like so many American companies of its time, through the 1970s IR built up a diversified portfolio of operating businesses, including not only semiconductors but also pharmaceuticals, metallurgical technology, and medical devices. By the mid-1980s the company had focused entirely on semiconductors, thanks largely to its proprietary MOSFET technology, a transistor in both analog and digital circuits.

It is worth underlining that even though it is the Average Joe of the trio, it was not necessarily a follow-the-leader, price-based competitor. In addition to leading-edge technology, IR astutely followed the diversification of the industry beyond government applications in the military and space programs into a wide variety of consumer and industrial applications. This, too, merits mention: how many companies that find early success in an evolving industry fail to change with the times and get left behind? In other words, IR was clearly able to innovate in an industry that demanded innovation, and to change dramatically in an industry that demanded dramatic change.

How, then, do we explain IR's entirely unremarkable performance? We will meet other AJs in our sample that were foiled by bad luck or avoidably poor choices. In contrast, IR provides a compelling example of attending to all the right issues, in largely the right way, yet failing to stand out.

Take R&D, for example. IR was hardly ignorant of the importance of R&D in semiconductors, but sought to find a way to reduce expenditures without sacrificing its competitiveness. To that end, it funded its R&D jointly with its customers. This allowed the company to remain a viable competitor with an R&D spend that was less than half Linear's relative spend: 4 percent of sales compared with 9 percent. However, by collaborating with customers in this way, IR was unable to command the sort of price premium that Linear could through extreme non-price value or that Micropac could through extreme customer focus.

International Rectifier's treatment of licensing was similarly reasonable, but ultimately counterproductive. The company's MOSFET breakthrough was marketed under the HEXFET trademark. The design proved so popular that IR was capacity constrained, and so licensed the technology to other manufacturers. This might have been a good stopgap measure, but IR—perhaps attracted by the seemingly high ROA associated with licensing revenue—made licensing a central part of its strategy. By the mid-1990s, 75 percent of the market was using its patents. This might have looked good on a stand-alone basis, but by licensing its key differentiating technology so extensively, IR proved unable to generate the profits (in absolute dollars) required to reinvest in its own capabilities. This eventually saw IR competing in product markets against its own technology, which left little latitude for non-price differentiation.

Recognizing the benefits of competing on non-price value, IR attempted to shift from discrete to analog semiconductors, where it was perhaps possible to carve out a more profitable niche. Differences in the necessary design and fabrication capabilities meant that IR had to shed many of its legacy assets while simultaneously acquiring new ones. The result was a string of eight major acquisitions between 2000 and 2004 that drove a 70 percent increase in its asset base and resulted in more than $400 million in restructuring charges.

International Rectifier's history suggests that it remained well attuned to its economic and industrial context. The company shed its nonsemiconductor businesses in the 1970s, in keeping with an economy-wide trend of declining diversification. Then, faced with price pressure in its legacy segment and a consolidating industry, IR sought out segments with opportunities for non-price differentiation and bulked up both to build capabilities and capture economies of scale.

So why did it not work? It is tempting to attribute Linear's and Micropac's superior performances to those old chestnuts of focus and organic growth. After all, there is a long tradition of research that has been distilled into folk wisdom: great companies stick to their knitting and avoid doing deals. Certainly the histories of the companies in this trio could be interpreted that way: Linear made not a single acquisition, and Micropac's focus makes a laser beam look like a flashlight.

But as we explained in chapter 1, some Miracle Workers have been active acquirers and had relatively diverse product portfolios while some Average Joes have been relatively focused. Even in the case of IR, the direct economic impact of its various gyrations was not as dramatic as you might think. For example, IR's restructuring charges accounted for less than 5 percent of Linear's performance advantage over IR, and the acquisitions, while sizable, gave rise to no obvious horror stories of gross overpayment.

Far more important, in our view, was that IR's movements seemed attuned to the dictates of industry structure and the need to "keep up." Success, however, is relative, and keeping up is not a recipe for getting ahead. In other words, a key to success is not focus versus diversification or organic versus acquisition-driven growth. Rather, the key is to build a non-price-based position via whatever means necessary.

> Linear had always been a well-run company, but it became a Miracle Worker only by moving into segments where it could differentiate itself on non-price value. Micropac's effective cost management earned it no better than Long Runner standing because of inherent limitations in its competitive position.

Note that both Linear and Micropac had superior ROS and TAT compared with IR, but that the composition of these advantages differs dramatically. Where Linear enjoyed an advantage in several drivers of both ROS and TAT, Micropac has a gross margin disadvantage that is then compensated for by advantages everywhere else. This signals the very different ways in which Linear and Micropac realized the value of their respective positions. Linear enjoyed higher prices and lower costs at higher relative volumes than IR, resulting in an across-the-board advantage. In short, Linear broke the trade-offs that constrained IR, able to deliver higher levels of non-price value and capture value through higher prices and greater asset efficiency through higher relative volumes.

Micropac, on the other hand, while still competing based on a non-price position relative to IR, did not capture value through higher prices. Rather, it relied on its focus on a single segment and a limited number of customers within that segment to keep indirect costs (such as SG&A and R&D) and asset base lower.

It bears repeating: average performance is not so bad. International

TABLE 9: **Linear's and Micropac's Elements of Advantage Versus IR**

Elements of ROA	Contribution to ROA Advantage in Percentage Points per Year	
	Linear Vs. IR	**Micropac Vs. IR**
	Period of Higher Performance: 1992–2010	**Period of Higher Performance: 1975–2010**
Gross Margin	19.9	−6.2
SG&A	3.8	5.1
R&D	−2.6	1.6
Other (incl. taxes)	−3.3	2.5
ROS	17.7	3.0
CAT	−1.2	0.7
FAT	0.8	1.8
Other	0.9	0.9
TAT	0.5	3.4
ROA	**18.3**	**6.3**

Source: Compustat; Deloitte analysis
Figures may not total due to rounding.

Rectifier should not be viewed as a "poor performer." Rather, it bobbed and weaved in response to a demanding and changing industry in ways that kept the company profitable and growing . . . but unremarkably so. In other words, its climb was nothing special and so there was little potential energy. We attribute this to having forgone the benefits of proprietary designs through joint R&D and extensive licensing, both of which made a better before cheaper position very difficult (IR has a price-based position compared with Micropac and Linear). Furthermore, much of IR's kinetic energy was dissipated as friction generated by changing industry segments and extensive M&A activity, both of which made a revenue advantage elusive (IR has lower prices than Micropac and lower volume than Linear). The result was average performance.

Execution: Kinetic Energy

Linear reveals the necessity of having a strong position in order to realize the benefits of strong execution. Our next trio, taken from the medical devices industry, shows how equally indispensable strong execution is to realizing the benefits of a strong position.

Founded in 1949 by Earl Bakken and his brother-in-law Palmer Hermundslie, and still headquartered in Minneapolis, Medtronic has long been a pioneer in the field of medical devices.[13] Starting out as a repair facility, the company began to take its modern form in 1960 with the introduction of an external cardiac pacemaker. Although still a leader in this field, the company has diversified significantly, but always within health care and devices, and always maintaining its emphasis on basic research and highly differentiated products: between 1969 and 1998 Medtronic was awarded more patents in medical devices than any other company in the world. Since the late 1960s, Medtronic has recognized the importance of close relationships between its engineers and leading medical schools, and has long invested in providing training and instruction to physicians, not just in Medtronic products, but in leading surgical techniques. A Found It Miracle Worker, Medtronic maintains a position as a non-price-based competitor that is about as unambiguous as it gets.

The Long Runner in this trio is Stryker, named by and for its founder, Dr. Homer Stryker, who, in 1941, got into the medical devices business to address more effectively the unmet needs he experienced as a doctor. Based in Kalamazoo, Michigan, Stryker has an emphasis on innovation comparable to Medtronic's. For example, between 1960 and 1999 there were approximately nineteen major new product introductions by Medtronic but

TABLE 10: **Descriptive Statistics for the Medical Devices Trio**

Company	Category (Trajectory)	Year Founded	Observation Period	Revenue Growth	Average Annual ROA	Compounded Annual TSR	Compounded Annual Revenue Growth
Medtronic	Miracle Worker [Found It]	1949	1966 to 2010	$5MM to $16BN	12.6%	14.4%	20.1%
Stryker	Long Runner [Kept It]	1941	1978 to 2010	$26MM to $7.3BN	12.0%	23.0%	19.3%
Invacare	Average Joe (N/A)	1971	1983 to 2010	$70MM to $1.7BN	3.2%	13.9%	12.6%

Source: Company documents; Compustat; Deloitte analysis

twenty-three by Stryker.[14] What separates the two is the level of sophistication and differentiation of their respective products. Where Medtronic was a pioneer in cardiac pacemakers—products of extraordinary and very nearly unique complexity—Stryker concentrated on relatively low-tech products such as mobile hospital beds and cast cutters, where clever design and close attention to the minutiae of daily use made the difference.

Competing on some dimensions of non-price value, but forced to be more price conscious than Medtronic, Stryker has an in-the-middle position when compared with the trio's Average Joe, Invacare. Based in Elyria, Ohio, Invacare entered our database in 1983. Although its product portfolio has expanded considerably over the years, it has consistently focused on nonacute care products such as wheelchairs, power scooters, and walkers.

Recall that in semiconductors, Linear broke through to Miracle Worker performance level as a consequence of establishing a sufficiently distinct non-price position. Like Linear, Medtronic has not always delivered the kind of profitability that leads to Miracle Worker status. We have data on the company from the start of our observation period in 1966, but it was not until 1986 that Medtronic delivered its first 9th-decile year, a level of relative profitability it maintained for all but seven of the subsequent twenty-four years through 2010.[15]

Unlike with Linear, however, it was not a change in position that drove the improvement in relative performance. Medtronic very clearly had established a non-price position very early in its history and never lost that focus. Stryker was just as clearly a more price-based competitor, especially through the mid-1980s, prior to Medtronic's breaking into the 9th decile. Yet when we compare Medtronic and Stryker during this initial period of overlap, from 1978 to 1985, it is Stryker that has superior performance, with an average decile rank of 7.9 versus 5.1, and an ROA that was on average 1.4 pp/year better. In other words, our in-the-middle competitor was doing better than our non-price-based one.

The causes of Medtronic's unfulfilled promise can be seen most clearly by looking for changes in behavior across the company's two streaks of relative performance, 1978 to 1985 (lower relative performance) and 1986 to 2010 (higher relative performance). Compared with Stryker, Medtronic improved its performance by 3.4 pp/year, moving from an annual deficit to a lead of 2.0 pp/year.

The structure of Medtronic's performance difference is especially telling. During its lower relative performance streak Medtronic suffered a 16.5 pp/year deficit because of across-the-board higher relative indirect costs (SG&A, R&D, other) and a relatively higher asset base (current, fixed, other). During the streak of higher relative performance this deficit is

TABLE 11: **Medtronic's Elements of Advantage Versus Stryker**

Elements of ROA	Contribution to ROA Advantage in Percentage Points per Year	
	Period of Lower Performance: 1978–1985	Period of Higher Performance: 1986–2010
Gross Margin	15.1	11.8
SG&A	−5.8	0.5
R&D	−4.7	−3.1
Other (incl. taxes)	−0.4	−4.2
ROS	4.2	4.9
CAT	−3.1	0.2
FAT	−1.6	−0.4
Other	−0.8	−2.7
TAT	−5.5	−2.9
ROA	**−1.4**	**2.0**

Source: Compustat; Deloitte analysis
Figures may not total due to rounding.

10.7 pp/year. Consequently, even though Medtronic's gross margin lead falls from 15.1 pp/year to 11.8 pp/year, it pulls ahead on ROA because its costs and assets are falling faster.

What did Medtronic do differently? Nothing about its relative position changed; rather, it got dramatically better at capturing the benefits of its position. For starters, the company improved product quality, avoiding expensive and reputation-damaging recalls, such as its Xytron pacemaker in 1975 and the 6972 pacemaker lead in 1984. This latter event was a major contributor to losing 3 percentage points of market share in a single year. In addition, reduced sales and increased expenses attributable to this recall depressed ROA by approximately 6.4 pp that year alone, which was 59 percent of Medtronic's entire performance deficit for its period of lower relative performance.

Changes to the company's R&D processes dramatically improved productivity. New product development cycle times fell from four years to approximately eighteen months, and the company earned 1,388 patents between 1991 and 2000, compared with 371 between 1979 and 1990. During this time, Medtronic's relative R&D spending compared with Stryker's was essentially unchanged.

Cross-functional teams generated new breakthrough ideas. The Activitrex, introduced in 1986, stimulated the heart in response to the patient's activity level. A single-chambered device in a dual-chambered world, the Activitrex was more reliable and less costly to make. As a result, it could be sold at lower prices than competing devices (without having to compete on price) yet generated superior margins. This one product boosted Medtronic's global market share in pacemakers from 30 percent to 40 percent by 1988.

The creation of common product platforms reduced costs and allowed Medtronic to find profitable growth in adjacent markets. The Thera and Thera-i pacemaker lines, introduced in 1995, generated more than forty derivative product lines, driving market share to 50 percent by the mid-1990s. Each new product targeted specific segments ever more precisely—a key attribute of competing on non-price value. Yet development and manufacturing costs were lower than would have been required if the company had been developing bespoke products from scratch each time.

None of this should be mistaken for counterevidence to our claim that what matters is *better before cheaper*. Medtronic still maintained an overall non-price position versus Stryker. In fact, these efficiency improvements enabled, rather than detracted from, Medtronic's ability to develop new leading-edge products such as the Kappa 400 and Kappa 700 series, introduced in 1996 and 1999 respectively, which commanded $300/unit price premiums in the market. In terms of our roller-coaster analogy, Medtronic kept climbing just as high, but it had stopped losing so much kinetic energy to friction.

For all the significance of Medtronic's changes, there is a second act to Stryker's story that also illustrates the importance of position. Although Stryker's relative performance is statistically a steady stream of 6th-to-8th-decile ranks—hence its Kept It trajectory—there are two distinct periods in absolute performance: 1978 to 1997 and 1998 to 2010. The break point is marked by the company's acquisition of Howmedica in 1998 for $1.6 billion, a deal that almost doubled Stryker's revenue and completed the company's years-long transition from a relatively low-tech maker of less differentiated products into a high-tech implantable medical device player.

Our statistical analysis points us in particular directions that both suggest and lend credence to commonsense interpretations of the narrative surrounding the numbers. On its own, there is a defensible hypothesis that a dip in ROA in 1998 was the short-run accounting consequence of an acquisition, a short-run spike in goodwill, but our algorithms are reasonably resistant to such aberrations.

Note instead a nascent but highly suggestive shift in Stryker's relative performance that follows the acquisitions: seven 9th-decile ranks in the thirteen years from 1998 to 2010, compared with none from 1978 to 1997. This recent run has not been enough to raise the company's lifetime performance level above the thresholds established for Long Runners, but it would be willful blindness to ignore those results. Stryker seems to have raised its game during this period.

The qualitative record supports this hypothesis. Prior to 1990 the company had 48 patents to its name, to which it added 278 more by 2000. By 1996, orthopedic implants were 38 percent of Stryker's revenue thanks to a string of a dozen small acquisitions, none exceeding 3 percent of Stryker's preacquisition revenue, including Osteonics (1978), Advanced Biomedical (1981), and Hexcel Medical (1987). Each of these allowed Stryker to test the waters and determine if it had the wherewithal to execute successfully what was to become a profound change in competitive position. The Howmedica deal signaled Stryker's commitment to the transformation, and by 2000 implantables were 58 percent of the company's revenue. By 2006 the company had made six more acquisitions of high-tech device companies, each one bigger than any of the deals struck prior to 1998.

The impact of this shift in position on Stryker's performance can be seen in the structure of Medtronic's performance advantage. During Medtronic's streak of lower relative performance (1978–1985) it enjoyed a gross margin advantage over Stryker of 15.1 pp/year of ROA, but gave it all back and then some thanks to weak execution. During its period of higher relative performance (1986–2010), the contribution of gross margin to Medtronic's ROA advantage over Stryker fell to 11.8 pp/year even though Medtronic's gross margin steadily improved from under 70 percent to over 80 percent. The reason? Stryker's gross margin was improving *more*, rising from the mid-50-percent range to over 70 percent.

However, Medtronic captured an overall performance lead despite a smaller gross margin advantage because it improved the other elements of its profitability formula.

Specifically, Medtronic's TAT disadvantage fell by almost half during its period of higher relative performance, from -5.5 pp/year to -2.9 pp/year. One could find this astonishing because Medtronic's asset turnover only gets *worse*, falling from about 1 to around 0.6 turns per year. The critical factor is that Stryker's asset turnover deteriorates even more, from 1.6 to about 0.8 even though Stryker's performance improves in both absolute and relative terms!

So did Stryker lose its ability to execute? There is no evidence of that. The more plausible explanation is that a different set of trade-offs was required to compete in the design and manufacture of more complex, highly differentiated medical devices. Medtronic continued to drive its non-price position. For all its efforts to be more cost effective and efficient, it still consistently chose *better before cheaper*. It is perhaps no surprise, then, that its asset turnover fell even as its execution improved. In this industry, at least, low turnover, as an empirical matter, seems to be an unavoidable consequence of competing effectively on non-price value.

Medtronic (Miracle Worker) built itself a strong non-price position but was unable to reap the full benefits until it improved its operations. Stryker (Long Runner) has long been a strong operator yet has seen signs of greatness only since a shift to a non-price position.

Stryker's shift in product portfolio—essentially from hospital beds to artificial hips—required it to accept similar trade-offs in order to compete effectively. The gradual erosion of Stryker's asset turnover tracks quite closely its transformation into a non-price-based competitor. The period of Medtronic's greatest lead in absolute ROA is from 1991 to 2001, when

Medtronic had pulled up its socks on execution but before Stryker had begun realizing the benefits of its change in position.

An inspection of the two companies' relative and absolute performance from 2001 to 2010 suggests a convergence. They are both delivering largely 9th-decile ranks while Stryker is actually outperforming Medtronic in absolute ROA by a point or two per year. Although it is too early to tell, Stryker might well be on a path to establishing a Miracle Worker performance profile—and for reasons largely attributable to adopting a non-price position. Medtronic and Stryker seem to have arrived at the same destination but via different routes: Medtronic found its position, and then improved its execution; Stryker established solid execution, and then found its way to the necessary position.

The backdrop that allows us to see still more sharply the contours of this dynamic is Invacare, our Average Joe. With one third the revenue of Stryker and one tenth that of Medtronic, Invacare's asset turnover is better than Medtronic's and on average just a hair better than Stryker's, indicating its ability to work its assets more efficiently. However, it has long operated at a significant gross margin disadvantage. Certainly the markets it competes in (wheelchairs, walkers, home care beds) tend not to lend themselves as obviously to the sort of non-price value that distinguishes Medtronic and to a lesser extent Stryker, but in a sense that is the point. When companies are unable to find material non-price value, they also seem systematically unable to find compensating efficiencies that lead to exceptional profitability.

This is not to say that Invacare was either incompetent or idle in the face of changes in its industry. To the contrary, many of its behaviors over this period are credible responses to important shifts in the structure of the health care sector. For example, increasing pressure to reduce health care costs, which began in the late 1980s and continues today, gave rise to consolidation in hospital groups and a drive to reduce the number of suppliers they dealt with. Medical device companies of all types often responded by expanding the range of products they supplied in order not to get squeezed out.

Other responses to industry trends included entering new customer segments or new geographic markets, typically outside the United States, either because they were less subject to increasing cost pressures or because they provided opportunities to increase revenue to capture economies of scale, scope, or increased asset efficiency.

Invacare entered fewer product categories and fewer market segments, but had a similar increase in geographic diversity and made a comparable number of acquisitions. The significance of these seeming differences and similarities is difficult to gauge, given the gross nature of the measures. Increasing levels of detail add little to the discussion, however, for it is not clear that there are direct causal links between these responses to industry pressures and the performance differences among the three companies. Was Medtronic's greater number of new product categories a driver of superior performance, or did that become a drag on profitability as complexity overwhelmed negotiating power with customers? Were Invacare's acquisitions, which were systematically smaller in both absolute and relative terms than Stryker's and Medtronic's, too small to make the necessary difference?

TABLE 12: **Responses to Industry Pressures, 1980–2010**

	New Product Categories	**New Market Segments**	**Rise in Non-U.S. Sales**	**Number of Acquisitions**
Medtronic (MW)	8	6	37% → 44%	32
Stryker (LR)	6	5	25% → 45%	20
Invacare (AJ)	7	4	26% → 55%	39

Source: Company documents; authors' analysis

One way in which these actions differed that does seem to make a difference in performance is the connection to creating or capturing non-price value. Medtronic remained committed to—and Stryker became committed to—differentiating itself on non-price value, sometimes via organic growth, sometimes via acquisition; sometimes in domestic markets, sometimes in international markets. In contrast, Invacare seems to have adapted to the shifts in the industry, but only insofar as required to maintain a viable price-based position. As it expanded its product scope, its asset turns fell, just as Medtronic's and Stryker's did as their scope and complexity increased. Because the company's return on sales remained flat, the company's overall ROA necessarily fell, and its relative performance fell also.

Industry: Frame of Reference

The IR and Invacare cases reinforce what has been observed in detail and repeatedly by others: there really is a "Red Queen" effect.[16] Doing merely what makes sense from the perspective of industry-level forces amounts to running simply to stand still. To get anywhere at all, one has to run at least twice as fast as that.

In the two trios reviewed in this chapter so far, Average Joes managed to "keep up" and were rewarded with consistently average performance. The third trio in this chapter, from the electrical wiring industry, demonstrates a still more nefarious implication; namely, that moving in what seems to be the right direction can actually undermine exceptional performance dramatically when it compromises a once-successful position.

We met Thomas & Betts (T&B) briefly in chapter 1. Founded in 1898, public since 1962, and headquartered in Memphis, T&B is the lone Miracle Worker in its industry. Hubbell is one of three Long Runners and Emrise is one of ten Average Joes.

What makes this trio so instructive is that both exceptional companies

TABLE 13: **Descriptive Statistics for the Electrical Wiring Trio**

Company	Category (Trajectory)	Year Founded	Observation Period	Revenue Growth	Average Annual ROA	Compounded Annual TSR	Compounded Annual Revenue Growth
Thomas & Betts	Miracle Worker (Lost It)	1898	1966 to 2010	$49MM to $2BN	9.8%	8.9%	8.8%
Hubbell	Long Runner (Lost It)	1888	1966 to 2010	$41MM to $2.5BN	11.0%	13.3%	9.8%
Emrise	Average Joe (N/A)	1983	1986 to 2010	$11MM to $31MM	-8.9%	-19.9%	7.7%

Source: Company documents; Compustat; Deloitte analysis

have Lost It trajectories, but our Miracle Worker's decline sets in much sooner (1985 versus 2001), is far more dramatic (T&B has lower ROA than Hubbell from 1982 to 2009), and is far more destructive of overall profitability (a drop in ROA from 20 percent to -5 percent versus a drop from 12 percent to 8 percent), thanks largely to T&B's inability to maintain its once highly profitable non-price position in the face of industry-level change. Although Hubbell's in-the-middle position denied it Miracle Worker status, it was able to maintain superior absolute and relative performance compared with T&B from 1985 on by avoiding T&B's long slide into price-based competition.

At the beginning of our observation period in 1966, T&B enjoyed remarkable profitability. The market for electrical wiring supplies had been growing rapidly thanks to increases in both the intensity and the extent of the electrification of America. Not only were new households being formed at a rapid rate, but each household went from an average of six to twelve electric appliances in the decade ending in 1960. In response, electric utilities were on a construction binge, with electricity generation increasing at 6 to 8 percent per year from 1960 to 1971, when it dropped to near 0 percent thanks to the OPEC oil embargo. (Today increases run at about 2 percent per year.) As a key supplier to residential and commercial construction and utilities, T&B was well positioned to profit and grow with the industry.

As is clear from the company's string of 9th-decile performances, however, T&B did far more than simply ride the rising tide. From 1966 to 1969 Hubbell was delivering 9th-decile performances as well, but T&B enjoyed absolute ROA nearly 50 percent higher and through 1984 racked up seventeen 9th-decile years while Hubbell never got above the 8th decile from 1970 to 1984.

This edge is attributable largely to T&B's non-price position. Consistent with its long history of innovation, through the 1960s and 1970s the company introduced a large number of new products based on advances both large and small that served to make the installation, servicing, or operation of electrical infrastructure that much easier and better.

Superior innovation does not happen on its own, however. Thomas & Betts spent an average of 5 percent of revenue annually on R&D versus Hubbell's 3 percent or less. This commitment to new products was manifested in part through nearly three hundred active patents by 1984, a portfolio nearly 60 percent larger than Hubbell's.

Adding to the company's relative success was its careful expansion into overseas markets, where its non-price-value proposition translated well. Revenue from its non-U.S. markets was limited to Canada, Europe, Australia, and Japan and generated just over a quarter of total sales by the mid-1970s at an ROA that flirted with the mid-20-percent range, compared with domestic sales that ran in the mid-teens. In contrast, the profitability of Hubbell's overseas operations during the 1970s proved much more fragile, and was ultimately a drag on average profitability thanks to foreign exchange losses due to currency devaluations in the United Kingdom and Brazil.

The structure of T&B's performance advantage reflects these behavioral differences. An average annual ROA advantage over Hubbell of 3.5 pp was driven by an average annual gross margin advantage of 11.4 pp, made possible by innovative products that allowed higher prices. The trade-off was lower asset turnover, which contributed an average of -1 pp/year to ROA. This was primarily a consequence of the higher inventory levels (a current asset) required to provide superior customer service.

The decline in T&B's absolute ROA from 1966 to 1984 is similar to what we saw Heartland go through in trucking (see chapter 1), and seems to have had many of the same high-level causes. Both companies enjoyed very high absolute ROA thanks in part to favorable industry forces, which they exploited more effectively than their competition through savvy non-price positioning. As with Heartland, the subsequent erosion of T&B's ROA was not, in itself, a signal that something was terribly amiss. Where Heartland was faced with an increasingly efficient trucking industry, T&B was wrestling with slowing growth in electrical products.

Recall that Heartland began exploring alternative service delivery models by building a small number of distribution centers, gradually increasing its reliance on employee drivers over owner/operators, and slowly expanding its geographic coverage. These tentative but purposeful moves were pointed at finding ways of sustaining and if possible extending Heartland's non-price position in trucking, even if that meant profound change to what had been some of the company's defining characteristics.

Thomas & Betts was similarly tentative but purposeful in exploring avenues of growth and renewed profitability, but rather than seek new high ground in the electrical wiring industry it began probing in entirely new directions, specifically into electronic infrastructure. Beginning with the acquisitions of Arthur Ansley Manufacturing Co. in 1966 and Cable Scan in 1970—which were combined to create T&B's Ansley division—by 1977 electronic components were 5 percent of total revenue. Annual reports from the period tout the company's disproportionate R&D investment in electronics, suggesting that T&B was targeting a non-price position in electronics, just as it had enjoyed in the electrical segment.

At this point, the two companies' paths diverge. Heartland successfully made the transition to a new model and preserved its relative superiority, even if its absolute ROA stabilized at a lower level than it had enjoyed in the past. Thomas & Betts, however, continued to suffer declines in absolute ROA—dipping below Hubbell in 1982—and, far more telling, its relative ROA also declined, falling below the 9th decile and below Hubbell in 1985, ending its streak of relative high performance in 1985. Profitability was down to single digits by 1992 and bottomed out with three consecutive years in the red from 2000 to 2002.

The cause of this nearly twenty-year deterioration can be summed up in a single phrase: a failure to take the hint. Thomas & Betts's initial push into electronics was arguably consistent with its longtime non-price position, and by avoiding significant commitments at the outset the company showed commendable prudence consistent with what has become conventional wisdom when it comes to trying something new.

However, T&B's performance reveals that this shift from electrical to electronic components simply was not working. Return on assets declined as the company's emphasis on electronics increased, reaching 50 percent of total revenue by 1992. Unable to find a non-price position that insulated it from intense price pressure from low-cost overseas competitors, T&B doubled down on electronics with a string of acquisitions through 1997: Vitramon (1987), Holmberg Electronics (1990), Eaton Corporation and Leviton Manufacturing (1994), Catamount Manufacturing (1995), Amerace (1996), WJ Furse and LE Mason (1997). The largest of its purchases was Augat in 1996, which doubled the company's electronics business.

The explicit intent, stated in management's pronouncements at the time, was to increase scale and scope in order to reduce cost and be more price competitive in the hotly contested global electronics market. In an attempt to achieve the scale that might permit successful price-based competition, T&B's expansion into overseas markets—now dominated by Singapore, Malaysia, Taiwan, Hong Kong, and South Korea—approached 50 percent of total revenue, but had an ROA that was indistinguishable from the now-depressed ROA of the company's domestic operations.

The story was hardly better in the electrical business. A number of deals maintained the company's presence in that sector, but the 1992 acquisition of American Electric, which nearly doubled the company's size, proved especially disastrous. New management spearheaded a shift to a lower-margin, higher-volume position, which undermined the company's historical non-price footing. With a declining electrical business and an electronics business that never really got off the ground, average ROA continued to fall, reaching its nadir in 2001.

As ROA plummeted, shareholders filed suit and there was a through-and-through top management change. New leadership shed Augat in 2000, which at the time was nearly 30 percent of the company's total revenue, and by 2001 the company had exited the electronics sector entirely.

By the late 2000s T&B and Hubbell had similar, and similarly unremarkable, absolute and relative ROA. Through the 1980s and 1990s, Hubbell executed a series of small acquisitions, very often of private companies competing in the electrical and lighting segments, leaving the two companies by 2010 essentially the same size. Thomas & Betts's spending on R&D had dropped to under 3 percent of sales versus Hubbell's 1 to 2 percent while Hubbell now had the larger active patent portfolio at more than six hundred, compared with fewer than five hundred for T&B.

Thomas & Betts's Elements of Advantage during its streak of lower relative performance (1986 onward) must be interpreted with care. The key is to remember that T&B's results are an amalgam of a slowly eroding non-price position in electrical with a price-based position in electronics.

The company's annual gross margin advantage over Hubbell declined dramatically between the two streaks. This is remarkable, for Hubbell's absolute ROA was falling during much of this period, especially from 1992 onward. It maintains a gross margin advantage very likely because half or more of T&B's revenue was still generated by its electrical business, which maintained a more nearly non-price position versus Hubbell.

Thomas & Betts ended up with an overall ROS disadvantage during its streak of lower relative performance thanks to its other costs: SG&A, R&D, depreciation, and nonoperating income. (The other cost element is less of a disadvantage thanks to lower relative taxes, which fell due to lower pretax profitability.) These cost disadvantages seem largely to have

TABLE 14: **T&B's Elements of Advantage Versus Hubbell**

Elements of ROA	Contribution to ROA Advantage in Percentage Points per Year	
	Period of Higher Performance: 1966–1985	Period of Lower Performance: 1986–2010
Gross Margin	18.1	4.6
SG&A	−9.8	−5.0
R&D	−0.3	−0.4
Other (incl. taxes)	−3.8	−2.4
ROS	4.2	−3.2
CAT	−1.5	−0.6
FAT	−0.5	−0.7
Other	0.9	−0.1
TAT	−1.1	−1.5
ROA	3.1	−4.7

Source: Compustat; Deloitte analysis
Figures may not total due to rounding.

been a consequence of the company's inability to execute its price-driven position in electronics. Although it still suffered a TAT disadvantage versus Hubbell, the elements of that difference had a different balance. An inventory turnover disadvantage, a consequence of T&B's service-driven differentiation when it was a purely electrical components company, fell, even as its fixed asset turnover deficit widened. This makes sense, given all the new assets T&B was bringing onto the books as part of its bid for scale in electronics while the higher inventory turns were consistent with the desire to compete on price rather than service and to reap profits through efficiencies rather than differentiation.

In short, although Hubbell did not deliberately abandon those non-price elements of value that defined its in-the-middle position, they eroded over time and the company lost its Long Runner level of performance. T&B's movement away from non-price differentiation was deliberate. Faced with unsatisfactory results, T&B reversed course, attempting to return to its roots in the electrical business, and its profitability appeared to be rebounding when the company was acquired in 2012 by ABB Ltd.

> When an industry slowdown depressed T&B's absolute ROA, the company began looking for greener pastures, even though its relative performance remained strong. Choosing to compete on price in the cutthroat electronic components business resulted in a continued deterioration in performance and the end of its streak of high relative performance, making it a Lost It Miracle Worker.

The Average Joe of this doleful trio is Emrise, an electronics manufacturer based in Rancho Cucamonga, California. At its debut as a public company in 1986 the company was a niche player in the telecommunications equipment sector focusing on analog technology, and grew rapidly from $5 million to $30 million in revenue in just five years. Declining ROA during this time could easily be attributed to the demands of growth, except that the company's second act was largely cheerless. A shift to digital technologies required introducing a raft of new products, which ended up late to market, while increased R&D spending that was intended, perhaps, to compensate for these shortcomings failed to deliver results: Emrise received its first patent in 2006.

Keenly aware that it was competing on price, through the 1990s Emrise outsourced much of its manufacturing, attributing improvements in its gross margin from 34 percent to 67 percent to aggressive cost cutting of this sort. Of late, the company has diversified into aerospace and defense, but here it finds itself—like Micropac in semiconductors—constrained by tightly defined product specifications and fixed-price contracts, which make non-price positions difficult to establish.

Emrise remains a small competitor in a global market, unable to build a cost structure appropriate to a price-based competitor. This is reflected in the Elements of Advantage of Hubbell over Emrise.[17] The gross margin disadvantage reflects Emrise's cost-cutting focus, but the disadvantage it suffers in essentially all other elements cumulates in inferior ROS and inferior TAT. When you are a price leader but not a cost leader, the result is Average Joe performance . . . at best.

The falls of T&B and Hubbell illustrate the dangers, even to exceptional companies, of attempting to capitalize on or even merely react to

TABLE 15: **Hubbell's Elements of Advantage Versus Emrise**

Elements of ROA	Contribution to ROA Advantage in Percentage Points per Year	
	Period of Higher Performance: 1986–2004	**Period of Lower Performance: 2005–2010**
Gross Margin	−9.4	−8.0
SG&A	20.7	18.9
R&D	4.7	1.2
Other (incl. taxes)	−0.4	1.2
ROS	15.6	13.3
CAT	0.3	1.1
FAT	1.4	−0.3
Other	3.2	0.9
TAT	4.8	1.7
ROA	**20.4**	**15.0**

Source: Compustat; Deloitte analysis
Figures may not total due to rounding.

industry trends without creating the non-price positions that drive superior performance. Like International Rectifier in semiconductors and Invacare in medical devices, T&B and Hubbell found themselves bulking up and branching out in order to keep up with what were reasonably seen to be defining trends in their industry: the shift to electronics, globalization, and increasing cost pressures. But in responding to these pressures they abandoned—T&B more than Hubbell—the non-price positions that had earned them exceptional profitability for decades.

Linear managed to create the position—the potential energy—that its strong operations—kinetic energy—were able to capture, and Medtronic was able to improve its execution to capture the profits that its position had long made possible. In contrast, T&B and Hubbell lost much of both. Changes in position that were aligned to the dictates of industry forces at the expense of the requirements of a non-price position, compounded by challenges in execution, left both struggling to regain lost glory.

The most general attributes of profitable positions can be stated only in uninformative truisms, such as create value for customers, be difficult for competitors to imitate, and be practical for your organization. The specifics of profitable positions cannot be generalized at all. They will be a function of, among other factors, your industry, the technologies of the day, your organization's capabilities, your competitors' capabilities, the customers you seek to serve, and the circumstances in which you operate. There simply cannot be any specific and generally applicable recipe for precisely how you can create a non-price position for your organization today.

Between these two extremes, we hope there is room for useful insight. This chapter has provided evidence that non-price positions are systematically more profitable and more sustainable than in-the-middle or price-based positions. This falls far short of a complete blueprint for success, but it does, we hope, provide valuable guidance when you have to make tough choices among equally viable alternatives.

For example, when your customers are yelling for price cuts, you can drop prices and then squeeze your company elsewhere to try to preserve profitability, or you can see through their complaints on price to the more difficult truth that maybe you have gotten lazy or lost focus or that the competition has upped its game and you no longer provide the superior value you once did. Addressing that problem means taking on the challenge of increasing and perhaps even changing the value you provide; it could mean changing any or all of your technologies, processes, markets, or customers. Both courses of action—cutting price or increasing value—can be difficult to pursue successfully, and each of them can make equally good sense.

It is in just these circumstances that *better before cheaper* proves its worth. Faced with a choice between two difficult, similarly plausible, but mutually exclusive solutions to what can be an existential challenge, the best you can do is play the odds. Our research suggests strongly that the most profitable course of action is to devote your resources to tackling the hard problem of creating anew the non-price value your customers will pay for, not the hard problem of how to remain profitable at lower prices.

Linear understood this, at least implicitly, abandoning a profitable but relatively undifferentiated position for an ultimately more rewarding non-price position in a wide range of markets. Medtronic remained dedicated to its industry-leading differentiation even as it invested in more efficient operations so that it could capture more of the value it was creating. Stryker has set itself up for a run at Miracle Worker status thanks to a change in position. And T&B slipped out of the top echelon of performance not because it could not renew its non-price position, but because it abandoned the quest even when it had the resources to persist.

Position comes first. It is the height to which your roller coaster climbs, and so it defines the upper limit of the profitability you can aspire to. Execution comes second, for it defines the thrill of the ride promised by that climb, or how much of that potential you capture as kinetic energy. Poor execution wastes potential energy in the form of noise and heat. So execution matters, but no level of greatness in execution can make up for poor positioning, any more than a smooth ride can compensate for a short climb.

Industry, of course, is critical: it is difficult to imagine how any company could hope to be successful running clearly counter to the dictates of its context. All of our exceptional companies, in their heydays, were astute surfers of industry waves. But the key to winning is standing out from the background noise, not blending in. Our Average Joes and our exceptional companies that fell from grace very often did so not by misreading industry forces or failing to respond to them; that level of benightedness typically results in bankruptcy or being acquired by someone else. Rather, what afflicted them was an inability to do what was required to get ahead, very often as a consequence of spending too much time trying not to be left behind.

CHAPTER 4

Revenue Before Cost

How best to create value for customers is a question that can be usefully seen as a choice between competitive positions defined by an emphasis on price value (that is, low price) or non-price value. Perhaps somewhat unusually, seeing the question in these high-contrast terms is not a dangerous oversimplification. It is instead an accurate distillation of an underlying structure that is too often hidden beneath unnecessary complexity. Sometimes the world is nuanced and complex and colored with shades of gray. But sometimes there are clear choices to be made, and we simply do not want to face up to them. *Better before cheaper* is an unambiguous answer to a straightforward but too often ignored question.

Creating value for customers is a necessary condition for exceptional performance, but it is not sufficient. The value you create is only the "size of the pie." Whether or not a given company is an exceptional performer is also a function of the "size of their slice," or how value is divided between customers and the corporation.[1] In other words, exceptional companies must not only create value, but also capture it in the form of profits.[2]

A company can increase its ROA by increasing price or volume or both, or by decreasing overall cost, the sum of cost of goods sold (COGS) and other costs, or reducing assets (see Appendix I, "The Structure of Profitability Advantages," for a discussion of the arithmetic of ROA). As with the trade-offs among the dimensions of performance that define position, however, there are typically trade-offs among the variables that determine a company's profitability. For example, increases in both price and volume increase revenue, which increases income, and hence ROA. However, price and volume can be negatively correlated, making it difficult to increase both simultaneously.

On the other hand, although higher cost (which reduces ROA) can be a consequence of inefficiency, it can also be a function of using higher-quality materials or more skilled labor, each of which can contribute to non-price value, thus justifying a higher price (which increases ROA). Consequently, price and cost can move in the same direction. Volume and assets also often move together yet exert contradictory pressures on ROA: higher volume can increase asset turnover, which increases ROA but only if the higher volume does not require disproportionately more assets.

The key to superior profitability, then, is not how well a company manages any one variable in the ROA equation, but how it manages the interdependencies among them in light of often unavoidable trade-offs. We call this a company's profitability formula.

We discovered that exceptional companies, by an overwhelming margin, have a common profitability formula, which we have summarized in our second rule, *revenue before cost*. This means that when exceptional companies face a trade-off between increasing profitability by increasing revenue or by decreasing cost, they systematically choose increasing revenue *even if that means incurring higher cost*. We have never seen an exceptional company spend with abandon. Rather, we have concluded that sustained profitability advantages are rarely driven by disproportionately lower cost or asset bases when compared with the competition, and instead are very often driven by disproportionately higher revenues.

A large part of the significance of this finding lies in the fact that our data could have revealed the opposite, namely, that superior profitability is typically driven by relatively lower cost. But it is not. Profitability advantages driven by higher revenue, even when they incur higher cost, prove to be more valuable than advantages driven by lower cost.

The Structure of Differences in Profitability

The ROA decomposition analysis on our case study companies suggests very strongly that Miracle Workers rely most heavily on a gross margin advantage for their overall ROA lead. Disadvantages in other costs (SG&A, R&D, and so on), asset turnover, or both are often simply the consequence of unavoidable trade-offs, the cost of the differentiated products or services that earn the higher gross margins.

We wanted to know if this pattern was reflected in a meaningful way in our full population of 174 Miracle Workers, 170 Long Runners, and 1,208 Average Joes. To figure that out, for each year that each company is in our database, we calculated the difference in gross margin, other costs, and asset turnover between that company and the industry median. We then regressed each of these differences against each company's ROA difference from the industry median in that year (see Appendix I). This allowed us to see how changes in advantages in these three drivers of ROA translated into ROA advantage. In other words, we could see how much an additional point's lead in gross margin percentage over the industry median affected the ROA lead over the industry median for Miracle Workers, Long Runners, and Average Joes.

The results were telling and entirely consistent with the patterns revealed in our case study analysis. For each additional point in gross margin percentage advantage, Miracle Workers realized 0.51 percentage points in additional ROA advantage. The same increase in a Miracle Worker's advantage in other costs, however, yielded only 0.47 percentage points in additional ROA advantage. The implication is that Miracle Workers tend to have a profitability formula that is more efficient at translating a relative gross margin improvement into a relative ROA advantage than it is at translating a relative reduction in other costs into a relative ROA advantage. In more practical terms, it means that Miracle Workers have positions and profitability formulas that favor revenue before cost.

Companies classified as Long Runners will necessarily have a smaller ROA advantage over the industry median than Miracle Workers since these categories are defined by their different profitability levels. This does not say anything, however, about how efficiently they turn gross margin or other cost advantages into ROA advantage. Long Runners could easily have been more efficient at translating advantage in one or more of the drivers of ROA but simply have been unable to generate a similar magnitude of advantage. Neither does a difference in the magnitude of ROA advantage say anything about the differences in efficiency for the various drivers. It is therefore telling both that Long Runners are less efficient than Miracle Workers and that Long Runners show no real difference in how efficiently they translate changes in advantages in either gross margin or other costs into additional ROA advantage: for an additional percentage point of advantage in either one, Long Runners realize about 0.40 percentage points of ROA advantage.

Average Joes, not surprising (but by no means necessarily), are the least efficient of the three performance categories, but, like Miracle Workers, are more efficient with respect to gross margin than other costs.

Finally, there are revealing differences in the relationship between changes in advantages in asset turnover and ROA advantage. All three performance types show a statistically significant negative relationship, which means that for an increase in asset turnover all three types see their ROA advantage go down. In practical terms, the effect size is small: Miracle Workers see their ROA edge slip by 0.023 percentage points for an additional asset turn annually—a significant achievement in just about any industry, and in some, all but impossible. Long Runners and Average Joes

TABLE 16: The Drivers of Differences in Profitability

| Advantage in | Gross Margin Percentage | | Other Costs Percentage | | Asset Turnover Advantage | |
	Efficiency Ratio	Median/Range	Efficiency Ratio	Median/Range	Efficiency Ratio	Median/Range
Miracle Workers	0.51	0.09/0.18	0.47	0.02/0.15	−0.023	0/0.34
Long Runners	0.41	0.03/0.16	0.40	0/0.15	−0.014	−0.04/0.43
Average Joes	0.32	0/0.10	0.27	0/0.09	−0.016	0/0.31

Source: Authors' analysis

Median and range figures for Gross Margin Percentage and Other Costs Percentage are in percentage points. Median and range for asset turnover are in asset turns per year. Ranges are the interquartile ranges for each variable.

see their ROA advantage over the industry median fall by 0.016 percentage points for a similarly heroic increase in asset turnover advantage. Since differences in asset turns among companies in the same industry rarely shift by that much, it means that differences in asset turns do not explain much of the differences in ROA.

An analysis of the distributions of the ranges for the three drivers reveals further that Miracle Workers tend to be more likely to have a gross margin advantage than Long Runners, but also more likely than Long Runners to have a *disadvantage* in other costs.[3] Since Miracle Workers, by definition, have higher ROA, it is no surprise that their gross margin advantage outweighs their cost disadvantage. This means the structure of the ROA advantage for our population of Miracle Workers is consistent with the sort of costly non-price differentiation that earns higher revenue through higher price rather than volume increases that drive asset efficiency. In short, revenue before cost, and when it comes to revenue, price before volume.

Of course, our population-level analysis is driven solely by the income statement and balance sheet. To get a finer-grained understanding of what is driving these results, we must turn to our trios. Based first on the ROA decomposition and then on our in-depth analysis of each company's behaviors, we identify the drivers of gross margin advantage.

The Revenue-versus-COGS splits for the Miracle Worker comparisons

TABLE 17: **The Drivers of Gross Margin Advantage in Trio Companies by Type of Pair-Wise Comparison**

	Revenue		COGS
	Price	Volume	
Miracle Worker Vs. Average Joe	7	1	1
Miracle Worker Vs. Long Runner	5	3	1
Long Runner Vs. Average Joe	5	1	3

Source: Authors' analysis

are both highly statistically significant (a 98 percent change of a relationship). For Long Runners there is a 25 percent chance that the 6:3 split is drawn from a uniform underlying distribution, which is consistent with our finding that Long Runners are quite likely to have in-the-middle or price-based positions which are likely to require COGS-driven profitability advantages.

Within the revenue-driven profitability formulas, price is the dominant driver of a revenue advantage versus Average Joes: for Miracle Workers, the 7:1 split has a 96.5 percent chance of being nonuniform while for Long Runners there is an 89 percent chance of nonuniformity. When Miracle Workers stack up against Long Runners, however, there is only a 64 percent chance of the split being nonuniform.

Our sample was chosen randomly with respect to competitive position and the structures of profitability differences.[4] We therefore infer with some confidence that the finer-grained structure of profitability differences in the sample is at least suggestive of what one would find through a similarly detailed analysis of the full population. We therefore conclude that *revenue before cost* is most likely the profitability formula for most exceptional companies, not just the most frequent result in our sample. The observed structure of the profitability advantages also provides corroborating evidence for our claims about the importance and nature of competitive position. After all, it would require some explaining if the Miracle Workers that we see as competing on non-price value (*better before cheaper*) tended to have profitability formulas driven by lower costs that compensated for lower gross margin; it would imply that they were better, but not getting paid for it, *and* cheaper. That is certainly not impossible, but far more satisfying is a non-price position that incurs higher cost yet translates into a revenue advantage and ultimately superior profitability.

Finally, there would be something deeply wrong with our method if companies to which we ascribed a price-based position were driving profitability through higher prices. Competing against a company on the basis of having lower prices while enjoying better profitability through higher prices is a logical impossibility.

If your advantage is driven by:	Then you most likely have higher:	And not lower:
Gross Margin	Price	Cost
Asset Turnover	Volume	Assets

The Bottom Line: Revenue Before Cost

What we see instead are two independent variables, position and profitability formula, that we can measure independent of performance and each other, but that have strong and consistent relationships with performance and each other. A non-price position is systematically associated with exceptional performance; a revenue-driven profitability formula is systematically associated with exceptional performance; and a non-price position and a revenue-driven profitability formula typically go together.

To beat the odds, you want to focus on creating value using *better before cheaper*, and on capturing value with *revenue before cost*.

To better understand how this can be done, we will take a closer look at Abercrombie & Fitch (A&F), introduced in chapter 1. We observe two Miracle Workers in our sample that rely on volume more than price, but in both cases that volume is driven by superior non-price value, not lower price. We touched briefly on one of them, Merck, in chapter 1, and we will return to Merck in the next chapter; here we will focus on Wrigley, the gum and candy company.

Finally, although the odds lie strongly with revenue-driven profitability, some Miracle Workers do rely on cost advantages. One of them, Weis

Markets (Weis), is in our sample. Our investigation of how it did this, and the pitfalls this reliance on cost reduction created, reveals much about the limitations of cost-driven superior profitability.[5]

Sustaining Profitability: Revenue Through Pricing Premiums

Position and profitability formula are closely connected. That is why the previous chapter, although focused on the question of position, also explored how Linear, Medtronic, and T&B translated their non-price positions into a profitability advantage, and each achieved that through higher price. In this chapter we will focus on trios in which the Miracle Workers used different profitability formulas. In clothing, A&F exploited its non-price position to earn higher prices; in confectionary, Wrigley similarly relied on a non-price position but extracted superior profitability through higher volume. And in groceries, Weis competed on price and drives profitability through lower cost.

In addition to A&F, our clothing trio includes Finish Line, the Long Runner and a retailer primarily of branded sports apparel from companies such as Nike and Adidas, and the Average Joe, Syms, an off-price retailer of branded fashion clothing.

Of the three, A&F is perhaps the one you are most familiar with, since it is the one that relied most heavily on its own brand to create value for customers. Its advertising campaigns won a good deal of notice, not all of it positive, and have long featured more skin than cloth.[6] The insight that "sex sells" was hardly its own, but for more than a decade A&F was a master at leveraging this fundamental feature of the human psyche.

It is easy, however, to make too much of this high-profile feature of the company's public image. If being exceptionally profitable required nothing more than pictures of pretty people not wearing your product, everyone in the industry would be a Miracle Worker.[7] What set A&F apart is a

TABLE 18: Descriptive Statistics for the Clothing Trio

Company	Category (Trajectory)	Year Founded	Observation Period	Revenue Growth	Average Annual ROA	Compounded Annual TSR	Compounded Annual Revenue Growth
Abercrombie & Fitch	Miracle Worker (Kept II)	1982	1995 to 2010	$236MM to $3.5BN	18.8%	15.7%	19.6%
Finish Line	Long Runner (Kept II)	1976	1991 to 2010	$98MM to $1.2BN	7.9%	7.0%	14.2%
Syms	Average Joe (N/A)	1959	1982 to 2010	$147MM to $445MM	5.5%	–2.4%	4.0%

Source: Company documents; Compustat; Deloitte analysis

tightly knit weave of several critical and mutually reinforcing choices, with a common thread running from design to manufacturing through to distribution and the in-store customer experience. These carefully coordinated activities served to establish a strong non-price position that earned the company its price premium.

A Kept It Miracle Worker, A&F's two eras in absolute performance illustrate both the boom-and-bust cycle that often characterizes the retail sector and A&F's ability to defy that gravitational pull longer than most. From 1995 to 1999 the company's ROA doubled from around 15 percent to over 30 percent even as revenue, too, had more than doubled. Investors, enamored of rapid and increasingly profitable growth, bid up the company's stock more than threefold.

The company not only coped with but exploited the interdependence among position, execution, and industry we saw in the previous chapter. At the industry level, two factors featured prominently. First, the fifteen-to-twenty-four-year-old cohort was growing twice as fast as the overall U.S. population, and clothing was the single largest spending category of this age group's rising disposable income.[8,9] As a result, A&F could focus even more narrowly, on eighteen-to-twenty-two-year-olds, yet still have in its sights a large, growing, and relatively affluent segment.

TABLE 19: **Abercrombie & Fitch's Eras in Absolute Performance**

	Years	Average Annual ROA	Compounded Annual TSR	Compounded Annual Revenue Growth
Era 1	1995 to 1999	26%	48%	45%
Era 2	2000 to 2010	15%	12%	11%

Source: Compustat; Deloitte analysis

Second, A&F sold only its own branded clothing, rather than selling others' brands, such as Calvin Klein, Hugo Boss, and so on. By building its own premium store brand, A&F was a particularly successful instance of a secular shift in the "store-brand" phenomenon. Historically, brand equity lay with clothing manufacturers while the retailers' brands were far less important. Store brands, or private labels, were a lower-cost, lower-priced alternative to "name" brands, waxing and waning in inverse proportion to the strength of the general economy.[10]

Perhaps somewhat ironically, while customers had historically been drawn to private labels by lower prices, retailers, by capturing wholesale and retail margins without spending on brand-building advertising, typically enjoyed gross margins on store labels that were almost twice what they earned on national brands.[11] Those economics have been difficult to ignore, and store brands have become a central feature of major retailers' strategies at every price point.[12]

Abercrombie & Fitch was not the only clothing retailer seeking to ride these industry-level currents, of course. American Eagle, Banana Republic, Pacific Sunwear, and others all pursued competitive positions that seem quite similar to A&F's.

Even so, A&F managed to differentiate itself. The company's extreme focus permitted it to make trade-offs most other retailers were reluctant to make. For example, the advertising campaigns that built A&F's racy image were a bull's-eye for the company's targeted demographic, and any possible offense taken by those outside of that narrow band was of little consequence. Better still, with such a focused message, the company tended to spend relatively little on national advertising, instead pioneering more targeted approaches such as its "magalog," carefully managed "word-of-mouth," viral campaigns, and social media.[13, 14]

(A&F's marketing and advertising was even deemed, after a fashion, competitively differentiated by the Sixth Circuit Court of Appeals. The company sued American Eagle Outfitters for "intentional and systematic copying" of its magalog. The court ruled that, unlike A&F, American Eagle's advertising "presents a decidedly wholesome image, with people of various ages in non-suggestive, often family oriented situations; nudity is absent.")

Similarly, that its dimly lit stores, loud, youth-oriented music, and strong in-store scents made its locations essentially intolerable to anyone over thirty was, if anything, a welcome side effect. Sales personnel were called models and hired with an eye to their physical attractiveness; they wore A&F clothing as a matter of policy and were carefully chosen to serve as exemplars of A&F's aspirational aesthetic.[15] Not unlike sales clerks in chic Manhattan boutiques, they were not there so much to serve you as to show you who you should want to be—and could be, with only a $30 T-shirt.[16] This unique in-store experience was most often set in higher-rent locations kitted out with the sorts of furnishings and decorations typically found in nightclubs.[17]

Creating that kind of hipness consistently and at scale was, not surprisingly, no accident. Even as the number of A&F stores rose from 127 in 1996 to more than 350 by 2001, the company's streak of 9th-decile performances continued uninterrupted—in defiance of the bust that so typically follows the early boom in fashion retailing. The corporate center maintained tight control over all aspects of the brand, providing store managers with detailed specifications and photographs of prototype stores for them to replicate, and direction on the appropriate volume levels for in-store music.[18] Location, too, was critical. Although typically located in high-rent, fashionable malls, flagship locations were also important for the halo effect they created for A&F stores across the country and around the world, including a Fifth Avenue store in New York City.[19]

These positioning choices manifested themselves in a strong price premium over several close competitors. Abercrombie & Fitch was able to

TABLE 20: **Percentage of A&F's Retail Price Realized by Similar Clothing Retailers on Comparable Goods**

	The Gap	**American Eagle**	**Aeropostale**
Men's Clothing	63%	60%	62%
Women's Clothing	58%	52%	60%
Other	74%	78%	53%
Total Basket	66%	63%	59%

Source: William Blair & Company, LLC; Deloitte analysis

charge from over 30 percent to almost 100 percent more for a similar basket of goods.[20]

Finally, A&F's execution had at least one defining element. A key component of the store-brand strategy is a lower cost of goods sold than when selling nationally branded products. In keeping with long-term trends in textiles generally, this typically meant sourcing products from a shifting array of contract manufacturers scattered about South America and Asia, driven by cost considerations.[21]

In contrast, A&F followed a more balanced, combined approach, sourcing 29 percent of its merchandise through Mast Industries, a wholly owned subsidiary of The Limited, which was in turn a major shareholder in A&F.[22] The rest of its product mix was sourced more in keeping with common industry practice: 270 vendors, none of which provided more than 6 percent of A&F's total volume.[23]

Maintaining its own in-house design capability, coupled with ownership of a material portion of its manufacturing capacity, meant that A&F had shorter lead times than its major competitors, allowing it to respond more effectively to fast-changing fashion trends.[24] This both supports a price premium—a more on-trend product—and reduces the frequency and volume of potentially damaging markdowns by keeping inventories lower.[25]

Finish Line is a Lost It Long Runner, with its streak in the 6th-to-8th-decile range coming to an unmistakable end in 2006, and a single era in absolute performance characterized by a downward slope and high variation. Not atypical of a successful retailer, during its streak of higher relative performance from 1991 to 2005 the company enjoyed strong but declining profitability as it ran to the end of its real estate runway, increasing its store count from 251 to 789. Unfortunately, its ROA had, by then, fallen from above 10 percent into the low single digits, and its decile ranks were as low as 0.

As a retailer of national brands, Finish Line had relatively little pricing flexibility. Its cost of goods sold was determined largely by the manufacturers of the brands it chose to stock—Nike, Adidas, Reebok, Saucony, and so on. These manufacturers invested heavily in their own brands through advertising, celebrity athlete endorsements, and all manner of other promotions. When you buy an A&F T-shirt everyone knows it's an A&F T-shirt—that's the point. But once someone has bought branded athletic footwear, the place of purchase is essentially irrelevant.

This does not mean, however, that Finish Line paid no attention to non-price dimensions of value. The company set up "The Lab" at its headquarters to test new décor, displays, and designs, and commissioned custom-made mannequins cast in various fitness or yoga poses.[26] With anchor products that were no different and prices that were no lower than those of its closest competitors, such as Foot Locker, Finish Line was fundamentally unable to establish anything like A&F's non-price position. And although being price competitive, and where possible a price leader, was important, Finish Line sought to establish some non-price differentiators. Consequently, Finish Line has an in-the-middle competitive position.

Consistent with an in-the-middle position, Finish Line targeted a relatively broad market segment, identified as "the whole family," with subsegments such as "12-to-24-year-old men" and "women." Activities designed to appeal to these subsegments were typically limited to shifts in advertising messaging and media outlets, rather than fundamental and substantive change in product mix, store layout, and so on.[27] So, for example, much of its advertising focused on national cable networks, with ad hoc specific initiatives tied to the NCAA basketball tournament or magazines such as *Sports Illustrated, Teen People,* or *Seventeen.*

Finish Line's exceptional profitability seems to have come to an end largely as a result of an inability to adapt to shifts in industry context. One such significant blow was the consumer shift away from sports apparel and shoes (a "preppy" look) toward either the "grunge" look, which featured loose-fitting flannel shirts, tattered jeans, and sandals, or the "fashion-forward" look of A&F. This trend is seen as a major factor in a 25 percent fall in Nike's sales between 1998 and 2000.[28]

In 2003, Finish Line attempted to get on the private label bandwagon, but its core product category—athletic footwear and apparel—has proven uniquely resistant to this trend. Consequently, private label products could only be at best a prop to profitability, not a driver.

Perhaps recognizing the limitations of its brand and product mix, in 2006 Finish Line acquired Man Alive, a more fashion-oriented chain that focused on hip-hop and rap-inspired clothing, shoes, and accessories. This put Finish Line in the casual apparel segment, but fully a decade after the trend had begun.

Through 2006, the story of A&F and Finish Line is more a study in the benefits of strong non-price positioning. But over the following four years, through 2010 (the end of our observation period), we begin to see the merits of sticking with a revenue-driven profit formula based on higher price even in the face of potentially severe competitive pressure and a shifting industry landscape.

Note that during A&F's first era in absolute performance it has both

TABLE 21: **A&F's Elements of Advantage Versus Finish Line**

Elements of ROA	Contribution to ROA Advantage in Percentage Points per Year	
	Era 1: 1995–1999	Era 2: 2000–2010
Gross Margin	24.9	42.0
SG&A	−0.1	−20.7
R&D	0.0	0.0
Other (incl. taxes)	−12.3	−9.6
ROS	12.6	11.6
CAT	5.0	−0.3
FAT	−0.3	−1.1
Other	0.8	0.0
TAT	5.5	−1.4
ROA	**18.1**	**10.2**

Source: Compustat; Deloitte analysis
Figures may not total due to rounding.

ROS and TAT advantages over Finish Line. Abercrombie & Fitch's non-price position allowed for the higher prices that drove superior gross margin. Its targeted advertising allowed it to keep relative SG&A spend lower, and its vertical integration permitted the kinds of efficiencies in execution that drove inventory turns, which shows up in higher current asset turn-over. The lower fixed asset turnover is consistent with the higher levels of investment A&F made in its stores.

The company's decline in absolute profitability was not inevitable, but it was predictable and expected. In fashion retail, utter newness is a powerful differentiator, and the passage of time inevitably erodes it. Abercrombie & Fitch's response, however, was not a desperate attempt to put lightning back in a bottle. Instead, it seems to have preserved its relative profitability by accepting the very trade-offs it once appeared to break. From 2000 to 2010, A&F's reliance on gross margin increased, even as the company's actual ROA values from 2003 through 2008 not only stabilized but increased. At the same time, A&F's SG&A advantage disappeared, becoming a significant drag on profitability, as did current asset turnover and asset turnover in total.

These shifts in the structure of A&F's profitability reflect the diversification of formats and customer segments explored briefly in chapter 1. Accepting the possibility that the A&F brand might wax and wane with unpredictable fashion trends, the company began launching new retail concepts long before the flagship was under any real stress. First came "abercrombie" in 1997, targeting grade schoolers (ages seven to fourteen), then Hollister Co. in 2000, aimed at fourteen-to-eighteen-year-olds, Ruehl No.925 in 2004, courting the postcollegiate crowd (ages twenty-two to thirty-four), and finally Gilly Hicks in 2008, which focused on women's lingerie and accessories.

This diversity could only increase the complexity of A&F's overall operations, and thus increased relative SG&A is not necessarily a sign of inefficiency. It is instead more likely a consequence of having to fund multiple advertising campaigns, expanding design capabilities, and the unavoidable increase in corporate overhead of all types that comes with increased operational scope. The lower asset turnover can almost certainly be attributed to the same phenomenon.

Of the new ventures, abercrombie was a modest success, Ruehl was shuttered in 2010, and it is perhaps still too early to tell with Gilly Hicks. Hollister was a significant hit, however, and by 2006 accounted for 41 percent of total company sales and generated 90 percent of the revenue per square foot that the core A&F stores produced, although at lower price points than A&F.[29] But not necessarily at lower price points *than its competition in those segments.*

Sticking to its pricing guns is not something that A&F did by accident; it was an explicit and consistent priority. Abercrombie & Fitch has avoided markdowns and promotions, and has typically sold its clothing at about 70 percent of full price, which is higher than many comparable clothing retailers.[30] Even during the 2001 recession, A&F maintained its price premium, with a degree of discounting that was 17 percent higher than in 2000, whereas key competitors increased their discounting by 26 percent.[31]

With the onset of the 2008 recession, A&F again stuck to its guns. The company's profitability dropped in both absolute and relative terms, and 2008 through 2010 have seen decile ranks of 6, 2, and 4. The financial and popular press claimed both that A&F has failed to realize that steep discounting was required and that its brand had become tired and passé.[32, 33] Yet, by late 2012, A&F was recovering smartly thanks to profitable international expansion and a revitalization of its U.S. operations.[34] Reasonable, informed people (both A&F's competitors and commentators) came to dramatically different conclusions about what to do and why with the onset of the recession. As it has turned out, in this case as in so many others we have examined, the steadfast application of *revenue before cost* seems to have carried the day despite the prescriptions of the conventional wisdom.

Finish Line might well be on track to begin a new streak of exceptional performance as well. From 2007 to 2009 the percentage of total sales from footwear rose from 79 to 86 percent, as the company shifted away from clothing and equipment. In 2009 the company disposed of the Man Alive chain, which never accounted for more than 6 percent of total sales, at a loss of $18 million.

In an attempt to increase its non-price differentiation, Finish Line has been exploring brand-specific stores that feature, for example, only the latest Nike products. With strong co-op advertising support, these outlets typically have higher prices than other outlets, but since the pricing power lies largely with the manufacturer (in this case, Nike) the profitability of this revenue will probably turn largely on cost control—a strategy consistent with the profitability formula of many Long Runners.

The runt of this litter is Syms, and we have said little about it largely because there is little to be said. At first blush, the company seems a case study in strategic focus, the kind of consistent, pure-play price position that strategy theorists salivate over. It sold out-of-fashion branded clothing at low prices in no-frills stores in low-cost locations. It never even dabbled in private labels, and its advertising message was as consistent as it was straightforward. If you wanted unfashionable fashions on the cheap, Syms was your answer. As it had been in business for almost thirty years prior to going public in 1982, Syms was clearly on to something valuable and knew how to deliver it.

Despite all these points in its favor, the company's performance was anything but exceptional. An unbroken and steady downward trajectory in absolute ROA is reflected in only six years above the 6th decile of relative performance. With negative net income in six of the last twelve years despite closing a fifth of its stores, the company filed for bankruptcy protection in 2011. Then-CEO Marcy Syms pointed to increased competition from other discounters and from department stores with their own low-price private labels. Perhaps more debilitating has been the improved inventory management by the national brands, which left Syms relatively little overstock to fill its shelves.[35] In short, the company's low-price position and low-cost profitability formula allowed it to survive, but never to thrive.[36]

Abercrombie & Fitch (Miracle Worker) staked out a valuable non-price position and captured value through higher prices. The 2008 recession tested the merits of this combination, but recent results suggest the company made the right choice in sticking with *revenue before cost*.

Of course, there is no reason that a price-based position and a cost-driven profitability formula *cannot* work. That is not our claim. Our claim is that in general such combinations do not lead to exceptional performance. What Syms shows us is that when you depend on low price and low cost, you are far more vulnerable to competitive imitation (in this case, by discounters) and to forces entirely beyond your control (improved inventory management by the fashion labels). This is but one of the doubtless innumerable ways in which a price-and-cost combination can come undone.

Similarly, it is entirely possible that creating a business around someone else's brand can be a path to the highest levels of profitability, but Finish Line illustrates how difficult that can be by revealing how few degrees of freedom you have in the face of industry-level shifts, such as the demise of preppiness and the rise of casual fashion and grunge.

Neither can A&F's behavior serve as too specific a template for your own pursuit of a non-price position and a high-price profitability formula. Abercrombie & Fitch reveals the possibility of breaking financial trade-offs by embracing positioning trade-offs, and the eventual need to allow the dictates of your position to drive your financial performance. Abercrombie & Fitch's experience through the 2008 recession is testament to the difficulty of adhering to the rules while the robustness of the company's recovery is testament to their validity.

Increasing Profitability: Revenue Through Higher Volume

Wrigley is a Found It Miracle Worker with a history in confectionary that goes back to 1891. Tootsie Roll, our Long Runner for this trio, has a Kept It trajectory, was founded in 1896, and has been a public company since 1922. With forty-one and forty-six years of observations in our database,

TABLE 22: **Descriptive Statistics for the Confectionary Trio**

Company	Category (Trajectory)	Year Founded	Observation Period	Revenue Growth	Average Annual ROA	Compounded Annual TSR	Compounded Annual Revenue Growth
Wm. Wrigley Jr. Company	Miracle Worker (Found It)	1891	1966 to 2007	$140MM to $5.4BN	15.2%	15.7%	9.3%
Tootsie Roll Industries	Long Runner (Kept It)	1896	1966 to 2010	$28MM to $521MM	10.5%	13.1%	6.9%
Rocky Mountain Chocolate Factory	Average Joe (N/A)	1981	1984 to 2010	$4MM to $31MM	7.6%	7.6%	8.6%

Source: Company documents; Compustat; Deloitte analysis

respectively, Wrigley and Tootsie are one of our most closely matched Miracle Worker/Long Runner pairings. The third company in this trio is Rocky Mountain Chocolate Factory (RMCF), a maker and retailer of higher-end chocolates and a far less storied organization, as befits an Average Joe.

Wrigley and Tootsie Roll are included in our database from the first observation in 1966. For almost twenty years they had comparable performance, with gradually increasing ROA and decile ranks in the 6-to-8 range. It was not until the late 1980s that their profitability diverged. Tootsie flirted with Miracle Worker status, turning in a few 9th-decile years, but the mid-1980s proved its zenith. Since then its absolute performance has deteriorated to the point that its Long Runner status is increasingly shaky. In contrast, in 1986 Wrigley began an unbroken eighteen-year run of 9th-decile performances, earning it a Found It Miracle Worker trajectory. Its acquisition by another large, privately held confectionary company in 2008 came just as that streak was beginning to wobble.

Like our groceries trio in the next section of this chapter, our confectionary trio has an Average Joe with a non-price competitive position. Rocky Mountain Chocolate Factory was founded by a former CIA officer in search of a quieter life (one imagines that almost anything would have met that criterion). Through the end of our observation period in 2010, almost 50 percent of all products were confected on site in its own retail locations. The company has long focused on delivering a fresh and unique product sold in an evocative and compelling retail environment. Creating and sustaining that combination has clearly proved challenging, as revealed by the company's entirely average performance, but its desired positioning in the candy market is clear.

By comparison, Wrigley and Tootsie Roll are much more traditional mass-production confectionary companies. Their products depend on branding at least as much as their intrinsic features to stand out, and distribution has been almost exclusively through conventional retail channels controlled by others, such as vending machines, convenience stores, and grocery stores. Wrigley typically dealt with these channels directly while Tootsie Roll often worked through distributors. Where RMCF sells its chocolate wonders for dollars per piece, Wrigley and Tootsie Roll sell their minor indulgences for less than a dollar per pack.

Within this narrower slice of the candy business, Wrigley and Tootsie Roll occupy different competitive positions due to a different relative emphasis on advertising and distribution management, a parting of the strategic ways that goes back to the earliest days of both companies.

For example, faced with economic depression in 1907, founder William Wrigley Jr. took out a $250,000 loan (equivalent to something in excess of $6 million today) to launch an ad campaign. William's son, Philip, took over the company in 1932, but, if anything, upped the advertising ante, at one point placing 117 billboards along a seventy-five-mile stretch of railroad track between Trenton and Atlantic City, New Jersey—one billboard every thousand yards or so.[37]

Both Wrigley and Tootsie Roll candies were pulled from consumer markets during World War II and included in GI rations, creating for both brands a powerful connection with U.S. soldiers and European civilian markets. Only Wrigley, however, launched a major advertising initiative, building the campaign on the tagline "Remember this wrapper." Wrigley spared little expense in an effort to support future sales—even though no one in the United States could buy the product.

This dedication to brand building has continued largely unabated. Wrigley typically spent approximately 15 percent of revenue on advertising and only 2 percent on trade promotions and "slotting fees," the payments made to retailers to, among other things, secure favorable shelf space.[38] This has contributed to making Wrigley, at times, one of the most valuable brands in the world.[39]

Wrigley's branding efforts allowed it to control its packaging and pricing in ways other companies could not. For example, in the 1980s many distributors priced most candy and gum at 50 cents. In response, Wrigley reduced its pack size and preprinted its desired price of 25 cents on the packaging, making less obvious the price premium Wrigley was charging as a result. Many retailers resisted this move, and the 7-Eleven chain stopped carrying Wrigley products for almost a decade.[40] More recently, one analyst estimated that Wrigley's products are between 7 percent and 15 percent more expensive than direct category competitors.[41]

These actions should be seen only as a commitment to pricing control, however, not a lack of concern for its distributors. Confectionary products are sold through hundreds of thousands of small retailers, and Wrigley worked with many of them to provide guidance and counsel on how best to organize and display candy, which is perhaps the stereotypical impulse purchase. Neither was Wrigley entirely self-serving in providing this advice, often suggesting ways retailers could increase their sales of competing products in ways that benefited the retailer. The company pioneered the effort to turn the checkout into a major "profit zone," and subsidized the cost of the shelving units, even though these units were used to display products other than Wrigley's. It could afford this sort of largesse because, thanks to its higher prices, Wrigley has often been the most profitable confectionary for the retailer, generating retail margins of 50 percent or more.[42]

Tootsie Roll, in contrast, typically spent only 2 percent of revenue on advertising, devoting the rest of its smaller marketing budget to coupons and trade promotions in an effort to spur consumer adoption through lower prices. Where Wrigley created what amounted to educational materials on the science of impulse retail, Tootsie Roll economized, providing little more than utilitarian catalogs of product photographs and UPC codes for ordering. Cost-consciousness pervades every aspect of the company to this day, to the point that the free candy samples on offer at Tootsie Roll's corporate headquarters have long consisted primarily of product in misprinted packaging that is unsuitable for retail sale.[43]

Through the mid-1980s Wrigley enjoyed an economically material performance advantage over Tootsie Roll of just over two percentage points of ROA per year. But in relative terms, Wrigley and Tootsie Roll were not statistically significantly different. Wrigley had an average decile rank of 6.7 for the period, with a range from 2 to 8, while Tootsie Roll had an average decile rank of 6.2, with a range from 2 to 9. Had Wrigley continued on that trajectory it would have been a Long Runner essentially indistinguishable from Tootsie Roll.

Up to that point Wrigley and Tootsie Roll were examples of different ways to be profitable. Wrigley had a gross margin advantage made possible largely by higher marketing expenditures, which showed up in an SG&A disadvantage. Tootsie Roll's greater emphasis on thrift shows up in an asset turnover advantage thanks to operational efficiencies and cost savings in plant, equipment, headquarters, and so on. The net result was very similar results. In short, Wrigley was "spending money to make money" while Tootsie took the view that "a penny saved is a penny earned." And they were both right.

It is from 1986 onward that Wrigley separated itself from Tootsie Roll, tripling its average annual ROA advantage and creating a significant lead in relative performance. The shift in the structure of Wrigley's advantage helps us pin down the specific behavioral differences that drove Wrigley's improved absolute and relative performance.

First, note that Wrigley's gross margin advantage persists, but shrinks, and is actually more than offset by higher relative SG&A spend. A contributing factor was very likely a push to develop new products and brands. The introduction of Freedent in 1975, a gum touted as one that would not stick to dentures or other dental work, was the first new brand

TABLE 23: **Wrigley's Elements of Advantage Versus Tootsie Roll**

Elements of ROA	Contribution to ROA Advantage in Percentage Points per Year	
	Period of Lower Performance: 1966–1985	**Period of Higher Performance: 1986–2007**
Gross Margin	15.1	8.2
SG&A	–9.2	–10.8
R&D	0.0	0.0
Other (incl. taxes)	–2.6	1.1
ROS	3.4	–1.5
CAT	–0.4	2.1
FAT	–0.7	0.5
Other	–0.1	5.3
TAT	–1.2	7.9
ROA	**2.1**	**6.4**

Source: Compustat; Deloitte analysis
Figures may not total due to rounding.

for the company in more than sixty years, its first attempt to move beyond Wrigley's Spearmint, Doublemint, and Juicy Fruit.

In an industry characterized by products with legacies going back generations, this marked the beginning of a relative burst of creativity. Wrigley introduced Big Red, Hubba Bubba, Extra, Winterfresh, Eclipse, and Orbit through 2001. In addition, the company experimented with gum as a medium for delivering medications, such as antacid, with the ultimately unsuccessful Surpass. The costs of developing, launching, and sustaining an increasing number of new products, all of which were highly dependent on the same advertising-heavy strategy, ultimately left Wrigley with a net ROS disadvantage compared with Tootsie Roll. And so, although we might like to have seen Wrigley's sustained commitment to product development and innovation be a driver of superior profitability—as it was for Linear, Medtronic, and A&F—we cannot make that connection.

Instead, Wrigley's more nearly non-price position and higher prices were a necessary but not sufficient condition of its Miracle Worker status.[44] We must find the rest of its recipe in behavior that turned what had been a 1.2 pp/year TAT disadvantage into an advantage of almost 8 pp/year. We have identified three contributing factors, each ultimately attributable to Wrigley's volume advantage, which was in turn made possible by its strong non-price position.

First, the correspondence between the two companies' international expansion and Wrigley's streaks of relatively lower and higher performance becomes salient. We lack reliable data for years prior to 1978, but that year Wrigley earned 44 percent of its revenue in non-U.S. markets. Through 1985, the end of Wrigley's lower performance streak, this fell to 32 percent while Tootsie Roll's held steady at 15 percent. During this period, Tootsie Roll's overall growth rate was almost twice that of Wrigley's.

Beginning in 1986, the onset of Wrigley's higher performance streak, Wrigley's sales from non-U.S. markets increased steadily, and in 2006 accounted for 63 percent of total revenue compared with only 9 percent for Tootsie Roll. From its much larger base, Wrigley grew at over 10 percent per year while Tootsie Roll's growth rate fell to 7.6 percent annually.

Wrigley patterned its international expansion on its domestic operations. For example, the company's entry into China was preceded by significant advertising campaigns on radio, television, and outdoor media. In addition, a large sales force was deployed to ensure extensive retail distribution.[45] Avoiding both joint ventures and acquisitions, Wrigley was singularly successful in venturing abroad. Chinese operations began in 1989, and by 1999 China was second only to the United States in sales for the company. Perhaps most remarkable of all, by 2005 Wrigley had a 60

TABLE 24: **Wrigley and Tootsie Roll Sales Growth Rates for Domestic and Foreign Markets**

| | | Wrigley's Lower Performance Period: 1978–1985* | | Wrigley's Higher Performance Period: 1986–2007 | |
		Wrigley	Tootsie Roll	Wrigley	Tootsie Roll
Sales Growth	U.S.	7.6%	8.3%	6.2%	7.4%
	Non-U.S.	0.1%	9.5%	14.0%	6.19%
	Overall	4.8%	8.5%	10.2%	7.3%
End of Period Sales		$620 million	$107 million	$5.4 billion	$493 million

Source: Compustat; company documents; Deloitte analysis
*For which we have data on non-U.S. sales.

percent market share and had driven the largest domestic candy company, Guangdong Fanyu Candy Co., to close.[46]

Second, differences in merger and acquisition activity come to the fore. Neither company executed any material deals from 1966 through 1985. From 1986 onward, however, Tootsie Roll becomes a serial acquirer of sorts, picking up Charms, Warner-Lambert's candy operations, Andes/OTEC, and Concord Confections between 1987 and 2004. The total sales of these companies in the year Tootsie Roll acquired them is 48 percent of Tootsie Roll's top line in 2006.

In contrast, Wrigley does only two deals of note: in 2004 it acquired Joyco, which was 8 percent of Wrigley's revenue at the time, and in 2005 it purchased Kraft's confectionary division, which was 14 percent of Wrigley's total revenue. Combined, these two deals accounted for 20 percent of Wrigley's total 2006 revenue. Said differently, Wrigley's organic annual revenue growth increased from 4.8 to 8.7 percent across the two streaks while Tootsie Roll's fell from 8.2 to 4.3 percent.[47] The difference in deal making drove significant differences in the goodwill assets carried on each company's balance sheet, which showed up as a higher "Other" asset turnover for Wrigley.

Wrigley might have done relatively few deals largely because of its industry-leading gross margins: when anything you might buy appears dilutive, you end up buying very little. The drive for growth can be powerful, however, and this factor would quite likely have been overlooked but for Wrigley's ability to drive growth in non-U.S. markets thanks to its powerful brands—a consequence of its long-term investment in brand building and distribution management. Not only does Wrigley earn most of its revenue outside the United States, it is dominant in many of the major non-U.S. markets in which it competes, with number two status in Canada and number one in Europe.[48]

In other words, Wrigley ended up avoiding deals and expanding beyond the United States because those were the choices that were consistent with its *better before cheaper* position and *revenue before cost* profitability formula. Its growth surge was driven by unit volumes enabled by a non-price position. That might seem at odds with what you might have learned in economics class, namely, that the key to higher volumes is lower prices. That principle, however, applies to highly efficient markets of substitutable goods. Exceptional companies avoid those kinds of battles, and so are able to grow while still commanding a price premium.

Tootsie Roll, on the other hand, was focused on profitability through cost reduction and relied on its brand legacy to drive revenue. It could only drive its own costs so low, and so it turned to finding "diamonds in the rough": smaller companies with solid brands but relatively higher costs. Trading on the slowly eroding nature of brand equity in the interstices of the North American candy market, Tootsie Roll was able to improve the profitability of these companies through cost reduction while avoiding any material investments. The company is, after all, a Long Runner.

However, that strategy eventually was a victim of its own success. The premiums paid for acquisitions steadily increased the goodwill on the balance sheet while the complexity of product diversification put a constant upward pressure on costs. Consistent with our overall thesis, price-based positions and cost-driven profitability formulas can work, they just work less well than non-price-based positions and revenue-driven profitability formulas.

Third and finally, Tootsie Roll carried much higher cash balances than Wrigley. High cash balances are not systematically associated with lower relative performance. Heartland, our Miracle Worker in trucking, consistently carried higher cash balances than Werner, the Long Runner, and we believe this contributed to Heartland's advantage in ways we will explore in the next chapter.[49] In this case, however, we believe Tootsie Roll's cash balances were a consequence of an inability to deploy those assets profitably. Sitting on the money is better than wasting it, but putting it to work is better still. And that is what Wrigley was able to do, and so its profits fueled profitable growth rather than piling up on the balance sheet.

From all this emerges the explanation we sought. Wrigley grew much more rapidly, and from a larger base, primarily through organic international expansion. This strategy was expensive, as it required spending on brand building and assets globally. But Wrigley's growth, enabled by its strong non-price position (rather than by low prices), paid off: overall ROA rose as higher revenue more than compensated for the rising asset base.

Tootsie Roll, on the other hand, unable to put its cash to work effectively and driving growth primarily through relatively expensive M&A, found itself with a balance sheet bogged down by current assets and goodwill and a cost base subject to an upward creep driven by a broad and complex product portfolio. The result was a dramatic relative decline in asset turnover versus Wrigley and an increasingly severe gross margin disadvantage.

Does this mean that acquisitions are always a bad idea? Or that international expansion is always a good idea? Not at all. What we learn from this detailed exegesis is how the specific actions that drove differences in profitability in this case are ultimately the consequence of the adherence—whether deliberate or not—to the three rules.

> Wrigley earned Miracle Worker status only when it leveraged its non-price position in its segment, built on valuable brands, to drive volume through international expansion. Tootsie Roll's strategy of "frugal acquisition" was inherently limited, resulting in a Lost It Long Runner trajectory, thanks to steadily increasing assets and rising costs associated with a portfolio of ever-greater complexity.

We have not forgotten our Average Joe, RMCF. As has been typical of companies in this category, the story here is not nearly as nuanced or revealing. Rocky Mountain Chocolate Factory started out focused on increasing its retail locations with a small number of franchisees. The company's weak revenue growth and low profitability defy the sort of explanation that emerged from our analysis of Wrigley and Tootsie Roll. When a non-price position and price-based profitability formula fail, at the most general level one is forced to observe merely that there was insufficient non-price value to justify the price levels required to be successful.

In RMCF we see a clear illustration of the challenges associated with pursuing a *better before cheaper* position and seeking profitability with a *revenue before cost* formula. From 1984 to 1988 it lost money in four out of five years before transitioning to a largely franchise-based model. Two years of strong profitability seemed to spur a rapid build-out of both franchisee and corporate-owned stores, and profitability plunged. Diversification into new formats and distribution channels followed, all of which were reversed when performance continued to deteriorate. The company then returned to a franchise-only model, but remained committed to the underlying position of high-end chocolates handcrafted on site.

This dedication to solving the hard problem of how to be better—instead of bolting for a low-price, low-cost solution—could well be on the verge of paying off. Despite its difficult beginning, RMCF has enjoyed steadily increasing absolute performance, culminating in a recent and highly suggestive run of 9th-decile years, making it the only Average Joe with even a glimmer of the sort of performance that defines an exceptional company. More intriguing still, Whole Foods, which we will discuss presently, is the only other Average Joe with a non-price position and revenue-driven profitability formula, and the only other Average Joe with systematically increasing ROA.

Committing to solving the *better before cheaper* problem does not guarantee success, for the simple reason that looking for an answer to a tough problem is not a sufficient condition for finding one. But it would appear to be an almost necessary condition for doing so.

Declining Profitability: The Limits of Lower Cost

However convincing you might find our observation that revenue trumps cost as a driver of exceptional profitability, it beggars belief that lower cost is *never* a driver of superior performance. It is somewhat reassuring, then, that our sample has at least one Miracle Worker that swam upstream, delivering standout profitability with *cheaper before better* and *cost before revenue*.

Our corporate sockeye is Weis Markets (Weis). Its thirty-year streak of relatively higher performance and twenty-eight consecutive 9th-decile years is the longest and most consistent in our sample. However, for the fifteen years through 2010 the company suffered steadily declining absolute and relative performance, putting it on a Lost It lifetime trajectory, but its remarkable run in the sun suggests pretty strongly that, although rare, cost-based exceptionalism can deliver enviable outcomes.

Publix Super Markets (Publix), today a much larger chain than Weis, is the only Found It Long Runner in our sample while Whole Foods Market (Whole Foods), the high-end organic and specialty grocery chain, is the Average Joe.

Of the three, Whole Foods has perhaps the most obvious relative competitive position, clearly competing on non-price dimensions of performance through a focus on specialty items, organic produce, meats, and personal care products, and attuned to such movements as local sourcing. Whole Foods has become a nationwide and international chain with mostly urban locations providing unique items of superior quality, with prices to match: the company is widely referred to as "Whole Paycheck."[50] Corporate leadership, not surprisingly, finds the sobriquet objectionable,

TABLE 25: Descriptive Statistics for the Groceries Trio

Company	Category (Trajectory)	Year Founded	Observation Period	Revenue Growth	Average Annual ROA	Compounded Annual TSR	Compounded Annual Revenue Growth
Weis Markets	Miracle Worker (Lost It)	1912	1966 to 2010	$126MM to $2.6BN	11.7%	11.6%	7.1%
Publix Super Markets	Long Runner (Found It)	1930	1974 to 2010	$1BN to $2.5BN	10.8%	9.7%	9.4%
Whole Foods Market	Average Joe (N/A)	1980	1991 to 2010	$93MM to $9BN	5.7%	16.3%	27.2%

Source: Compustat; company documents; Deloitte analysis

but does not deny that the company's prices are often higher than those at other stores, even other specialty grocery chains.[51]

Despite its non-price position, Whole Foods has not turned in noteworthy profitability overall, notwithstanding a gradual upward trend and occasional flashes of brilliance. Although investing for growth can certainly be a drag on ROA, Whole Foods has been in operation for more than thirty years, more than twenty of them as a public company, and its decile ranks have been 5 or less as often as not. This steady mediocrity belies the wild swings in investor expectations. The stock tracked the broader market through 2000, and then for five years outperformed by a factor of six, only to plummet back to long-term market parity by 2008, followed by a sevenfold run-up versus the market through 2012. At some point, financial theory tells us, Whole Foods will have to show investors the money.

Weis is the price-based competitor of this trio. With approximately 80 percent of its store locations in Pennsylvania, and mostly in more rural locations, Weis's period of relatively higher performance was driven by its industry leadership in such trends as private-label products, which it sold at lower prices than nationally advertised brands. Its product mix was entirely unremarkable, offering the standard selection of food staples, meat and deli, vegetables, and produce. Unlike its leadership in private label, it followed industry trends such as introducing an in-store pharmacy, and only ever dabbled in alternative grocery segments such as organic or ethnic foods.

In the middle is Publix, a Found It Long Runner. Expanding from its base in Florida, Publix has steadily increased its ROA in both absolute and relative terms. Since the 1970s, its ROA has steadily increased from the 7 to 9 percent range to the 12 to 14 percent range, and between 1999 and 2010 inclusive the company has delivered nothing but 9th-decile ranks. Like Stryker in the previous chapter, its profitability has improved so much and so consistently that one cannot help but think the company is on track to Miracle Worker status.

This seeming improvement in performance tracks its changing competitive position over the decades. For perhaps the first fifteen years of our observation period Publix was a more traditional price-based competitor, focusing on driving profitability through cost reduction and efficiencies—the company was among the first to adopt aggressively Universal Product Code (UPC, or "bar code")–based inventory control. Through the mid-1990s its performance was solid, but also solidly in the shadow of Weis's, for reasons we will explore below.

For some time now, however, it has sought ways to compete on an increasing number of non-price dimensions and with increasingly positive results. For example, the company initially moved to private-label products in the more traditional pursuit of lower price, lower cost, and higher margin. More recently, however, it introduced its own store brand of organic products, GreenWise, seeking out a niche among the interstices of inexpensive traditional private-label products, nationally advertised brands, and premium-priced branded organic products available at retailers such as Whole Foods. It has also invested in ethnic-specific formats and stores-within-stores such as Publix Sabor (Spanish for "flavor"), which target specific demographic groups with identifiable food preferences.

These relative competitive positions suggest that lower cost was at the root of Weis's superior profitability. After all, a company competing on the basis of lower prices is unlikely to be driving profitability with prices that are simultaneously *higher*. Further, while Weis grew at a respectable 7.3 percent per year for the period, Publix grew at 11.3 percent annually, making a volume-driven explanation (as with Wrigley) highly unlikely.

In light of its competitive position, the structure of Weis's advantage over Publix is also suggestive. With no evidence that Weis could command a price premium, its gross margin advantage and lower relative SG&A spending is entirely consistent with a lower-COGS, lower-cost model.

To this circumstantial evidence we can add two specific differences

TABLE 26: **Weis's Elements of Advantage Versus Publix**

Elements of ROA	Contribution to ROA Advantage in Percentage Points per Year	
	Period of Higher Performance: 1974–1995	Period of Lower Performance: 1996–2010
Gross Margin	12.1	−0.7
SG&A	0.4	−4.4
R&D	0.0	0.0
Other (incl. taxes)	−4.3	1.9
ROS	8.2	−3.2
CAT	−4.5	−2.0
FAT	−0.1	−1.0
Other	0.1	0.9
TAT	−4.5	−2.1
ROA	3.7	−5.4

Source: Compustat; Deloitte analysis
Figures may not total due to rounding.

between Weis and Publix that support this hypothesis. First, and perhaps most compelling, is Weis's greater reliance on private-label products. Private-label products were identified as early as the 1940s as a source of increased profitability for grocery retailers.[52] Historically, they have been of lower quality and lower price than nationally advertised brands, but also disproportionately lower cost, and hence higher margin.[53]

Despite these seeming advantages, few grocery retailers pursued a private-label strategy with much vigor prior to the 1990s. Weis was a notable exception, introducing its own brand of potato chips and ice cream in the early 1960s. Given the relative dearth of suppliers of private-label products, Weis backward-integrated, setting up its own manufacturing plants.

Weis's private-label strategy was so important that it created a private-label department, and by 1965 Weis had 433 private items, many of which it manufactured itself, a number that had almost doubled to 809 by 1969.

Publix did not launch its private-label strategy until 1979. Despite starting its push into private label more than fifteen years after Weis, Publix did not accelerate its rollout of this initiative. Private labels would not become a staple of grocery retailers' strategies until the late 1980s, and so there remained a challenge in sourcing products and a relative resistance on the part of consumers. Consequently, like Weis before it and as had become typical among early adopters of private-label strategies, Publix began with dairy, a category that generally has relatively fewer strong national brands. Success in that foothold segment would earn the company the ability to slowly expand the range of private-label products it offered. Consequently, despite the attractiveness of private label, there was only a slow convergence of the fraction of grocery sales generated by each company from lower-cost, higher-margin private-label offerings.[54]

TABLE 27: **Percentage of Total Sales Generated by Private-Label Products**

	Weis	**Publix**
1975	14%	–
1980	14%	2%
1985	15%	6%
1990	15%	10%
1995	17%	14%
2000	17%	16%

Source: Company documents; Deloitte analysis

TABLE 28: **Sales and Income per Square Foot**

	Sales per Square Foot		Net Income per Square Foot	
	Weis	Publix	Weis	Publix
1974	$149	$144	$6	$2
1980	$254	$246	$12	$4
1990	$310	$394	$21	$10
1997	$293	$443	$13	$14
2006	$307	$534	$8	$27

Source: Compustat; company documents; Deloitte analysis

Second, for the decade ending in 1983, Weis and Publix had essentially identical sales per square foot, as both companies rose from $135 to about $285. Yet Weis enjoys a significant profitability advantage, with an income per square foot edge of $4 in 1974, which widens to $12 by 1990, even as Publix takes the lead in sales per square foot in the period from 1983 to 1990. In such similar product categories it is difficult to see how Weis was able to increase its relative profitability even as its relative productivity decreased, without concluding that Weis enjoyed a significant cost advantage.

Although none of these arguments is conclusive on its own, we find the cumulative weight of the evidence compelling. Weis's greater focus on lower-priced, higher-margin private labels, similar or lower sales per square foot but higher net income per foot, lower growth, and lack of any clear non-price differentiation that might earn a price premium, and relatively lower SG&A spending, all point to a cost-driven profitability formula during its period of relative high performance.

Weis's streak of relative high performance, at fully thirty years, is, in absolute terms, one of the longest in our entire database. *Better before cheaper* and *revenue before cost* might well be the rule; clearly these maxims are far from inviolable laws. That Weis's streak ended, and the company is now a Lost It Miracle Worker, in no way negates the merits of its achievement.

Even so, it is worth understanding why Weis's streak ended, and perhaps more important, what it was that allowed Publix to establish both an absolute and a relative performance advantage over Weis. For what we see in the performance profiles of these two companies is not simply the perhaps inevitable erosion of a dominant position, but a dramatic and steady decline by a onetime industry leader coincident with an equally dramatic and steady ascension by its onetime imitator.

From 1985 to 1995, grocery stores were enjoying structural growth, increasing their collective share of total at-home food expenditures, largely at the expense of "other grocery" outlets—essentially one-off, small "mom-and-pop" stores. Thanks to lower costs, driven by greater economies of scale and higher levels of investment in technology, grocery stores were able to offer greater selection at lower prices, yet still prove more profitable, than these smaller, subscale retail channels.

In the late 1980s discount supercenters got into grocery retail. Walmart, the largest such entrant, opened its first supercenter offering meats, produce, dairy products, and baked goods in 1988. By 2000 it had nearly eight hundred, a number that more than doubled by 2005.[55] By 2010, supercenters had collectively increased their share of the retail grocery business to just over 16 percent, and almost all of that growth came at the expense of traditional grocery retailers.[56]

These new competitors tended to take share through price-based competition. They often enjoyed lower costs thanks to greater scale, often enabled by investment in technology and more efficient distribution. They also often saw groceries as a way to increase traffic to their stores, which drove sales of higher-margin general merchandise.[57] Grocery chains typically fought fire with fire by bulking up through acquisition in the pursuit of economies of scale and expanding the range of merchandise they offered in order to create a more profitable product mix.[58]

But even before the rise of supercenters began putting pressure on

TABLE 29: **Percentage of Sales of At-Home Food by Outlet**

	Supermarkets	**Other Grocery**	**Supercenters**	**All Other Grocery**
1985	66.0%	18.6%	0.2%	15.3%
1990	63.4%	13.7%	1.4%	21.4%
1995	75.4%	1.5%	3.2%	19.8%
2000	70.9%	1.4%	7.2%	20.5%
2005	65.8%	0.7%	14.1%	19.5%
2010	64.4%	0.9%	16.1%	18.5%

Source: U.S. Department of Agriculture, Economic Research Service; authors' analysis

Figures may not total due to rounding.

supermarkets on an industry-wide basis, Weis's profitability was waning. Between 1988 and 1992 the company's ROA fell from over 15 percent to under 10 percent, about the same as Publix's. This was precipitated by a collapse in Weis's ROS, stemming from a reduced COGS advantage and higher SG&A spending. These changes were most likely a consequence of the widespread adoption of private labeling by its competitors, generally lower prices in the grocery segment due to increased competition, and the need to increase other costs, such as advertising.[59] Its decline was symptomatic of the industry as a whole, as the grocery industry's average ROA had been steadily eroding for decades: from about 8 percent in the 1960s, by the late 2000s it was hovering around 4 percent.[60]

Weis's response to its declining profitability has been demonstrably ineffective and arguably both unfocused and halfhearted. In 1993 the company acquired Superpetz, a pet supply business. Leaving existing management in place, Weis funded the expansion of operations from two stores to forty-three by 1996. With a top line of $73 million, the division was barely more than 4 percent of total revenue that year, yet its $3.5

million after-tax loss more than wiped out what would have been a $3 million increase in earnings on grocery sales of $1.75 billion.

In an attempt to improve performance, Weis management took on a more active role in the pet supplies division, centralizing accounting and financial functions. The number of locations was reduced from forty-three to thirty-six by 1998. By 2009 the number of locations was down to twenty-five, and in 2011 the remaining locations were sold or closed.

The direct financial impact of this failed diversification attempt is quite minor, but many commentators have noted that diversification, however limited its scope, can be dangerously dilutive of management time, one of the most valuable resources in any corporation.[61] Management's possible distraction by the continuing need to stabilize a venture that had been intended to drive growth and compensate for declines in the grocery business could have tightened the grip of senescence on the core business. As evidence, consider that in an industry characterized by a drive for scale, Weis grew at a nominal 3.2 percent per year, barely more than the rate of inflation.

This seeming inability or unwillingness to grow was not new for Weis. Through 2007, the company had 125 stores in its home state of Pennsylvania. It entered Maryland in 1967 and had 24 stores there forty years later, which was markedly better than its growth rate in New York: the single store that opened the year Weis entered Maryland was still its only Empire State location after four decades. The 1982 entry into West Virginia maxed out at 2 locations, and the 1993 expansion into New Jersey did little better, at 3.

From the perspective of Weis's streak of relative high performance, staying close to home can easily be seen as prudence. We cannot know if an appetite for expansion would have positioned Weis to cope better with industry forces in the 1990s or simply have brought its run of exceptional profitability to an end during the Carter administration. Forced to choose, we would argue for the latter. Either way, Weis proved unable to cope with the increased cost and price pressures of twenty years ago.

Over this same period Publix pulled away. Despite its late start—its first store outside its base in Florida was not opened until it entered Georgia in 1991—by 2006 the company had 892 locations, 615 in Florida and the rest distributed throughout Tennessee (14), Alabama (26), Georgia (107), and South Carolina (38). This increasing scale is in our view a material part of the explanation for Publix's sustained cost-competitiveness.

It was also during this period that Publix began exploring those dimensions of non-price differentiation that earned it the in-the-middle competitive position: in-store deli and pharmacy, organic products, and ethnic-focused store formats. These actions seem to have kept Publix both cost competitive and sufficiently differentiated that it did not need to rely on cost and price leadership to drive profitability.

What are we to make of Whole Foods? With its consistent focus on a clear non-price position and a strong revenue-driven profit formula, it seems to be three for three in its adherence to the rules. What has been missing?

Perhaps nothing. The structure of Weis's and Publix's profitability advantage over Whole Foods during their respective streaks of lower and higher performance provides a framework for understanding what Whole Foods's future might hold.

The consistent gross margin advantage Whole Foods has held over its higher-performing trio members suggests that it is more than getting recompensed for the higher COGS it must incur sourcing organic and other specialty products. However, its much higher SG&A costs more than offset that advantage. These higher costs, however, are not likely due to inefficiencies. For example, Whole Foods typically operates in higher-rent locations. Whole Foods has 6 to 8 employees per 1,000 square feet of retail space versus 4.5 for Publix and fewer than 3 for Weis. This higher personnel load is

TABLE 30: **Weis's and Publix's Elements of Advantage Versus Whole Foods**

Elements of ROA	Contribution to ROA Advantage in Percentage Points per Year		
	Weis Vs. Whole Foods		Publix Vs. Whole Foods
	Period of Higher Performance: 1991–1995	Period of Lower Performance: 1996–2010	Period of Higher Performance: 1991–2010
Gross Margin	-10.2	-20.6	-26.3
SG&A	14.0	16.1	25.1
R&D	0.0	0.0	0.0
Other (incl. taxes)	2.3	5.8	5.5
ROS	6.1	1.4	4.3
CAT	-2.8	-0.7	0.0
FAT	0.0	0.3	1.4
Other	0.6	0.7	0.5
TAT	-2.3	0.2	1.9
ROA	**3.8**	**1.6**	**6.2**

Source: Compustat; Deloitte analysis
Figures may not total due to rounding.

likely a function of several features of Whole Foods's model, including the challenges of sourcing unique or specialty items and the higher levels of customer service required to help customers navigate the relatively rapidly and constantly changing local brands that feature in Whole Foods stores. Higher levels of depreciation (an element of other costs) speak to higher-cost facilities. Intriguingly, although Whole Foods has expanded rapidly and largely through acquisition, which has accounted for more than half of its growth, there is not a significant ROA deficit due to other asset turnover, which is where the impact of goodwill would be felt. It would seem the company has been a savvy acquirer, giving the lie to any suggestion that acquisitions are a necessary drag on profitability.

Whole Foods has not yet delivered the performance required to be exceptional, even by Long Runner standards, despite decades of exploring and developing its model. The question is whether the tide is about to turn for Whole Foods, and its non-price position is about to pay off, or against it, in which case its thirty-year experiment might be at risk.

> Weis's price-based position and cost-based profitability formula earned it solid Miracle Worker status, but was ultimately undermined by competition from adjacent industries with structural cost advantages. In contrast to Weis's Lost It trajectory, Publix (Long Runner) created a Found It trajectory by shifting to a non-price position.

As the supply chain for organic and other specialty items improves, Whole Foods's costs will fall. However, it has very likely been the complexity and frustrations of that supply chain that have kept other major players at bay, allowing Whole Foods a nearly unique non-price position in groceries. Ironically, then, it is possible that the very efficiencies Whole Foods needs in order to break through to exceptional performance might also allow other players to more nearly mimic Whole Foods's position, as evidenced by the relatively recent entry of, among others, Publix, Walmart, and other major grocery retailers into the segment.

It seems to us that Whole Foods's experience, like that of RMCF, reveals the peril, but also the promise, associated with a non-price, revenue-driven pursuit of exceptional profitability. Weis's price-based competition and cost-driven profitability proved unable to cope with the dramatically different cost structures of nontraditional competitors and industry consolidation. In contrast, the question for Whole Foods is whether it can continue to find valuable ways to differentiate itself in order to preserve its enviable gross margins even as industry-level change threatens to create a host of new competitors.

These three trios, like the three in the previous chapter, illustrate the diversity of exceptional companies' specific recipes for profitability. For example, growth was a key driver of Wrigley's rise to Miracle Worker status while its lack was a contributing factor in Weis's demise. Abercrombie & Fitch's growth was noteworthy, but it came as a consequence of the company's success, as it did with Publix. The erosion of Finish Line's position limited its growth options while growth seems to be both cause and consequence of Whole Foods's potentially brightening prospects.

Ownership structure differed radically among the companies. Miracle Worker A&F had a dominant shareholder in the form of another corporation, The Limited. Miracle Worker Weis, Long Runner Finish Line, and Average Joe Syms were all majority owned by their founders while Miracle Worker Wrigley and Average Joe Whole Foods, although strongly influenced by their founders, had a widely dispersed ownership.

As Weis makes clear, price and cost leadership can drive profitability that is just as remarkable and durable as non-price, revenue-driven approaches. It is, however, the only company with that particular combination of traits.

Since our sample was chosen independent of any knowledge of what was driving companies' performance, we take this as evidence that this particular combination is at least less common than revenue-driven exceptional profitability, and perhaps dramatically so.

The prevalence of revenue-driven profitability among exceptional companies is perhaps most significant for what it says about how best to use ROA as a guide to strategic action.

As we explored briefly in chapter 1, since ROA is a ratio, there is no mathematical difference when ROA is increased by adjusting any of its constituent elements. Raise price or volume, reduce costs or assets . . . the arithmetic cannot tell the difference.

But in practice there seems to be a very real difference. Miracle Workers are not wastrels, but they do not rely on cost leadership to drive their performance. Both in our population of exceptional companies and in our sample, Miracle Worker status is a consequence of gross margin advantage driven by higher price or volume—and as often as not enabled by higher costs and frequently assets. In other words, exceptional profitability demands, beyond a point, making trade-offs, accepting higher costs as the price of being truly exceptional. Driving profitability from merely good to truly great by reducing either costs or assets is not something we see, as an entirely empirical matter, to be the most likely route to Miracle Worker performance.

Long Runners, on the other hand, are much more likely to rely on cost leadership. At the population level, they count on cost leadership for a much greater proportion of their performance advantage, and in our sample, in four cases out of nine it is cost leadership that we observe driving essentially all of their profitability lead.

It is on the basis of these findings that we conclude *revenue before cost*.

CHAPTER 5

There Are No Other Rules

It might seem somewhat precious to posit "there are no other rules" as our third rule, but we feel it serves two important purposes. First, it is our admission that we were unable to find any other meaningful patterns in the behaviors of our case study companies that were associated with differences in performance. We cannot prove a negative, but in what follows we will explore at greater length why we dismissed such perennial favorites as M&A or diversification as systematic drivers of performance. The irretrievably idiosyncratic and contingent nature of how these and many other behaviors contribute to performance led us to conclude that exceptional companies all have the same recipe (*better before cheaper, revenue before cost*) but use different ingredients.

Second, in addition to creating superior levels of performance, exceptional companies deliver superior levels of performance for longer than anyone has a right to expect. It seems worth exploring, then, if and how exceptional companies adapt. Is exceptional performance a function of deep moats and thick ramparts, or does it require agility and flexibility to cope with competitors' attempts to imitate a winning formula, or with the technological, regulatory, or other environmental changes that can render onetime advantages useless, or even turn them into liabilities?

We found that not only were there no patterns *between* companies from different performance categories, there were no patterns across time *within* individual companies. So not only did Miracle Workers and Average Joes show no differences in their appetites for M&A, but individual Miracle

Workers were just as likely to adopt M&A as to abandon it over time. In short, what mattered when assessing how a behavior affected performance was not the behavior or even its implementation, but the contribution made to a company's adherence to or deviation from the first two rules. Where Lost It Miracle Workers typically changed in ways that violated the rules, Found It Miracle Workers became more aligned with the rules. Most revealing, Kept It Miracle Workers often showed evidence of the greatest degree of change in their specific behaviors, but always in the service of remaining in alignment with the rules. We conclude from this that exceptional performance demands an ability to change in order to stay the same.

Same Recipe, Different Ingredients

We shared with you in chapter 1 some of the frustrations born of our search for patterns in behavior at the level of relatively specific activities, many of which are the subject of ongoing and extensive research and often feature prominently on managerial agendas. Take, for example, mergers and acquisitions. The conventional wisdom has crystallized into "buyer beware," which is certainly not bad advice, but not particularly helpful. (When would one ever think it is good not to beware?) Research on the topic is largely consistent with this view, observing that acquirers, on average, earn about the going rate of return on their investments, but are subject to wide variation, sometimes doing very well, sometimes spectacularly poorly.[1]

Unfortunately, the demonstrated riskiness of deals is not reason enough to eschew them. Mergers and acquisitions are critical to many initiatives that can be essential to a company's success and even its survival, from gaining access to new technologies to international expansion to competitive preemption to creating strategic options. Consequently, the question is not "Does M&A help?" but "Given my circumstances, and given the details of this deal, is this particular acquisition the best mechanism for achieving my goals as I understand them now, and how can I employ it most effectively?" Since circumstances and goals vary widely from company to company, and within a particular company over time, it comes as no surprise that evidence of a first-order relationship between M&A and performance is weak and elusive.

In our sample we saw Miracle Workers and Long Runners doing no deals (Linear and Micropac in semiconductors) and using M&A to transform themselves (Medtronic and Stryker in medical devices), nearly driving themselves to ruin (T&B in electrical wiring), and attempting to reverse a long-term decline (Finish Line and Weis). The deals that worked were in accord with the rules. The ones that didn't, weren't.

The relationship between business line diversification and performance is only slightly less ambiguous, despite the recurring finding that companies with more business units do worse than those with fewer.[2] As with M&A and much else, an "on average" result hides as much as it reveals. For example, consider a company that has found a highly profitable but slow-growing niche. This company might see opportunities in an adjacent market that are less profitable than its current business, but such diversification can still make perfect sense if those new opportunities are profitable enough. Diversification therefore lowers the company's performance yet still makes good economic sense.[3]

This was arguably the dilemma that faced A&F: its core business was rapidly filling its niche in the retail landscape, yet new opportunities were not as profitable. Part of what makes our research helpful is that it differentiates between declines in absolute and relative profitability. Where more conventional research approaches would see only a negative relationship between diversification and profitability in A&F's chosen path, we see its diversification as making a key contribution to exceptional performance by extending the run of 9th-decile results even as absolute profitability declined.

Also running counter to expectations, we saw focus associated with mediocre performance: International Rectifier abandoned medical devices and pharmaceuticals to concentrate its efforts on semiconductors, yet its performance only deteriorated. We therefore conclude that focus is not what matters. *Better before cheaper* and *revenue before cost* are what matters, and it was along these fronts that IR failed to distinguish itself.

Vertical integration is another type of diversification that has multiple determinants and wide variation in outcomes. For example, in nineteenth-century America several major manufacturing companies expanded into distribution in order to compensate for the inadequate capabilities of the "jobber"-based channels of the day.[4] More recently, the rise of highly diversified business groups in emerging economies such as China and India has been seen as a response to all manner of "missing markets" for inputs in everything from capital to labor.[5] Theoretical models show that vertical integration can serve both non-price and cost-based competitive positions.[6] Empirical investigations have shown in a variety of contexts that vertical integration is profitable, unprofitable, and that changes in degree of vertical integration in either direction can improve performance.[7] In an attempt to reconcile these findings, there have been repeated efforts to define relevant contingencies that might guide us in determining when vertical integration makes sense and when it does not.[8] But here, too, there are credible competing views. For example, some argue that vertical integration is an effective way to cope with uncertainty while others hold that uncertainty undermines its effectiveness.[9]

In our sample, A&F's vertical integration was a way to create a more responsive supply chain, which was central to its non-price competitive position. Weis, in contrast, vertically integrated in the service of its lower-cost, lower-price private-label strategy. Both companies enjoyed notable success, but A&F has seemed able to renew its performance through continued commitment to the first two rules where Weis seems less likely to recapture its past glory.

Additionally, business line diversification can sometimes be not a cause of poor performance but instead a consequence.[10] Weis did not diversify into pet supplies until after the performance of its core grocery business had deteriorated significantly. The same can be said of Finish Line's ill-fated expansion into hip-hop fashion with its Man Alive franchise.

A form of diversification that seems to have a less ambiguous relationship with performance is international expansion. Several studies have found consistent and positive relationships, suggesting that going abroad is a good idea, and especially so for companies with diverse product portfolios.[11] Our sample seems largely consistent with these findings, for although internationalization was a drag on Hubbell's profitability, it seems to have helped Thomas & Betts and was central to success for Wrigley and Merck while the lack of a global footprint seems to have been part of Maytag's decline.

In light of these contradictory, or at least highly nuanced, findings on these and other dimensions of behavior, we felt it made sense to explore whether our case study data showed evidence of any consistent patterns. Appendix J, "Behavioral Differences by Pair-Wise Comparison," shows the differences for all twenty-seven pair-wise comparisons across five behaviors. Sometimes Miracle Workers do more M&A, sometimes less, and on average there is no real difference. Sometimes Miracle Workers are more diversified, sometimes less, and on average there is no real difference. We reached similar conclusions for Miracle Worker–Average Joe and Long Runner–Average Joe comparisons. The absence of any compelling patterns for these or other behaviors we were able to analyze led us to believe that anything goes. We could find no other behaviors where the contingencies did not swamp the prescriptions, and so the third rule is *there are no other rules*.

Change to Stay the Same

The absence of any rules beyond the first two has important implications for how exceptional companies adapt. As with questions of position (*better before cheaper*) and profitability (*revenue before cost*), whether exceptional companies change over time is an empirical matter. It could have been that exceptional performance is typically achieved through relative intransigence: find a winning formula and stick with it. Eventually it will be overtaken by events or the competition, but little matter; nothing lasts forever. On the other hand, superior performers might be characterized by change. In this case, we would like to know if there are any guiding principles that might help determine when and what to change.

> No behaviors we studied suggested any significant association with performance. The only thing that seemed to matter was whether a given behavior contributed to *better before cheaper* or *revenue before cost*.
> ### The Bottom Line: There Are No Other Rules

We found that, just as the specific recipes for exceptional performance were unique to each Miracle Worker, the nature of the changes each employed in order to create or sustain its exceptional performance defied meaningful generalization. There was neither a small, consistent subset of activities that responded to competitive or environmental shifts, nor did "everything" have to be reinvented. About all that seemed to matter was the first two rules. Consider this brief summary of the trios we have discussed so far.

Semiconductors: When Linear shifted to non-price differentiation, its performance improved while Micropac's focus on cost containment capped its upside. International Rectifier never found the plot, playing a scale and scope game at the industry level and never distinguishing itself at the product level.

Medical devices: Medtronic and Stryker both saw their performance improve, one by retooling its ability to deliver non-price value, one by metamorphosing into a non-price player. Invacare was stuck in a segment that precluded the sort of non-price value associated with exceptional performance.

Electrical wiring: Thomas & Betts drove itself almost over the edge by abandoning its non-price position in wiring while Hubbell suffered a watered-down version of the same fate. Emrise struggled to increase profitability in nearly monopsonistic markets.

Clothing: Abercrombie & Fitch focused on non-price differentiation and captured value with higher prices through thick and thin. Its profitability suffered as a result, but its commitment to the rules has paid dividends: A&F, almost alone among fashion retailers, is not struggling to cure customers of a "discount addiction." Finish Line's muted and seemingly halfhearted attempt to differentiate itself proved ineffective while Syms, the most clearly price-based competitor of the three, declared bankruptcy.

Confectionary: Wrigley began to realize the full value of its competitive position only when it expanded internationally yet remained focused on brand building. Tootsie's cost focus has limited both its profitability and its growth while RMCF seems, after several false starts, to have found its own particular non-price position and price-driven profitability.

Groceries: Our sole price- and cost-based competitor, Weis, enjoyed an admirable run, but, unlike Stryker in medical devices or its retail grocery counterpart Publix, was unable to adopt a non-price position when circumstances required. Whole Foods, like RMCF, is perhaps on an upward glide path as it works out the kinks in what is clearly a non-price position and price-driven profitability formula.

There remain three trios to examine in detail, each of which was reviewed briefly in chapter 1. Merck and Heartland will show us how much and how dramatically companies can change yet still prosper provided they follow the first two rules. Maytag will highlight how strategically sound reactions at just about every level can actually undermine success when those two rules are not followed.

Proactive Change: Leading the Charge

Both Merck and Eli Lilly have long histories and had been public for over a decade prior to the beginning of our observation period in 1966. They were within 15 percent of each other by revenue that year, and for the subsequent forty-five years both established themselves as leading research-based drug companies focused on patented, so-called ethical pharmaceuticals (that is, dispensed only with a prescription from a qualified medical professional). They both relied on the efficacy and uniqueness of their medicines to drive their success, and so both companies have had consistently non-price competitive positions.

The Average Joe, KV Pharmaceutical (KVP), entered our database as essentially a generic drug manufacturer. That is, it synthesized chemical compounds that had been discovered and initially commercialized by others that had come off patent. The company's own drug-delivery technologies, for example, coatings on pills that control the release of the drug in the digestive tract ("enteric" coatings), provided a modicum of non-price value for some of its products; it also licensed these technologies to others. Even so, its competitive position compared with Merck and Eli Lilly was clearly one of price-based value.[12] In the mid-1990s, KVP shifted its emphasis to original research and drug development in an attempt to

TABLE 31: **Descriptive Statistics for the Pharmaceuticals Trio**

Company	Category (Trajectory)	Year Founded	Observation Period	Revenue Growth	Average Annual ROA	Compounded Annual TSR	Compounded Annual Revenue Growth
Merck & Co.	Miracle Worker (Other)	1891	1966 to 2010	$418MM to $46BN	15.2%	11.4%	11.3%
Eli Lilly & Co.	Long Runner (Kept It)	1876	1966 to 2010	$367MM to $23.1BN	12.7%	10.7%	9.9%
K V Pharmaceutical	Average Joe (N/A)	1942	1971 to 2010	$5MM to $27MM	-0.3%	3.8%	4.6%

Source: Compustat; company documents; Deloitte analysis

develop its own patented medications. This shifted its position toward the non-price end of the spectrum, giving it a more nearly in-the-middle competitive position by the end of our observation period in 2010.

Until the 1970s, the pharmaceutical industry discovered drugs almost exclusively through a process known as "random screening." New chemical entities (NCEs) were discovered or synthesized, and then tested in vitro or in vivo to determine whether they were chemically active in potentially useful ways. Those with a glimmer of promise were fed into a long and typically fruitless process of isolating specific compounds with relatively predictable therapeutic effects. Scientists had little understanding of the underlying mechanisms of action, and so the discovery of effective and reliable drugs was essentially a numbers game: whoever identified and assayed more compounds would likely end up with more drugs to take to market.

Prior to the 1960s, random screening was a viable drug discovery process for many relatively small and scientifically unsophisticated companies. Government regulation at the time was, compared with today's regime, undemanding, with no standards for preclinical, in-human trials and no requirements of demonstrated efficacy. About the only requirements were fairly rudimentary demonstrations that an alleged medication "did no harm."[13]

The "thalidomide tragedy" changed all that as effective government regulation prevented the drug's widespread sale in the United States.[14] This gave rise to the Kefauver-Harris (K-H) Amendments of 1962, which significantly expanded the Food and Drug Administration's (FDA) authority. The most salient elements were new standards of evidence for safety, proof of efficacy, the demonstration of good manufacturing practices, and a premarket testing requirement. In addition, the Drug Efficacy Study (DES), launched in 1966, subjected 3,443 drugs already on the market to the new safety and efficacy requirements, which resulted in the removal from the market of 30 percent of all drugs reviewed and a dramatic revision in the therapeutic claims of many other medications.[15]

Companies such as Merck and Eli Lilly did not so much respond to these shifts as find themselves well positioned to benefit from them. As early as the 1930s these two companies had begun transforming themselves into the large, science-based companies we recognize today. Both were highly active in the fields of antibiotics and vaccines and had enjoyed significant breakthroughs.

The K-H Amendments served to increase the development time for new compounds by 240 percent between 1960 and 1970 while development costs increased sevenfold.[16] These increased costs drove many smaller operations from the industry, resulting in a dramatic concentration of revenue among much larger, better-capitalized companies.[17]

For as long as the remaining players could recoup the costs of the required investment, these changes in market structure were an unalloyed boon. However, included in the K-H legislation were provisions for the elimination of branded drugs and mandatory licensing of compounds prior to patent expiration. Fearful that this would undermine the profitability of their pharmaceutical operations, many companies looked for less-regulated industries where they might exploit their scientific capabilities.[18] Popular choices were cosmetics, agricultural chemicals, animal health products, and medical devices.[19] Merck and Eli Lilly were no exception, as each acquired a number of companies outside of pharmaceuticals. Eli Lilly, however, made larger acquisitions that grew strongly, and so rapidly became more diversified than Merck: from 1966 to 1980, Merck's share of total revenue from nonpharmaceutical businesses ranged between 11 percent and 28 percent while Eli Lilly's rose from 17 percent to almost 52 percent.[20]

There are at least two reasons that Eli Lilly, our Long Runner, diversified so much more than Merck, the Miracle Worker. First, Eli Lilly's nonpharmaceutical businesses enjoyed an ROA in the low teens and were consistently within a percentage point or two of the ROA of Eli Lilly's core pharmaceutical business. In contrast, Merck's nonpharmaceutical businesses were in the mid–single digits and typically underperformed the pharmaceutical division by ten percentage points or more.[21] As a result, where Eli Lilly could justifiably see diversifying outside of pharmaceuticals as a profitable course of action, Merck would likely have seen such efforts as options at best—investments to be ramped up in the event that pharmaceuticals really did lose its underlying attractiveness as a result of regulatory changes.

Second, Merck was in the vanguard of geographic diversification, exploiting a profitable avenue of growth sooner and more aggressively than did Eli Lilly. From 1966 to 1975, Merck generated nearly 50 percent of its total sales from non-U.S. markets while Eli Lilly's share crept up slowly from 25 percent; the two companies converged at just over 60 percent of sales from non-U.S. markets in 1980.[22] The relative delay in Eli Lilly's international expansion is perhaps surprising, since both companies seemed to earn five to ten percentage points of ROA more on non-U.S. sales than on domestic revenue.

Merck is the only Miracle Worker in our sample with an "Other" trajectory: it enjoys a streak of relative high performance from 1966 to 1977, even as its absolute ROA falls steadily from the low-twenties to mid-teens. Meanwhile, Eli Lilly has a very steady ROA in the mid-teens and a series of sevens and eights in relative performance. By the late 1970s the companies' performances are almost identical.

Merck's success from, say, 1966 to 1970 is entirely consistent with *better before cheaper*, for although it enjoyed no demonstrable superiority over Eli Lilly in pharmaceuticals, it had a lower level of diversification into nonpharmaceutical businesses where its *better before cheaper* position was less clear. Eli Lilly, on the other hand, was strongly diversified into businesses where it was relatively less able to stake out as strong a non-price-value position as it could in pharmaceuticals: Elizabeth Arden was not as clearly a non-price player in cosmetics as Eli Lilly was in antibiotics.

As for profitability formula, Merck's total revenue by 1976 was just over 1.2 times Eli Lilly's ($1.66 billion versus $1.34 billion), but in pharmaceuticals Merck had clearly driven growth much more aggressively: its overall pharmaceuticals business was more than 1.7 times larger than Eli Lilly's ($1.40 billion versus $803 million). By remaining focused on pharmaceuticals and diversifying earlier and more aggressively into more profitable non-U.S. markets, Merck's higher ROA during this period is largely attributable to *revenue before cost*.

The two companies' performances had converged by the mid-1970s thanks to declining ROA in the U.S. pharmaceutical business, an increase in Eli Lilly's exposure to more profitable non-U.S. pharmaceutical markets, and savvy management by Eli Lilly of its nonpharmaceutical interests. Consequently, Eli Lilly's corporate ROA held essentially steady while Merck's declined dramatically: 1978 marked the beginning of a statistically significant streak of non-9th-decile years.

Now begins our story of corporate reinvention. For Merck, the period from 1978 to 1985 would prove to be an interregnum in performance characterized by a transformation of the company's fundamental processes of drug discovery, changes that would eventually be emulated throughout the industry. In the face of declining profitability in its pharmaceutical business, both at home and abroad, Merck would invest heavily in its R&D function, adopting an entirely new approach that, beginning in 1986, would deliver seventeen of eighteen years in the 9th decile.

In reconstructing events of so long ago for an organization as complex as Merck, it is tempting to make actual outcomes look inevitable. The most plausible explanation we can see is that Merck's senior management observed the company's declining profitability along with its inability to find profitable opportunities outside of pharmaceuticals. There was very likely, therefore, an appetite to explore ways to reinvigorate its research and development.

It was not uncommon for pharmaceutical companies to engage academic researchers as consultants. During the early 1970s, Merck researchers worked with Roy Vagelos, then the chairman of the Department of Biochemistry and director of the Division of Biology and Biomedical Sciences at Washington University in St. Louis. Vagelos's views were valued because he had built his department into one of the most productive and respected in its field anywhere in the world.[23] Through this work, he came to have some insight into Merck's drug discovery techniques, noting that a deeper understanding of the underlying biological mechanisms for action might inform the drug discovery process.

After coming to the attention of then-CEO Henry Gadsden, Vagelos became the head of Merck Research Laboratories (MRL) in 1974. Vagelos's explicit intention was to remake Merck's R&D labs after the academic model, shifting the drug discovery process from "random screening," based in chemistry, to "directed discovery," which is based in biology. It was a revolution at the time, a dramatic departure from centuries of tradition in drug discovery. Merck was the first major pharmaceutical company to make a major bet on this new approach, and it was led by a person who, for all his credentials and accomplishments at the time, had never discovered a single drug.

Worse, the move for Vagelos was not considered by his colleagues in the scientific community to be a step up. Having built up a globally respected research laboratory only to leave it for the relatively lowbrow world of a commercial pharmaceutical company was seen, even by Vagelos's friends, as not just a mistake, but almost a betrayal. But Gadsden, and his successor John Horan, who took over as CEO in 1976, gave Vagelos enough confidence that he would have the freedom to manage the research function his way that he took the job.

Given the time it takes to transform any large organization, coupled with the lead times in the pharmaceutical industry—it can take decades to see a discovery translated into a drug—the commercial impact of this change in R&D strategy was not immediate. Other leading indicators, however, began to shift quite quickly. For example, through the mid-1970s Merck and Eli Lilly published approximately the same number of academic papers and were granted roughly equal numbers of patents. By the 1980s the two companies had diverged materially, and by 1990 the differences were dramatic: Merck was publishing four times as many papers, securing three times as many patents, and introducing three times as many products.[24, 25]

Merck's research output also changed the company's relationships with the U.S. National Institutes of Health and academic researchers. The development of Mevacor, a cholesterol inhibitor, is an early example of the benefits of these improved connections. In 1956 Merck had isolated mevalonic acid, a chemical link in the cholesterol chain. In 1974 Michael Brown and Joseph Goldstein of the University of Texas identified the key steps in the production of cholesterol, for which they got the Nobel Prize in 1985. This discovery was available to all, yet it was Merck that isolated lovastatin in 1978, which was approved for sale as Mevacor in 1987.

Following essentially random observations of therapeutic effectiveness made drug discovery time-consuming and expensive and often resulted in focusing on the effects of different compounds. So, for example, drug companies would develop specialties in vaccines or antibiotics. It turns out, however, that although the pathologies to which the human body is subject are legion, the biological mechanisms of action are relatively limited, if highly versatile. In other words, different mechanisms can result in similar pathologies while the same mechanisms can reveal themselves in very different ways. A fever, for example, can be evidence of the flu or lymphoma. Consequently, when Merck identified a particular target, for example, a protein that it wished to inhibit, it was able to follow the impact of that protein inhibition into a number of therapeutic areas, thus driving growth.

Although Eli Lilly made the transition to targeted discovery, it was constrained by its legacy of expertise in so-called large-molecule drugs and biotechnology products such as insulin. Unlike the "small-molecule" synthesis that characterized Merck's traditional strengths, these products did not lend themselves to the sort of adjacencies that Merck was able to exploit.

Worse still, large-molecule, protein-based therapies have relatively high initial costs compared with small molecules. This makes large-molecule therapies much more "front-end loaded," which reduces their optionality. Consequently, Merck could explore a number of alternatives at low cost, abandoning what did not work and investing further only in what showed promise; indeed, Merck was a leader in understanding and exploiting the option value of drug development. Eli Lilly, on the other hand, was forced to treat each research initiative as essentially a commitment.

We see the effects of these two factors in the diversity of Merck's and Eli Lilly's portfolios of therapeutic areas. The earliest data we have are from 1977, which is still too early for Merck's shift to targeted discovery to have had any real effect. By 1985, however, we see that not only is Merck in more than three times as many therapeutic areas—having expanded into ophthalmologicals, antibiotics, and antiulcerants, among others—but the spread of its sales across those categories was relatively even, as no therapeutic area accounted for more than 25 percent of total sales. In contrast, Eli Lilly relied on antibiotics for 75 percent of its total pharmaceutical revenue in 1985. These differences in balance are captured by the entropy measure of diversification, with higher values indicating a more diversified, more balanced portfolio. (Neither company engaged in any M&A activity that had a material bearing on its pharmaceutical businesses during this period.)

TABLE 32: **Therapeutic Area Portfolio Diversity**

	Number of Therapeutic Areas		Entropy Measure of Portfolio Diversity	
	Merck	Eli Lilly	Merck	Eli Lilly
1977	4	2	1.3	0.7
1980	4	2	1.3	0.6
1985	7	2	1.8	0.6
1990	8	4	1.8	1.3
1995	8	6	1.5	1.5
2000	11	6	1.7	1.5
2005	9	6	1.7	1.4

Source: Company documents; Deloitte analysis

By shifting to a focus on biological mechanisms of action, Merck ensured that its portfolio of drugs not only got broader, but got deeper as well. Understanding how mechanisms are affected by compounds allowed Merck scientists to develop variations on established compounds in order to attenuate some side effects under certain circumstances or to mitigate different interaction effects with other drugs, thereby making a compound's basic therapeutic effects available to a larger population of patients. For example, Mevacor was followed by Zocor, Vasotec, Prinivil, Cozaar, Hyzaar, Vytorin, and others, which collectively created a powerful franchise in the cardiovascular therapeutic area.[26]

Contrast Merck's ability to build on Mevacor with SmithKline's lack of follow-up to Tagamet. Launched in 1976, the heartburn and peptic ulcer medication became one of the most widely prescribed drugs in the world. In 1983, Glaxo launched a competitor, Zantac, which had fewer side effects and required fewer doses. SmithKline was unable to respond. It is impossible to say definitively why—perhaps the underlying science simply precluded the sort of "line extension" strategy that Merck executed so well. But it is telling that James Black and William Duncan, the discoverers of cimetidine—the active ingredient in Tagamet—left SmithKline soon after the research ended, and the company was unable to replace them with equally leading-edge scientists. In fact, SmithKline seems to have invested much of the profits generated by Tagamet in the acquisition of Beckman Instruments in 1982, essentially using success in pharmaceuticals to diversify away from pharmaceuticals.

This emphasis on science indirectly enhanced Merck's discovery capabilities in ways that were self-reinforcing. For example, Merck was perhaps unique in the permeability of the membrane between its R&D labs and top academic institutions. A Nobel laureate biochemistry department head at a top university told us in an interview that for decades Merck was easily the most attractive pharmaceutical company to work for. This school would often encourage its top students to work for a time in Merck's labs, confident that they would be able to continue to do cutting-edge, publishable research that would leave the door back to academia wide open.

By the late 1980s and early 1990s, the cost of developing new drugs was skyrocketing, and it was increasingly clear to all players that no company could rely solely on its own R&D capabilities.[27] One common response was to "buy pipeline" through major acquisitions. Through the late 2000s, Merck and Eli Lilly were essentially alone among major pharmaceutical companies in doing no major deals during the merger waves of the late 1980s (for example, SmithKline and Beecham, Bristol-Myers and Squibb) and the late 1990s (for example, Pfizer and Warner-Lambert, SmithKline and Glaxo).

These megadeals confer size and can stave off a so-called patent cliff but do little to improve a company's R&D productivity; generally, joint venture (JV) agreements and alliances are more effective.[28] Initially, such agreements were better seen as simply "in-licensing," in which one company with a drug would strike what amounted to a distribution arrangement with another company that had market access and a sales force. For example, Eli Lilly negotiated rights to Kefzol with Fujisawa Pharmaceutical, and Merck did something similar with Neo Pharmaceuticals of the Netherlands.

Merck was among the more successful companies at transforming JV arrangements into truly collaborative efforts that amplified both parties' R&D assets. For example, Merck was collaborating with an Italian company on bone cancer treatments. Becoming aware that they had reached a dead end, Merck scientists realized that they had hit upon a mechanism for rebuilding bone, useful in treating osteoporosis. But ability to prevent a disease is difficult to measure, so Merck, again in collaboration with partners, developed a diagnostic that allowed physicians to determine if the drug was working for each patient. The result was Fosamax, which generated $25 billion in revenue in the decade after its launch in 1995.[29]

More generally, Merck's deep internal scientific expertise, which under Vagelos's tenure went all the way to the top and has stayed there to this day in the world-class credentials of members of its top management committee, has tended to make the company, in the eyes of many industry insiders, a partner of choice. People who have worked at several pharmaceutical companies, including Merck and Eli Lilly, and continue to be active in the field as academic researchers, explained in interviews that spooling up a collaborative effort is a time-consuming undertaking. It requires a good-faith commitment of scarce resources, especially by the academics or the smaller of the two companies involved. Like the course of true love, no such effort ever runs smooth, and critical to the long-term success of such collaborations is the ability to take bad news in stride. The decision to press ahead or to abandon any given project in the face of adverse results is one that is rarely dictated unambiguously by the data.

Consequently, when senior management in the "big pharma" company pulls the plug, it is critical that the research partners involved feel that the decision, even if they disagree with it, was reasonable. When those making the decisions do not have the requisite relevant expertise, and instead see themselves as bringing objectivity to decision making and tempering the "enthusiasm" of the scientists, research partners can feel that they have been treated badly. In a small and tightly networked world, reputations take decades to build and even longer to repair.

Merck's willingness to bet big and bet consistently on a new approach to drug discovery allowed it to establish a second streak of high performance beginning in 1986 that lasted through 2010, the end of our observation period. Through the 1980s and early 1990s, this was driven largely by its deeper and broader product portfolio.

From the mid-1990s to today, however, the story gets increasingly ambiguous. From 1966 to 1977 Merck enjoyed a gross margin and SG&A advantage but owed two thirds of its ROA edge to higher asset turnover. We have attributed this to Merck's greater focus on pharmaceuticals and greater geographic diversification.

For the nine years that Merck is, on average, underperforming Eli Lilly, Merck sees the elements of every factor of its previous ROS advantage either dramatically diminished or entirely reversed, something we lay at the feet of Merck's restructuring of its R&D function.

The ROA lead that defines its second higher performance streak, from 1986 to 2010, is, statistically speaking, a single period of time but cannot, in good conscience, be qualitatively analyzed as such thanks to one acquisition: Medco.

In the early 1990s there was increasing pressure on health care costs in the United States, and several drug companies moved to vertically integrate into pharmaceutical benefits management (PBM) by acquiring high-volume distributors of prescription drugs. Merck moved first, buying the largest player at the time, Medco, in 1993. This followed three major deals in 1994: SmithKline Beecham's purchase of Diversified Pharmaceutical Services, Pfizer's joint venture with Value Health, Inc., and Eli Lilly's acquisition of PCS Health Systems (PCS).

The PBM business is fundamentally different from pharmaceuticals: it has much lower margins and much higher asset turnover. Luckily for our pair-wise comparison research design, Merck and Eli Lilly made essentially the same type of diversification move at essentially the same time. Rather less helpfully, Eli Lilly sold its (much smaller) PBM business in 1997 for $1.5 billion—$2.5 billion less than it had paid for it three years earlier. It was not alone in a loss of this magnitude, for SmithKline Beecham sold its PBM to Express Scripts in 1999 for $700 million, $1.6 billion less than it had paid.

But Merck would hang on to Medco until 2003, despite regulatory changes soon after the acquisition that had made it essentially an arm's-length division of the pharmaceutical business, which undermined most of the strategic rationale for having it.[30] Unlike its industry peers, however, Merck realized $8.6 billion on divestiture in the form of a $2 billion dividend and a $6.8 billion sale price, which compares favorably with the $6.2 billion Merck had paid.

From 1993 to 2003 Medco climbed from 3 percent to 58 percent of Merck's total revenue. Medco's very different economics mean that we must look at Merck's second period of higher performance in three sub-periods: pre-Medco, Medco, and post-Medco.

Prior to the Medco acquisition, we see that Merck's R&D transformation yielded a strong run of superior performance—its largest lead ever over Eli Lilly, with absolute ROA values in the high teens and low twenties. Merck's publication record, patent production, new product launches, and therapeutic and product diversity all strongly support the hypothesis

TABLE 33: Merck's Elements of Advantage Versus Eli Lilly

| Elements of ROA | Period of Higher Performance: 1966–1977 | Period of Lower Performance: 1978–1985 | Contribution to ROA Advantage in Percentage Points per Year | | |
| | | | Period of Higher Performance | | |
			Pre-Medco: 1986–1992	Medco: 1993–2003	Post-Medco: 2004–2010
Gross Margin	2.0	0.1	4.0	-16.1	0.3
SG&A	2.2	1.3	-2.7	6.2	0.7
R&D	0.5	-0.6	1.6	6.1	0.7
Other (incl. taxes)	-3.4	-0.8	-1.1	3.0	1.7
ROS	1.3	0.0	1.8	-0.9	3.4
CAT	1.6	0.4	0.3	2.5	-0.1
FAT	0.9	-1.4	1.9	1.5	-0.3
Other	-0.3	-0.1	1.5	-0.2	-2.1
TAT	2.2	-1.1	3.7	3.8	-2.6
ROA	3.5	-1.1	5.5	2.9	0.9

Source: Compustat; Deloitte analysis
Figures may not total due to rounding.

that better research led to both the gross margin and the growth that drove its ROA advantage.

We have been unable to isolate Medco's ROA within Merck. And although it can be an almost theological problem to accurately sort out the impact on ROA of each company's PBM deal, we estimate that the companies' respective PBM-related gains and losses account for approximately two thirds of Merck's ROA advantage over the period.[31] In other words, if neither company had gone down the PBM road, Merck's annual ROA advantage would have been about 1 pp/year. That lead would have been reduced as a consequence of Eli Lilly's having had an ROA up to 5 pp higher in years when its decile ranks were 6, 7, 9, 8, and 5. It is entirely possible that without these losses Eli Lilly would have delivered enough 9s to have qualified as a Miracle Worker—and we would have been comparing Merck with a different company! What this means is that Merck might well have held on to its lead over Eli Lilly not by virtue of having done anything particularly right, but by virtue of having avoided an expensive misstep.

With Medco out of the picture as of 2004, Merck's ROA advantage falls to very nearly what we estimated Merck's advantage would have been without Medco during the previous decade. On both absolute and relative ROA, Eli Lilly and Merck have converged, which is no great surprise. For the prior ten years, with the exception of PBMs, the two companies had pursued similar strategies with similar behavioral outcomes: focused on pharmaceuticals, a diversified product portfolio, science led, with a strong base of international sales. Since we have hypothesized that it was differences in these behaviors that drove Merck's advantages from 1966 to 1977 and from 1986 to 1992, it is comforting to observe that as the companies behave similarly along these dimensions their performance also converges.

> Merck (Miracle Worker) bested Eli Lilly (Long Runner) first by staying fo-
> cused on pharmaceuticals and expanding internationally, then by rein-
> venting its R&D function in ways that allowed it to diversify its product
> portfolio, and finally avoided a disadvantage by aggressively driving the
> growth of its PBM acquisition, Medco. It takes a lot of flexibility to stick to
> the rules.

Merck shows us, then, that there are almost always many different
routes to *better* and *revenue*, and they should all be on the table all the
time. Business line, product, and geographic diversification; mergers;
joint ventures; even unrelated diversification—it really does not matter.
These initiatives do not always work, but it would seem that they have the
best chance of working when they serve the first two rules. And in the
seemingly endless variation of ways in which those rules can be served,
we find the third rule: that there are no others.

What of our Average Joe, KV Pharmaceutical (KVP)? Its performance
profile suggests a "found and lost" pattern as the company's eroding ROA
from 1971 to 1994 gives way to dramatically higher but rapidly deteriorating performance through 2005, followed by a third era defined by three
years of dramatic losses.

These patterns in KVP's performance can be understood in the context of the structure, and shifts in the structure, of the pharmaceutical industry generally. When KVP entered our observation window it was a
contract researcher and manufacturer. Its customers tended to be the major pharmaceutical companies. The company's expertise lay in delivery
technologies such as sustained-release formulations, solid-dosage tablets,
and effervescent products. The K-H Amendments and DES, which gave
rise to the modern pharmaceutical industry, increased the importance of
these technologies, and KVP responded by increasing its R&D expendi-

ture as a percentage of sales—consistent with, but lagging behind, the behaviors of Merck and Eli Lilly.

In the mid-1980s, KVP entered into a series of licensing agreements that secured distribution for KVP products in Japan, Canada, Mexico, and India. This served to diversify the firm internationally—but again, later than Merck and Eli Lilly and, although data are scarce, seemingly to a far lesser extent.

The Waxman-Hatch Act of 1984 made a viable generics industry possible, and in 1990, KVP entered the generics manufacturing business with its ETHEX division. Finally, capitalizing on the tendency of large, postmerger pharmaceutical companies to rationalize their portfolios and divest smaller niche drugs, the company completed its journey up the industry's value chain by establishing Ther-Rx, its own branded, patent-protected pharmaceutical business, in 1999.

These initiatives served to increase KVP's sales and, perhaps more important, gross margins over time: from an average of 22 percent in 1972 to 1985, to 30 percent in 1986 to 1990, to 48 percent by 1999, to 70 percent by 2006. And yet, it was only for a brief period in the late 1990s that the company was able to reap the rewards of these efforts in anything like exceptional performance, breaking through with decile ranks in the 8s and 9s. What prevented KVP from delivering a more consistently strong performance?

One potentially relevant strategic difference between KVP and our two top performers was the timing and effectiveness of its various efforts. For example, Merck and Eli Lilly effectively anticipated the increasing importance of R&D: they had been ramping up spending almost a decade prior to the seismic shifts wrought by the K-H Amendments and the DES. By the beginning of our observation window, Merck and Eli Lilly were each spending between 8 and 10 percent of total revenues on R&D, about twice the industry average. KVP essentially reacted to these changes, increasing its R&D expenditure only after it was clear that a shift would be required in order to remain viable.

Similarly for the shift to internationalization: in our observation window, Merck never had less than a third of its sales outside of the United States, and Eli Lilly suffered relative to Merck through the 1980s largely as a result of failing to maintain a significant presence in global markets. Yet KVP did not start to go international until the mid-1980s. The company was at best in the middle of the pack in exploiting the rise of the generic market, and its shift into patent-protected branded pharmaceuticals seems largely to have been a "feast on the crumbs" strategy.

Finally, KVP fell victim to two significant setbacks. First, the company's move into selling its own drugs in the late 1980s required that it develop a marketing capability. To do this, KVP entered into a comarketing agreement with Bolar Pharmaceutical in 1987. KVP terminated the agreement in 1990 upon reports that Bolar was distributing adulterated drugs.[32] This both reduced revenue—since the drugs Bolar was marketing were no longer being sold—and increased costs, as KVP had to develop its own marketing and distribution capability.

Second, when KVP set up its ETHEX generics division, the company was cited by the FDA for noncompliance with Current Good Manufacturing Practices (cGMPs), which led to the seizure of most of KVP's products in 1993.[33] The requisite revalidation of the affected products was not complete until 1995. In the interim, the company lost contract manufacturing revenue and faced significant delays on pending Abbreviated New Drug Applications (ANDAs). It was during this period that KVP's performance fell into the 2nd decile.

One does not want to make too much of these events: both Merck and Eli Lilly have had their own difficulties that could have portended near-disaster.[34] However, incidents such as Merck's recall of Vioxx and Eli Lilly's litigation over Zyprexa appear to be "normal accidents"—the inevitable left tail of an unavoidably imperfect system.[35] Although these events were unfortunate, and in their specifics perhaps avoidable, a large, complex company operating at a high level in a complex and challenging environment over the course of decades will inevitably face a crisis of some sort.

In contrast, the Bolar and FDA compliance challenges appear to be indicative of a deeper, more systemic vulnerability; each spoke to a structural failing with respect to a key success factor: marketing (Bolar) and manufacturing (noncompliance with cGMP), respectively. In other words, KVP seems to have been ill equipped to execute its chosen strategy effectively.

Overall, KVP shifted its strategy—from a contract manufacturer to a research-based long-term supplier to a generic drugmaker to a provider of patent-protected products. Throughout, the company's performance remained, relatively speaking, mediocre. The relevant observation here appears to be that KVP merely kept up with shifts in industry structure and adapted to—rather than led—shifts in what was necessary to be a player in this industry.

Despite all this up and down, we must give KVP its due. Just as in our comparisons of Merck and Eli Lilly it is important to recall that Eli Lilly is an exceptional performer in its own right, KVP is middling only by the lights of fairly exacting standards. It has achieved what many—indeed most—companies do not: decades of survival. But exceptional performance has eluded it.

Reactive Change: Only If Necessary

Where Merck drove change in its industry, Heartland responded to it slowly and gradually. It started out with a contrary model that violated the conventional wisdom of its industry peers. The company then hung on to those differences, even in the face of declining profitability. Over time, it retooled just about every aspect of its business in ways that, perhaps surprisingly, reflected more nearly standard industry practices. Remarkably, Heartland remained sufficiently different that this seeming convergence in behavior did not undermine its relative profitability advantage. Our opportunity here is to observe how careful, incremental change can, over time, effect a dramatic transformation in the service of maintaining superior profitability.

Recall from chapter 1 the three companies in this trio: Heartland, the Kept It Miracle Worker; Werner, the Lost It Long Runner; and PAM, the Average Joe. Heartland enters the database, along with Werner and PAM, in 1986. Its performance was nothing short of astonishing, with an average ROA through 1994 of 17 percent to Werner's 7 percent. However, this era in Heartland's performance is characterized by a steep decline from the mid-twenties to the low teens. Heartland's second era in performance, from 1995 through 2010, remains consistently in the 9th decile, but is characterized by a relatively preternatural stability, averaging 13 percent within a range of plus or minus two percentage points.

Werner's Lost It performance profile is quite different: a single era of absolute performance characterized by a narrow range and a gradual decline. This erosion in absolute ROA sees the company's streak of 6th to 8th deciles end in 2001, and it has ranged between 0 and 4 ever since.

The behavioral differences between Heartland and Werner that seem to account best for the observed ROA differences during Heartland's first era in absolute performance are entirely consistent with the first two rules. Heartland, you might recall from the discussion in chapter 1, was focused on a smaller number of customers within a relatively compact geographic area. This permitted an asset-light point-to-point route structure, which obviated expensive distribution centers, even as the company invested heavily in trailers in order to maintain high service levels. Through a combination of higher wages and attractive perquisites such as university scholarships for drivers' children, Heartland had much higher-quality owner/operator drivers, which kept the company's asset intensity down even as service levels remained high.

Werner, with consistently twice Heartland's revenue through 1994, had a much more diverse customer base, a wider range of services (for example, many types of trailers, from refrigerated to flatbed), and a broader geographic footprint. With essentially no owner/operator drivers through the mid-1990s and a commitment to adopting new cost-cutting technologies such as GPS ahead of many others in the industry, Werner occupied a price-based position compared with Heartland's non-price position.

The net effect of these very different choices was reflected in three major drivers of Heartland's ROA advantage. Although Heartland had higher labor expenses, it enjoyed a gross margin advantage thanks to prices that ran 10 percent or more higher. Its lower asset base resulted in lower depreciation expense and higher fixed asset turnover. Heartland, unusually for Miracle Workers and in part due to its remarkably high ROA advantage, relied more on asset turnover and other costs than it did on gross margin for its superior profitability.[36]

As the industry consolidated and matured in the decades after deregulation, Heartland chose to grow through acquisition, increasing the company's geographic footprint and number of customers, resulting in a need to provide a wider range of services. This led the company to construct a dozen distribution centers between 1993 and 2004. Increased competition in the industry generally made it difficult to break the trade-off between quality service and the use of owner/operator drivers, resulting in a shift to employee drivers and a resulting need to invest heavily in its own fleet. Heartland's commitment to service meant having reliable rigs, but keeping purchasing costs down meant having to buy in quantity or countercyclically. To give itself that sort of flexibility, Heartland chose to run high cash balances, with cash and investments rising from 30 percent of total assets during era 1 to 50 percent of total assets during era 2. In contrast, Werner's cash and investments were typically 5 to 10 percent of total assets.[37]

With trucking a structurally competitive industry, Heartland's pricing power fell. Yet the company chose to maintain what non-price positioning it could by adopting a more asset-intensive model. This new set of trade-offs resulted in a smaller overall ROA advantage with a structure that was dramatically different from era 1. Heartland's fixed asset and depreciation expense advantages were both down by about 75 percent while its current asset turnover disadvantage more than doubled. Its gross margin

TABLE 34: **Heartland's Elements of Advantage Versus Werner**

Elements of ROA	Contribution to ROA Advantage in Percentage Points per Year	
	Era 1: 1985–1994	Era 2: 1995–2010
Gross Margin	2.3	7.4
SG&A	0.0	0.0
R&D	0.0	0.0
Other (incl. taxes)	4.2	0.3
ROS	6.5	7.7
CAT	–1.0	–2.5
FAT	4.1	1.4
Other	0.0	–0.3
TAT	3.1	–1.4
ROA	**9.6**	**6.2**

Source: Compustat; Deloitte analysis
Figures may not total due to rounding.

advantage, both in absolute and relative terms, was dramatically higher, increasing from 2.2 pp/year to 5.6 pp/year and accounting for 89 percent of Heartland's total ROA lead, up from 23 percent in era 1.

You might be wondering how a more competitive industry results in a greater reliance on superior gross margins for superior profitability. The key is to keep in mind that all success is relative. From 1995 to 2010 Werner's profitability is degrading in absolute terms: its relative rank falls from the 6th-to-8th-decile band and after 2003 is never higher than 5, and is often in the 0–2 range. In other words, in era 2 Heartland was doing worse than in era 1, but it was still doing better than Werner. And although its absolute ROA lead was fully a third smaller than during era 1, it relied for that lead on a gross margin advantage to a far greater extent than in era 1. In era 2 Heartland invested much more heavily in a particular sort of asset base in order to earn the price premiums that drove its gross margin advantage.

We can see which of the operational changes mattered most, and the sorts of trade-offs Heartland accepted that it had previously been able to break, by looking at the relative differences in key behaviors between Heartland and Werner across the two eras.

Start with owner/operator (O/O) drivers. In 1985–86, at the start of era 1, Heartland generated 56 percent of its revenue from O/Os. Werner's figure was 0 percent. As a proxy for the industry's relative reliance on this tactic, note that 32 percent of total industry miles were driven by O/Os. In 2000 these figures were 40 percent for Heartland, 16 percent for Werner, and 13 percent for the industry, and only four years later the figures were 12, 11, and 13 percent, respectively.[38] From a position of dramatic divergence—from each other and from industry averages—during era 1, the two companies ended up in essentially the same place as each other and the rest of their competitors. Use of O/Os had gone from a difference with a plausible connection to performance implications to a homogenizing influence, coincident with the compression of the performance differences among companies.

We also attributed much of Heartland's non-price position to its relative customer focus and the impact that had on its ability to provide superior service levels, which were reflected in higher prices. In 1986 Heartland's top five customers accounted for 62 percent of its revenue. By 1994 this number had fallen to 43 percent and by 2006 to 35 percent. Over this same period Werner's level of customer focus had increased, but only slightly. In 1994 its top 5 percent of customers (more than five customers) accounted for 9 percent of revenue while its top 50 percent accounted for 47 percent of revenue. In 2006 those numbers had risen to 11 and 54 percent, respectively. In other words, the magnitude of the difference in customer focus between the two companies was markedly lower, but Heartland was still considerably more focused than Werner. This is consistent with a lower absolute lead in ROA for Heartland over Werner.

In contrast to customer focus and geographic footprint, where Heartland began to look more like Werner (even if it remained meaningfully different), business unit diversification became a key behavioral difference. In 1993, Werner began moving beyond contract trucking services into dedicated fleet—taking on the assets and responsibilities of its customers' formerly in-house trucking operations—and what is referred to as "non-asset-based services" such as brokerage: that year, each of these new lines of business accounted for 1 percent of total revenue. By 2006, dedicated fleet was 43 percent of Werner's revenue and non-asset-based services were 13 percent of its top line. Interviews with Werner executives suggest that these new lines of business are more profitable for Werner than contract-based trucking services, and we have no evidence to the contrary.

Whatever the relative profitability of these services to Werner, however,

Heartland remained focused on contract trucking. Consistent with our hypothesis that contract trucking was subject to increasing pricing pressure as the industry consolidated, Heartland's absolute ROA is on average much lower in era 2. However, by remaining committed to delivering superior non-price value, it was able to resist price compression better than its competitors by investing in assets and capabilities that preserved its non-price position. Consequently, Heartland maintains an absolute ROA lead over Werner and its 9th-decile ranks, which are, you will recall, based on Heartland's performance compared with all other publicly traded companies.

We should be impressed with Heartland for at least two reasons during era 1. First, that it was able to enjoy such a high level of performance for so long: holding competitive pressures at bay for a decade through its dedication to a seemingly unique non-price position is truly remarkable. Second, Heartland seems to have appreciated that the dramatic decline in its absolute performance—a rate of almost 1.5 pp/year—was not evidence of any failing on its part. Its declines in ROA were not a problem to be fixed, in that getting ROA back up to its historical levels, while desirable, was not achievable. Return on assets percentages in the twenties and high teens when clearly well-run competitors such as Werner were making do with high single digits were unlikely to be sustainable.

As its absolute performance deteriorated, Heartland did not start flailing about blindly in a hopeless attempt to recapture past glory. Instead, it gradually explored an alternative model: allowing its O/O percentage to fluctuate as economics demanded, gradually adding distribution centers as required, and even moving boldly on occasion with transformative acquisitions. Through all this, however, it never wavered in its commitment to a position built on non-price value, and as a consequence it was able to preserve its revenue-driven, price-based profitability formula.

Heartland changed just about every aspect of its model: from point-to-point routes to a network of distribution centers; from O/O drivers to employee drivers; it expanded its geographic footprint and broadened its customer base. In the process, the structure of its profitability advantage shifted from an advantage in both ROS and TAT to a strong ROS advantage but a material TAT disadvantage. The only thing that didn't change was *better before cheaper* and *revenue before cost*.

Finally, PAM, the Average Joe of the three, spent the first five years of its existence as a public company recovering from the self-inflicted wound of a failed growth strategy. PAM found a path to profitability through dedicated fleet operations. With highly predictable volumes and routes, you would think that an efficiently run trucking company can at least ensure its survival through the effective exploitation of this niche. Once again, however, PAM found itself on the wrong side of a significant bet, having thrown in its lot with the auto industry: General Motors was among its largest customers through the early 1990s. This worked just fine while the U.S. auto sector was relatively flush through the late 1990s. However, when the carmakers' fortunes declined, PAM proved unable to find new customers or drive down costs enough to preserve its ten-year run of solid profitability. From 2007 onward, results were once again suggesting rather parlous circumstances, with an ROA hovering at or below 0 percent.

Compared with PAM, Werner is a salutary example of a trucking company that ran a tight ship. Non-price differences play far less of a role in explaining the performance gap between these two companies, but Werner still got to keep the money. Werner's consistent efficiency and avoidance of any apparent large-scale blunders might lack the appeal of Heartland's non-price differentiation, but it served to generate well over a decade of superior profitability. It is worth reminding ourselves that, as a

Long Runner, Werner's performance deserves our admiration. Balancing the competing demands of meeting necessary levels of customer service, remaining price competitive, and controlling costs was almost certainly no less challenging than Heartland's very different recipe. It had to be difficult; after all, Werner was an exceptional performer in its own right, and we should not expect exceptional performance to be easy.

It is worth noting, however, that Werner's performance also took a nosedive, essentially converging with PAM's. Perhaps it is not a surprise that their behaviors seem largely to have converged as well. By that time PAM had successfully diversified its customer base in dedicated fleet away from the U.S. automotive sector and added contract trucking services, which had historically been less price sensitive. It had also diversified into logistics services, which were less asset-intensive and promised higher ROA. During that same period, Werner moved into dedicated fleet, which promised more predictable and higher asset utilization while also adding logistics services to its portfolio.

In this case, at least, it seems clear that Heartland's non-price position is a key determinant of both the magnitude of its exceptional performance (its 9th-decile ranks) and the stability of its exceptional performance (its unbroken streak of 9th-decile years). Werner's well-executed, price-driven (compared with Heartland) position drove exceptional, if not quite as exceptional, performance, yet proved more susceptible to competitive pressures: its relative position seems to have deteriorated not due to any deep failings, but rather simply because others (such as PAM) caught up.

This qualitative narrative is reflected in changes in the structure of the profitability advantages enjoyed by Heartland and Werner over PAM during their respective relevant regime changes. During its era 1, Heartland enjoys both an ROS and a TAT advantage. During era 2, however, Heartland actually suffers a TAT disadvantage versus PAM, relying on its gross margin lead for all of its overall ROA advantage. As with Heartland's lead over Werner, these are the financial fingerprints of Heartland's dedication to a non-price position and a price-driven profitability formula.

Werner's profitability lead over PAM, however, shows no qualitative shifts between Werner's higher- and lower-performing streaks of relative performance. As Werner's performance deteriorates, its gross margin lead shrinks and it comes to rely more heavily on lower costs and higher asset turnover. This reflects the convergence in the two companies' positions. In short, when PAM was suffering through its disastrous growth campaign in the 1980s and 1990s, PAM was "the same as but worse than" Werner. From 2002 through 2010, PAM had somewhat righted the ship, but Werner's superior execution left it "the same as but better than" PAM.

Once again, the distinguishing characteristics of our Miracle Worker are *better before cheaper* and *revenue before cost*. Our Long Runner shows that a more price-driven position can work, and cost-dependent profitability is worth having, but it delivered neither the same magnitude nor duration of exceptional performance.

Ineffective Change: Dig a Hole to Fill a Hole

The last of our nine trios is taken from the household appliances industry. Maytag, a Lost It Miracle Worker, is still known for the Maytag Repairman character "Ol' Lonely," who idles away his days thanks to the reliability of Maytag washing machines.

The company's fortunes began to deteriorate in the mid-1980s, and its streak of higher relative performance ended in 1989. Despite the company's aggressive and seemingly entirely reasonable attempts to cope with dramatic industry-level change, financial results continued to disappoint and prospects failed to improve. In 2006 Maytag was acquired by Whirlpool, the Average Joe of the trio, which has delivered unremarkable financial results, but proved a noteworthy survivor in an increasingly competitive and global marketplace.

The Long Runner, HMI Industries (HMI), is perhaps best known for the FilterQueen line of vacuum cleaners, long sold door-to-door. Like Maytag, HMI has a Lost It trajectory: from 1996 to 2004 it suffered declines in performance so severe that the company was taken private in an attempt to find the breathing room required for a turnaround.

Since Maytag and Whirlpool are such close competitors, we begin the analysis of this trio somewhat uncharacteristically with a comparison of the Miracle Worker and the Average Joe. Although Maytag has two streaks of relative performance—one of higher relative performance from 1966 to 1989 and one of lower relative performance from 1990 to 2004—its absolute performance is a single era of continuous decline, with ROA dropping from nearly 20 percent to effectively 0 percent.

Average Joe Whirlpool's forty-five-year history in our database through 2010 shows no such recognizable pattern of relative performance. Its two eras in absolute ROA have gradual, positive slopes but suggestively different average levels: from 1966 to 1987 it runs an average ROA near 9 percent while from 1988 to 2010 average ROA is about 3 percent.

Our analysis of these performance profiles begins with the Elements of Advantage over the relevant periods. During Maytag's period of higher relative performance we see a suggestive and almost archetypal set of trade-offs among the different elements. Note first the trade-off between ROS and TAT, and within ROS, very strong gross margin compensating for relatively higher SG&A expenses.

During the period of lower relative performance we have a totally different picture: it is Whirlpool that has the gross margin advantage, and the minuscule ROA lead Maytag enjoys is driven by lower-cost elements, particularly SG&A, and higher asset turnover.

From the start of our observation period in 1966, Maytag and

TABLE 35: **Descriptive Statistics for the Appliances Trio**

Company	Category (Trajectory)	Year Founded	Observation Period	Revenue Growth	Average Annual ROA	Compounded Annual TSR	Compounded Annual Revenue Growth
Maytag	Miracle Worker (Lost It)	1893	1966 to 2005	$131MM to $4.9BN	12.3%	9.0%	9.7%
HMI Industries	Long Runner (Lost It)	1928	1967 to 2004	$9MM to $32MM	3.1%	–1.4%	4.1%
Whirlpool	Average Joe (N/A)	1911	1966 to 2010	$705MM to $18.4BN	6.0%	10.1%	7.7%

Source: Compustat; company documents; Deloitte analysis

TABLE 36: **Maytag's Elements of Advantage Versus Whirlpool**

Elements of ROA	Contribution to ROA Advantage in Percentage Points per Year	
	Period of Higher Performance: 1966–1991	**Period of Lower Performance: 1992–2005**
Gross Margin	24.3	–1.4
SG&A	–7.4	2.6
R&D	0.0	0.6
Other (incl. taxes)	–7.2	–1.2
ROS	9.7	0.5
CAT	–0.7	0.3
FAT	–0.9	0.0
Other	0.7	–0.1
TAT	–0.9	0.3
ROA	**8.8**	**0.8**

Source: Compustat; Deloitte analysis
Figures may not total due to rounding.

Whirlpool had distinct competitive positions and different profitability formulas.[39] Maytag generated two thirds or more of its revenue from washers and dryers, which were distinguished by their reliability, consistently earning the highest quality rating in *Consumer Reports*. The company built and supported its quality image by distributing its products through an extensive network of independent dealers and spending anywhere from two to four times as much on advertising, as a percentage of sales, as did Whirlpool. That commitment to advertising was made during a period when Whirlpool had only two to four times Maytag's total revenue, implying the same or higher absolute advertising expenditure.

In contrast, Whirlpool had a broader and more balanced product portfolio. Through 1979 fully half of its revenues were from sales to Sears that were then retailed under the Kenmore brand, which had a lower retail price than Maytag-branded appliances, and so generated less per-unit revenue and margin for Whirlpool. At the time, Sears was the largest retailer of appliances in the United States, and so enjoyed significant bargaining power, negotiating cost-plus contracts with its private-label suppliers.

The nature and magnitude of these behavioral differences explains the nature and magnitude of the differences in profitability. For Maytag, stronger focus on a narrower range of products was a key ingredient in designing and manufacturing higher-quality products; this, coupled with dedicated, independent distributors and an emphasis on brand building through advertising, earned Maytag a 10-to-15-percent price premium. This is reflected in its gross margin advantage of 13 pp per year. Maytag's incremental spending on advertising (3 pp of sales) shows up in the more than 5 pp per year disadvantage in SG&A, with the balance likely accounted for by Maytag's higher level of support for its distribution channel, for which, among other things, it paid shipping expenses. Maytag's lower asset turnover is likely not evidence of inefficiency, but rather a consequence of its more complex retail distribution network. This is as clear an example of *better before cheaper* and *revenue before cost* as we have in our sample, and perhaps as clear an example as one is likely to find.

Despite the strengths of its position and profitability formula, Maytag's absolute profitability was in long-term decline. Its rebound from the recessions of 1973 to 1975 and 1980 to 1982 were each lower than the prior recession, even as Whirlpool's absolute profitability through the mid-1980s was consistently increasing. Although a phenomenon this complex is unlikely to have a single cause, a key driver seems to have been consolidation in the retail channel.

Maytag's ability to charge premium prices depended on the ability and willingness of an army of smaller, independent, and often one-store appliance retailers to explain and promote the advantages of Maytag products.

Having higher-quality products and building brand awareness through advertising were indispensable ingredients, but "closing the deal" turned on the customer experience that was created through personal care and attention. However important appliances and the Kenmore brand might have been to Sears, it was only ever one department in its stores, and Whirlpool was only ever one supplier among many.

With each recession, this differentiated distribution channel came under increasing pressure. The network of 10,000 Maytag dealers in 1985 was down to 650 by 1996. In addition, a number of "big box" retailers that began life in other retail sectors began to see appliances as a growth opportunity. Circuit City, Best Buy, The Home Depot, and Sam's Club all entered the fray, and each of these companies competed with independent dealers and even traditional department stores, such as Sears, through lower prices. These retailers offered less retail assistance and tended to carry higher volume, full-line brands.

In these changes Maytag saw a key element of its profitability eroding. It responded by expanding the product line and the customer segments it served. Two major acquisitions essentially tripled the size of the company. Maytag was no stranger to acquisitions: it had expanded into cooking appliances in 1981 with the purchase of Hardwick Stove Company and Jenn-Air Corporation, but these were relatively small, as the two deals accounted for 16 percent and 27 percent, respectively, of Maytag's predeal revenue. In addition, both brands were premium products with a reputation for quality.[40]

The Magic Chef deal, in 1986, was a dramatic departure from this strategy. At one-and-a-half times Maytag's predeal revenue, this was a merger more than an acquisition, dramatically increased Maytag's long-term debt, and brought with it an asset base of outdated plant and equipment in need of refurbishment. Magic Chef's products traditionally had received low quality grades.

Despite these drawbacks, the deal was seen by senior leadership as crucial to Maytag's long-term prospects. Then-CEO Daniel Krumm explained, "Through consolidation, the competitors in the appliance industry had become fewer in number and larger in size. Consequently, we had increasing concern about Maytag's long-range future in the industry."[41] The need for a product line that covered all major appliance categories and market segments, coupled with a decreasing number of viable candidates, appears to have left company leadership feeling its hand had been forced.

In the wake of the acquisition, Maytag's return on sales declined, as gross margin fell more than SG&A, suggesting that any economies of scale were more than offset by price declines. Increases in asset turnover were unable to make up the difference, and average overall ROA dropped from 19 percent in the three years prior to the acquisition to 15 percent in the two years following.

In 1988 Maytag executed its second-largest relative acquisition, Chicago Pacific Corporation, the makers of the Hoover line of vacuum cleaners. This deal seemed to tack in the opposite direction, diversifying away from household appliances (in the newly consolidated channel, vacuum cleaners were considered a different product category), but appealed to a more upscale customer segment. It diversified the company geographically, but essentially only into the United Kingdom, as Hoover had little in the way of a continental European presence.

Worse, the deal was plagued with tactical errors. Hoover's plant and equipment, like Magic Chef's, required significant capital investment to increase quality and reduce costs, and Maytag's "free airline ticket" promotion, which offered a free flight to the United States from London upon the purchase of a Hoover vacuum cleaner, resulted in a $60 million writedown. By 1995 Maytag had sold its Hoover assets in Europe and Australia at a combined additional pretax loss of $154 million. Its 1997 acquisition of G. S. Blodgett, a commercial oven company, fared little better, and Blodgett was disposed of in 2001 at a pretax loss of $60 million.

As Maytag bumped into one sharp object after another, Whirlpool was proving itself a capable survivor. The long-term upward trend in Whirlpool's ROA from 1966 reflected its decreasing reliance on Sears as a distribution channel. Through the early 1970s fully 60 percent of Whirlpool's revenue came from the Chicago-based retailer. This began to decline, gradually at first, to just over 40 percent by 1980. This reduced the bargaining power of its channel partners and allowed Whirlpool to bolster its own brand image. The resulting higher price, coupled with Whirlpool's ingrained cost-consciousness (the legacy of having been beholden to Sears for so long), resulted in an increasing ROA. Although not a non-price competitor compared with Maytag, Whirlpool's shift in position toward the non-price end of the spectrum is the most plausible explanation for the company's increasing gross margin, which climbed from under 20 percent to just shy of 25 percent by the early 1980s.

Accustomed to dealing with a broader product line and seeing in the rise of big box retailers a relative diversification of its distribution channels, Whirlpool seemed on track to eclipse Maytag and achieve standout profitability.

Enter globalization. At first Korean (LG, Daewoo, Samsung) and then Chinese (Haier) companies entered the U.S. appliance market through the newly consolidated distribution channels. Somewhat atypically, they collectively covered the full range of product and customer segments, entering with price-competitive and high-end, feature-rich products. Building off their success in their home markets, and leveraging their capabilities in consumer electronics, the Korean makers in particular were well positioned to exploit the growing high-end appliance segment, which by 2001 had essentially quadrupled its market share between 1985 and 2001, rising from 8 percent to 23 percent. Mid-range appliances were down from

54 percent of the market to 41 percent while the low end was steady, falling from 38 to 36 percent over the same period.[42]

Fighting globalization with globalization, Whirlpool internationally diversified both its production and its markets. From 0 percent in 1984, 35 percent of sales were from non-U.S. markets by 1989, a number that has remained relatively stable since. In addition to the company's nine U.S. production facilities, by the mid-2000s, the company had plants in Italy (4), France (1), Germany (2), and Sweden (1) as part of its European strategy, and in Mexico (4), Brazil (3), India (3), China (2), Poland (1), and Slovakia (1), each to serve both local and global markets with lower-cost production. Through a series of partial equity stakes and joint venture agreements, the company learned about each new market and increased its ownership position as circumstances warranted. The effective management of the company's global strategy is credited with sustaining gross margins and increasing asset turnover despite an increasingly competitive landscape.[43]

Meanwhile, Maytag's globalization effort foundered. Non-U.S. sales spiked and then dived as a result of the Hoover fiasco, climbing from the low single digits in 1996 to perhaps 10 percent of sales by 2004. On the supply side, the company's seven U.S. plants were supplemented by four in Mexico.

Maytag's last gasps came in the late 1990s, with an attempt to return to its roots as a non-price-differentiated, higher-price, premium player. Ironically, Sears had become the relatively high-touch distribution channel in a world dominated by big box players, and in 1997 Maytag and Sears signed a distribution agreement. By spurning international expansion, Maytag avoided the expense of geographic diversification.

Prospects brightened further with the 1997 launch of the Neptune washer and dryer, an innovative front-loading appliance that retailed for $1,100, more than double the top retail price at the time. It was tremendously successful, generating $2.5 billion in sales over the following four years. In 1999, the company launched its own Maytag retail outlets, with thirty in operation by 2003, in an attempt to recapture the customer engagement that had been the linchpin of its historical success.

It was a false dawn, however. Quality problems plagued the Neptune, and in 2004 the company set aside more than $33 million as part of a class-action lawsuit associated with the product's defects. Ol' Lonely, it seemed, had a lot more to do than in days gone by. Maytag's channel strategy proved largely unsuccessful thanks to channel conflict with Sears coupled with Sears's own challenges in the retail space, and confusion among customers because the same Maytag products were still available, typically at lower prices, at big box retailers.[44]

Whirlpool, however unremarkable its profitability, was growing strongly, expanding internationally, and gradually improving its results through stable gross margins thanks to competitive products, consistent cost reductions, and increasing asset turnover through growth fueled by international expansion. By 2005, Maytag was less than one third of Whirlpool's size but had a valuable stable of brands, and so Whirlpool acquired it. Jeff Fettig, Whirlpool's CEO since 2004, said later that the turnaround strategy for the division was essentially to restore to Maytag all that had made it great: high-quality, differentiated products delivered through a unique customer experience in order to earn a price premium and customer loyalty.[45]

The only flaw in Maytag's responses to the challenges it faced was they didn't work. It's easy to blame "execution," but then Whirlpool adopted essentially the same responses, executed brilliantly, and ended up the Average Joe for its troubles. What should Maytag not have changed? *Better before cheaper* and *revenue before cost*.

The Long Runner of the trio, HMI, took its corporate name from "Health-Mor Sanitation Systems," the corporate name in 1930. Long focused on vacuum cleaners, the company's FilterQueen brand was the bedrock of the company through the late 1980s. Until then, HMI's strategy seemed in many ways to be an amped-up version of Maytag's: high-quality products sold through high-touch distribution at premium prices. HMI, however, took high-touch about as high as it could go, using a network of door-to-door salespeople. As a result, during Maytag's streak of higher relative performance, HMI's gross margins were comparable to Maytag's, but each dollar of sales was relatively expensive, and thus HMI's SG&A spend was relatively higher. With more complex and extensive

TABLE 37: **Maytag's Elements of Advantage Versus HMI, and HMI's Elements of Advantage Versus Whirlpool**

Elements of ROA	Contribution to ROA Advantage in Percentage Points per Year			
	Maytag Vs. HMI		HMI Vs. Whirlpool	
	HP: 1967–1991	LP: 1992–2004	HP: 1968–1995	LP: 1996–2004
Gross Margin	−1.4	−14.1	17.7	15.7
SG&A	7.0	34.7	−11.8	−38.5
R&D	0.0	−1.1	1.1	1.7
Other (incl. taxes)	−3.2	−6.2	−1.5	3.7
ROS	2.5	13.4	5.4	−17.4
CAT	3.4	0.7	−2.0	−1.8
FAT	−2.2	2.1	0.3	−4.4
Other	1.6	1.4	−0.3	−1.8
TAT	2.7	4.2	−2.0	−8.0
ROA	**5.2**	**17.5**	**3.4**	**−25.4**

HP = High Performance
LP = Low Performance

Source: Compustat; Deloitte analysis
Figures may not total due to rounding.

manufacturing assets, Maytag's fixed asset turnover was much lower, but HMI carried higher working capital, resulting in a total asset turnover advantage for Maytag.

We see a similar structure in HMI's lead over Whirlpool. During HMI's streak of higher relative performance it enjoyed a strong gross margin advantage, reflective of its non-price competitive position, but a significant SG&A disadvantage, consistent with HMI's more labor-intensive distribution. With greater volume and efficiency than Maytag, Whirlpool was able to match HMI's fixed asset turnover despite Whirlpool's asset-intensive model while it managed current assets more efficiently than HMI, leaving the vacuum cleaner company at an overall asset turnover disadvantage.

HMI's ROA declined through the early 1970s, and the company expanded into traditional retail distribution: by 1978, retail store sales accounted for 50 percent of revenue and seemed to be improving profitability through increasing gross margin and lower SG&A costs. However, growth lagged and the retail channel essentially cannibalized door-to-door sales, and in the retail channel the high-priced FilterQueen proved especially vulnerable to recessionary pressures in the early 1980s. In response, HMI introduced the Princess line for retail sale and shifted FilterQueen back to in-home solicitation exclusively.

It is perhaps telling that HMI, with its non-price position, had a relative R&D expense advantage over both Maytag and Whirlpool despite its much smaller size. It was therefore spending dramatically less in absolute dollars on product development. It is perhaps for this reason that the company proved unable to reverse, or even halt, its long-term decline in absolute ROA.

In 1987, a new CEO, Kirk Foley, was installed. Consistent with the view that business line diversification is a response to as much as a cause of poor performance, he began aggressively moving into new product markets. In the decade ending in 1995, HMI's revenues grew from $25 million to almost $125 million, but its complexion had changed utterly. The vacuum cleaner business had become merely a division of consumer products. Metal-formed tubing grew to a quarter of total revenue, only to be dropped in 1989, replaced by a more diversified floor-care division that included European operations and a carpet-cleaning rental business, Household Rental Systems (HRS).

None of these operations enjoyed a distinctive competitive position, and HMI's ROA continued to erode, even though its relative standing remained in the 6th-to-8th-decile band, as required for Long Runner status. Even so, the long-run trend was clear, and when a new CEO, James Malone, took over in 1997, he bet the business on a return to fundamentals. Malone discontinued six major product lines and reconstituted the FilterQueen vacuum cleaner business from what was left of it inside the HRS division. Sales plummeted to just $39 million as a result of these changes.

As the company's performance profile reveals, ROA continued to decline and became quite erratic. Losses were sufficiently dramatic and the downward pressure on share price so strong that the company was taken private in 2005.

Playing the Odds

Merck and Heartland owe their sustained exceptional performance to what they did right. Merck consistently moved first—to international markets, to targeted discovery, to a diversified product portfolio, to joint ventures, to PBM investments—and best, either achieving desired outcomes or avoiding unprofitable reversals. Heartland waited, adopting what had become common industry practice years after its competitors, and enjoyed the benefits of its unique position and operating model for nearly a decade. When it finally had to adapt, it did so in ways that upended just about every aspect of its business. But in both cases, *better before cheaper* and *revenue before cost* seem to be the only constants.

Eli Lilly, Werner, and Whirlpool all enjoyed relatively consistent performance. Greatness eluded them not because of any gross failings on their part but primarily because of what they did not do. Eli Lilly did not move aggressively enough or fast enough into new paradigms of research and new international markets. It had the capabilities, but was—compared with Merck—less committed to the rules. Werner, similarly, and ironically, chased profitability in dedicated fleet and non-asset-based services. But management time and attention are limited resources, and these initiatives did not lend themselves to a non-price position; consequently, exceptional profitability remained elusive. Whirlpool found itself caught in a rapidly globalizing industry and under extreme pressure from lower-cost foreign competitors. It took everything the company had to stay on an even keel.

Maytag, HMI, KVP, and PAM all owe their declines or average profitability to what they did wrong. Maytag and HMI were not arrogant; in fact, just the opposite: they gave up on what made them special seemingly in response to overwhelming industry pressures. KVP and PAM both made a grab for the brass ring in their respective industries, and both missed. Where KVP lacked the operational savvy to pull off its transformation, PAM made strategic bets that just turned out wrong.

The fascinating thing, of course, is that our successful companies did not manifest the opposite of the behaviors we see in our less outstanding performers. Merck made big bets that worked (discovery-driven planning) and big bets that did not (Medco). Heartland acceded to industry pressures, as did Maytag, but managed to sustain its Miracle Worker status. Werner's international expansion served it hardly at all while for Merck it was a primary contributing factor to the company's success. HMI changed its underlying distribution model, which served only to dig it into a deeper hole faster, while for Heartland a similar shift was essential. In short, we end where we started: with the observation that, beyond *better before cheaper* and *revenue before cost*, there really are no other compelling generalizations to be made.

Our hope is that our rules will serve you when making difficult, ambiguous decisions. After all, rarely are the data dispositive on any questions of moment. In such circumstances, one has a choice to make: follow your instincts or follow the rules.

And too many of us do not follow the rules. Instead, we place our faith in our intuitions. This is a mistake, because our intuitions seem programmed to see patterns in randomness, leading us systematically to make far worse decisions than we need to.

For example, in a lab experiment subjects are told that the next card they see will be either red or blue.[46] They are asked to predict which it will be. At first, subjects have no information to work with, so they simply guess. As the experiment continues, red and blue cards appear with a consistent frequency of 75 percent red and 25 percent blue. Some subjects never realize this and simply keep guessing based on intuition, attempting to tap into their perceived ESP talents, signals from the beyond, or whatever, and so have miserable luck. Some keep track of what they are seeing and infer the relative frequency of each color. These clever folks now have a choice to make: do they simply go with the most frequent color all the time, guessing red on every draw? Or do they attempt to match the frequency of their guesses of each color with the frequency with which the colors appear?

Curiously, rats often do quite well at this experiment. They figure out the frequency bit pretty quickly and then guess red 100 percent of the time. That limits their upside, but also their downside: for short stretches they might do better or worse than 75 percent accuracy, but their long-run average is guaranteed.

When it comes to people, the danger is that our innate and often irresistible urge to see patterns everywhere will overcome us. Our downfall is not that we do not recognize underlying patterns, but that we see patterns too quickly, or worse, see patterns where there are none. Once we understand the unconditional odds—that is, the relative frequency of red and blue—we start looking for conditional odds: the likelihood that the next card is blue *given* that the last card was red, or blue, or that the last sequence was *red, red, red, blue, red, red*.

If there is no pattern, this "matching" strategy has a long-run accuracy of 62.5 percent, materially worse than rats typically do. If the order in which the colors appear is random, the best strategy is simply to follow the odds and to guess red every time. Only if you can correctly discern a true underlying pattern to some reasonable approximation can a matching strategy based on that pattern improve your long-run accuracy.

The relationships between many variables of interest—say, M&A activity and share price, or diversification levels and profitability—are statistically significant and often economically material. Like the frequency of red and blue cards, one might argue that on average M&A or diversification are bad ideas. Based on that, we could do better than simply following our gut, because playing the odds based on the observed high-level associations is better than random guessing.

However, it would be foolish to stop there and only follow those odds by avoiding all M&A or never diversifying. We can plausibly and credibly specify the contingencies that bear on those relationships in ways that improve outcomes beyond the first-order correlation that we observe at the population level. In other words, we have figured out a reasonable approximation of the underlying pattern, so we are well served to go beyond the naïve strategy and exploit this additional knowledge.

The relationships we observe between each of the two rules—*better before cheaper* and *revenue before cost*—and exceptional performance are statistically significant and economically material. This means, as before, that we can now do better than guessing, following our intuition, or relying only on our own personal experience. If you seek exceptional performance for your company, your best bet is *better before cheaper* and *revenue before cost.*

However, there are counterexamples: some Miracle Workers have a price-based position and a cost-driven profitability formula. That is why we characterize them as *rules,* not *laws.* They are "on average" claims, and thus at their core are utterly contingent. Under some circumstances you should follow our rules, and under other circumstances you should not.

In that case, you might want to know how you can determine which circumstances you are in. The bad news is that we cannot specify the contingencies, that is, the underlying pattern, that would allow us to predict with sufficient accuracy which path is the best route to exceptional performance. Rather, our case study sample deliberately encompasses a wide range of industries with many and varied characteristics that might bear on the outcomes. The rules seem to apply just as strongly in medical devices and semiconductors as they do in electrical wiring and long-haul trucking. With so few counterexamples, it is very difficult even to suggest what that pattern might be. For now, we must conclude that there is no underlying pattern.

This statement, like all empirical statements, is provisional and subject to revision. Should it be determined that there is an underlying pattern that can be specified with sufficient accuracy, then this third rule will fall. At that point, *better before cheaper* and *revenue before cost* will no longer be rules either, but simply alternatives, and the relevant discussion will be to assess whether a company is operating under conditions that call for *better* before *cheaper* or under conditions that require *cheaper* before *better.* When we know the patterns, "it depends" is no longer a two-word sentence of surrender but a segue to our deeper understanding.

At the same time, we must not beg the question: we might never achieve the level of understanding we desire. Competition in reasonably efficient markets is a highly chaotic system, and even if we could specify all the causal relationships at work, as a practical matter dependency on unmeasurable initial conditions would make the eventual outcomes effectively random. With no discernible underlying pattern, we might forever be stuck observing only long-run frequencies, in which case the research project is to specify the relevant odds with ever-greater accuracy.

Even if that pattern exists, for now we do not know what it is. We cannot specify the conditions under which *better before cheaper* and *revenue before cost* are to be preferred over their alternatives, and so our best bet lies in following the odds.

In other words, *there are no other rules*.

CHAPTER 6

Why You Should Use the Three Rules

An efficient market depends on the ability of a buyer to assess the merits of a purchase, either before or after purchase and trial. The more completely and inexpensively one can make these assessments, the more efficient the market is.

By these criteria, the market for, say, instant coffee is likely to be relatively efficient. When faced with the challenge of deciding whether or not to try a new brand, you could explore the design and execution of the focus groups and surveys the coffee company undoubtedly conducted before launching its product. But you probably will not do that. Instead, because there is relatively little at stake in any given trial and few lingering aftereffects if it goes poorly, you will more likely listen to your friends or people who like what you typically like and try it out, or not. After all, the only focus group that really matters is the focus group of you, and finding out what you think requires that you try the product. If you are the victim of a false positive—trying something you should not have—there is no real harm done: at worst, a few bucks down the drain. If you are the victim of a false negative, and you erroneously forgo trying something you would have liked, there is no real harm done there, either: you cannot miss what you have never known.

The market for pharmaceuticals that treat life-threatening, chronic illnesses is very different. When it comes to figuring out whether you should take blood pressure medication, and if so, which one, listening only to your friends is a very bad idea. The cost of a false negative—not taking something you should—could materially shorten your life; but so could a false positive (taking something you should not). Worse, we often cannot know after the fact whether taking the drug was good or bad for you, because your condition and the drug are but two of many factors affecting your health, and we cannot redo the experiment *on you*. Consequently, the mechanisms of market efficiency are much more heavily skewed toward understanding what is likeliest to work *before* you try it out. That means experimental design, data collection, and analysis are absolutely critical to making an informed choice.

Our view is that the marketplace for the sort of management advice on offer in success studies, this one included, falls much closer to the pharmaceutical end of the spectrum than to the instant coffee end. The most relevant companies to look to for indications of what works are most likely your competitors, but if you do what they are doing you will not improve your relative performance. No individual can hope to have had a sufficient quantity or variety of experience—never mind the challenge of avoiding well-documented psychological biases that would render difficult an objective interpretation of that experience—to come to reliably correct conclusions on their own. Adopting any study's advice typically requires a commitment over time, often many years, and connecting outcomes to adoption of the advice can be very difficult since a company's performance is a function of many other variables. And, finally, we cannot replay your company's history with different advice and see what would have happened instead.

Yet the behavior of both purveyors and consumers of popular management advice, including and perhaps especially that on offer in success studies, suggests to us that we are treating what is more appropriately seen as a beta-blocker as if it were a caffeine-free breakfast blend. It is only too frequently that otherwise accomplished executives endorse and adopt the findings or prescriptions of a given work because the advice offered confirms what they already felt were the key drivers of corporate success. That is, they like what they have read precisely because it does not tell them anything fundamentally new.

Hence our emphasis on questions of research design and standards of evidence. We have been as complete and transparent in the presentation of our method and data as we felt a book permits. We have, somewhat uncharacteristically among business books, been explicit in comparing our approach to those adopted by others, in some cases offering side-by-side comparisons. We hope these aspects of our work are not seen as gratuitous or unnecessarily provocative, and we are keenly aware of many limitations and flaws in our work. To the extent that our efforts win notice, we have no doubt that more shortcomings will be brought to our attention.

However, progress, in research as in any competitive market, is a function of relative improvement, not the attainment of absolute excellence. It is certainly true that in pursuing the drivers of exceptional corporate performance we are much closer to the social than to the hard sciences, and the sorts of "double-blind, prospective, randomized, placebo-controlled trials" that the testing of pharmaceuticals requires are simply not possible.[1] But that does not mean that anything goes, or that all designs are equally valid or equally, or even sufficiently, likely to produce meaningful results. There are important differences in method that make some studies better than others, and certain features that completely disqualify some studies from serious consideration.

Unfortunately, there are no demonstrably true hard and fast rules that guarantee that the truth will emerge from a given effort. It falls to each of us to evaluate the evidence on our own and reach our own conclusions. We must accept that people of goodwill can differ on matters of substance, and that two reasonable people can look at the same facts and come to different, perhaps very different, conclusions.

Thankfully, there are criteria that can help us make these evaluations.

Organizational theorist Karl E. Weick posits that theories should be evaluated along three dimensions: simplicity, accuracy, and generality.[2] As an empirical matter, there appears to be a trade-off among these three characteristics, especially in the social sciences.[3] A simple theory is typically one with few variables, and so it often proves less accurate in accounting for the specifics of a particular case. Improving accuracy often requires introducing more variables, which compromises simplicity. The more accurately a theory explains a given case, the less generally applicable it is while more generally applicable theories must make allowances that undermine accuracy. Consequently, when evaluating the merits of a particular theory, one must not only attend to its relative position on each dimension but also the trade-offs among them. Whether a theory that is general and simple is better or worse than one that is accurate and general, or accurate and simple, is a question of the use to which it will be put.[4]

With these nuances in mind, we now make the case for the three rules as a worthy theory of exceptional corporate performance.

Simple

The world is a complicated place. The conscious determination of the course of action that has the best probability of achieving your desired aims based on all available data is not something we are able to do, and not something we are likely to be able to do. It is not only the ambiguity of the data, it is the volume and complexity of the required calculations. Chess, for example, is conceptually no different from tic-tac-toe in that it is a determined game. It is more interesting than tic-tac-toe because of its complexity. Other games are challenging not because of complexity but because of uncertainty, like backgammon, for example. Combine the two and the cognitive load can quickly become overwhelming.

Unfortunately, faced with a superabundance of alternatives and unable to choose using deliberative rationality, we very often do nothing at all, delaying action in ways that leave us worse off than making even a random choice.[5] This phenomenon has been observed in circumstances as trivial as deciding whether or not to buy jam. It is only too plausible that this deer-in-the-headlights phenomenon plays out, if anything, in sharper relief when addressing choices of far greater moment. It is not for nothing that we have the phrase "the paralysis of analysis."

This fact of human cognition has led to the increasing popularity of simple rules for action, heuristics that enable a response by specifying a "search strategy" as much as a choice algorithm. When you face clearly defined alternatives, but which is the better course cannot be readily determined, you should choose the alternative that is most closely aligned with your rules. When the task is to find or blaze a path forward, the three rules provide a guide for what is fundamentally a creative act. In either case, rules render tractable what would otherwise have been overwhelming.

The use of rules is often seen as an unavoidable trade-off. We lack both the completeness of data and the computational power required to make optimal choices, so we must "satisfice," that is, do the best we can, given those limitations.[6] The assumption is that we could get better outcomes with more complex models, but they are too much to cope with.

Second, it turns out that not only are simple rules more actionable, they can often give better results than more complex, seemingly complete models.[7] It is necessarily true, and hence uninformative, to posit that a completely correct model will do a better job than a less completely correct model. However, as a matter of fact, rather than theoretical necessity, we find that more complete models tend to introduce additional error with their increased specificity.[8] In other words, not only are simple rules more actionable, but even when complex rule sets can be used, they should probably be avoided because simple rules give better results.

Simplicity, then, seems to be an unalloyed virtue, one the three rules appear to possess. *Better before cheaper* and *revenue before cost* are not "dumbed down" simplifications of our findings, nor mnemonics connected to more elaborate formulations. These rules *are* the principles we inferred from our research, and so their simplicity does not come at the expense of completeness. In addition, there are only three rules—and the third is, in truth, proscriptive, not prescriptive, born of what we saw as a need to demonstrate that the first two rules are as far as the data allow us to go.

Better still, the three rules are falsifiable in a way that many other prescriptions are not, a topic we explored in chapter 1. You can know independently and in advance of observing your relative profitability whether you are competing on price or non-price dimensions of value. You can know whether your prices or volumes are higher than your competitors', and whether you are counting on lower costs to drive superior profitability.

This makes the three rules actionable in ways that longer or more nuanced recipes for success might not be. The daily routines of everyone in every organization of any complexity demand innumerable decisions. Very often the alternatives are unclear, the trade-offs unspecified, and the consequences unknown, but still one must act. With only three rules to appeal to, and relatively unambiguous criteria for determining if one is adhering to them, it is possible to create a widespread and shared consistency of action that is all but unachievable otherwise.

Accurate

Contrasting the substance and the number of our rules with, say, the eight principles of *Good to Great*, the "Seven S's" of *In Search of Excellence*, or the "4+2" of *What Really Works* leads us to conclude that our prescriptions for action are simpler than others'. It would be facile, however, to hold that merely because we have fewer rules we have a stronger claim on your allegiance. If that were true, then we would be trumped by someone with one rule. And having no rules would be best of all!

To be useful, a simple set of actionable rules needs to be right, or at least, right *enough*. Given the difficulties associated with testing these rules, one must often rely as much on the method and evidence used to derive them as on prospective tests of their efficacy. Hence our discussion of research design, data collection, and causal inference in chapter 2.

It is perhaps worth recapitulating briefly what we believe are the distinguishing features of our approach.

IDENTIFYING THE PHENOMENON. Every success study begins by specifying its *dependent variable*; that is, the outcome it hopes to explain. There are three features of how we define superior corporate performance that we believe are noteworthy.

First, no study we are aware of has used an explicitly statistically driven method to separate signal from noise. Based on our assessments of the samples used by a selection of high-profile and otherwise well-regarded efforts, none has had the good fortune to pick a compelling sample by luck alone. In contrast, we have used validated statistical techniques to quantify the probability that we are focused on companies that have delivered relative performance worthy of examination.

Second, we have identified patterns in performance based on similarly transparent and objective statistical tests of significance. This forces our explanations of performance to track more closely with the performance itself and limits the inevitable temptation to fit the performance to our explanations. (See Appendix C.)

Third, we use these first two features to define what it is we hope to explain—our *dependent variable*—more precisely than in most success studies: the difference in ROA between two carefully chosen companies over a relevant time period. Now, that might sound facile—who compares two haphazardly chosen companies over an irrelevant time period? But as we hope to have shown in chapter 2, despite the care and good intentions that were no doubt behind most of the others, for the most part they ended up with precisely that. (See Appendix B.)

CAUSE AND EFFECT. Eighteenth-century philosopher David Hume taught us that causation is only ever inferred, never observed.[9] This deep limitation on the validity of any causal claim does not necessarily undermine the notion that some causal claims are more plausible than others. It is therefore worth commenting on how we have attempted to establish causal connections between differences in behavior and differences in performance.

The most damaging criticism leveled against success studies as a genre is that much of the data relied upon to explain a company's performance is drawn from accounts that are colored by the performance itself. This is the so-called halo effect discussed in chapter 2.[10] The halo effect corrupts success study findings because the *independent variable* (differences in behavior)—that is, what explains movement in the *dependent variable* (differences in performance)—is not truly *independent* of what one hopes to explain.

By decomposing the ROA differences we hope to explain into differences in ROS and TAT, and thence into differences in gross margin, R&D, SG&A, current and fixed asset turnover, and so on, we provide some measure of insulation from halos. There is no necessary connection between the magnitude of one company's ROA advantage over another, and so the Elements of Advantage are independent variables. It turns out, as discussed in chapter 4, that there is a systematic relationship between structure and performance type, but there was nothing necessary about those findings. (See Appendixes A and J.)

The observed financial structure of one company's advantage over another forced us to find behavioral explanations that could account for those observed differences. And luckily for us, commentators on successful businesses do not typically gush over a company's relative gross margin advantage. Instead, we concentrated on quantifiable behavioral differences that we could connect to the drivers of ROA differences relevant to each case.

It is for these reasons that we attribute Linear's rise to Miracle Worker status to its shifts in product markets, Medtronic's to increased product quality, and T&B's fall to diversification. Abercrombie & Fitch's success is driven by its customer experience and branding, Wrigley's by its globalization while Weis's run ended due to competitive emulation to which it had no effective response. Merck owes its outperformance to international growth, a more diverse product portfolio, and having better managed the fallout from a strategic dead end that Eli Lilly had also pursued. Heartland first broke, and then accepted, the defining trade-offs of long-haul trucking while Maytag proved unable to stay the course, losing its product differentiation and distribution-driven advantages. In each case, we documented differences in behavior that were not colored by the performance we hoped to explain. In other words, our independent variables were truly independent.

Finally, we attempted to demonstrate the relevance and materiality of our explanations. It is one thing to observe that Heartland's ROA edge was driven by a gross margin advantage and to document a price premium as an explanation of that gross margin advantage. It is another to explore the extent to which that premium is a plausible explanation for the magnitude of the advantage observed. Our estimates of the materiality of specific behaviors to performance advantage are unavoidably crude, but they provide some confidence that the behaviors that seem to matter actually do. (See Appendix G.)

QUANTIFIED PROBABILITIES. The success study world has been somewhat chastened by its critics. Even its most successful standard bearers, who once sought, and claimed to have found, "the enduring physics of great organizations" have in subsequent work retreated to seeking "correlations not causes."[11] The evidence required to support a claim of correlation, however, is no less exigent than that required to support a causal claim. Statistical tests matter, even—and perhaps especially—with small sample sizes.

Our findings do not allow us to specify especially precisely your odds of success if you follow the rules. Rather, our claim is that the probabilities that emerge from our analysis are sufficiently compelling to identify the underlying trends in the full population of exceptional companies. We have done what we can to quantify the likelihood of our observations arising by chance alone. We feel that these probabilities are sufficiently low that our findings are real. As ever, it is up to you to draw your own conclusions. (See Appendixes H, I, and K.)

General

There are at least three dimensions along which findings based on case study analysis should be generalizable in order to be useful.

First, the sample companies studied should be representative of a population of companies of material interest. Very often, success studies set up selection criteria that are so demanding that the sample chosen *is* the population; that is, there are only a very few companies that meet all the desired benchmarks. This obviates demonstrating representativeness, but it dramatically limits the generalizability of the findings. At the limit, prescriptions for action would seem to apply only to companies seeking to replicate precisely the performance parameters that defined the sample.

Our sample selection criteria are certainly demanding, but they do admit of several hundreds of companies meeting them. We did not select our companies based on patterns of performance over time or a specific magnitude of outperformance. The rules we have inferred accommodate a wide range of possible performance outcomes—all of them demonstrably exceptional.

From this population of exceptional companies we have selected a sample. We did not choose our sample entirely randomly. We selected companies from a range of industries and we insisted on meaningful comparisons within each trio. We cannot, therefore, rely on this part of our method to support claims of generalizability. As with so much else, the final judgment in this matter is not categorical, and so instead we have described the degree to which our sample is representative of the population. To the extent you find this convincing, you will see our findings as more broadly applicable.

Second, the findings should apply beyond the population used to generate them; that is, they should have predictive power. There are generally accepted methods for testing the predictive power of a theory, but in light of the unavoidably qualitative nature of at least some of what emerges from any success study, the generators of that theory are almost always the last people you would want to test them.

The problem, once again, is inescapable cognitive biases. Thanks to this research, we have strong opinions about what accounts for a company's success. If you hand us a trio in an industry we have not examined and ask us to test whether the rules account for the performance differences, we are irretrievably contaminated simply because we generated the theory. It is not a question of individual honesty, but of the integrity of the process. For the same reason that no one should approve their own expenses, qualitative theories should not be tested by their creators.

Consequently, we, like the authors of every other success study we are aware of, cannot claim any demonstrated predictive accuracy. The most we can claim is that the more nearly quantifiable nature of our theory makes it easier for others to test our claims on new data, and therefore perhaps more likely that they will do so. Whether the strategy used by one company is simple and clear compared with that used by another is more subjective than whether one company is competing on price compared with another. Whether a company is abandoning its core prematurely strikes us as much more of a judgment call than whether one company is more profitable than another due to advantages in gross margin driven by higher unit volumes.

With these caveats tempering our enthusiasm, we can point to evidence of the rules at work in the actions of companies in a wide variety of circumstances as they wrestle with the challenges of improving their performance. For example, China Resources Enterprise Ltd. (CRE) operates 4,100 stores under ten retail brands across much of China.[12] It has been facing intense and increasing pressure from large U.S.- and European-based discount retailers, some of which have been steadily gaining market share.

China Resources Enterprise has fought back, but not, perhaps, in ways you might have expected. Its largest foreign competitors—none of which are Miracle Workers—are pursuing low-cost strategies with profit margins as low as 2 percent. But CRE, by emphasizing product selection and brand, is enjoying profit margins of up to 25 percent. Better still, the resulting popularity of its products makes for increased market share and an increased ability to secure space in newly opened malls. In other words, faced with price-based competition from lower-cost rivals, CRE has responded, seemingly successfully, with *better before cheaper* and *revenue before cost*.

Back in the United States, Goodyear Tire & Rubber Co. seems to be coming out of the doldrums by changing course in ways consistent with the three rules.[13] Under Rick Kramer, who took over as CEO in 2010, the company shifted its product mix from high-volume, low-price tires to much lower-volume, more differentiated, higher-priced products. In 2007, 40 percent of its tires sold for $60 each; today, 75 percent of its tires sell for $130 or more.

The transition has not been easy or painless. Goodyear closed or sold thirteen of twenty-nine plants while investing almost $1 billion to upgrade its remaining capacity. The company also had to take on the very difficult problem of determining precisely what sorts of attributes its tires would have to have in order to command such price premiums—from innovative tread design to reduced stopping distance and road noise to built-in air pumps that maintain tire pressure to increase fuel efficiency.

Non-price positions and revenue-driven profitability formulas are not prerequisites for exceptional performance or a guarantee of success, even in our sample. But the weight of the circumstantial evidence is, to us, convincing, and we hope it is to you, too. We encourage you to reevaluate your own intuition, your own personal library of examples of success and failure, and to determine for yourself if the three rules do as good a job— or better—at accounting for the facts as you know them.

Third, a new theory must either be consistent with the prescriptions of established theories or provide an alternative and at least equally compelling explanation for the contradictory findings.

The three rules are partly consistent with established theories of competitive advantage, something we explored at length in chapter 3. But there are many other theories out there addressing a large number of relationships between behavior and performance or other outcomes. Some of these theories have significant evidence supporting them, and if our prescriptions contradict theirs, then, as Ricky Ricardo might have put it, "we got some 'splaining to do."

At this point in our story, a review of even a representative sampling is beyond our scope and very likely your patience. For now, let us confine this discussion to a theory that we believe is correct and that, in the eyes of many with whom we have shared the three rules, seems to prescribe contradictory advice: Disruptive innovation.[14] Disruptors get their start by creating new business models that allow them to serve small or economically unattractive market segments more profitably than incumbent organizations. This is the "foothold" segment. Faced with a structural disadvantage in a relatively undesirable segment, incumbents do the rational thing and retreat upmarket. Disruptors, powered by an enabling technology, extend the advantage developed in their foothold segment and pursue the incumbents into those same segments.[15] Eventually, the incumbents have nowhere left to run and no effective way to fight back. By focusing on markets where they enjoy superior profitability, it would appear that victims of Disruption are following *better before cheaper* straight into oblivion.

We believe this formulation ignores the fact that Disruption and our three rules explain fundamentally different phenomena. The three rules apply at the level of relatively closely substitutable product markets while Disruption theory explains the collision of previously relatively unsubstitutable product markets.

Take, for example, the foundational example of Disruption: the disk-drive industry from the 1970s to the 1990s. Each wave of Disruption—14-inch drives supplanted by 8-inch drives supplanted by 5¼-inch drives supplanted by 3½-inch drives—saw companies in once entirely separate markets encroaching on more lucrative turf that had become, by virtue of technological advancement, increasingly adjacent turf. It is certainly the case that 14-inch drive makers, by ignoring the 8-inch drive market in the pursuit of *better before cheaper* in the 14-inch market, were Disrupted. But who disrupted them? It was the 8-inch drive makers who were determined to earn the business of the most demanding and profitable customer segments that their technology permitted them to pursue. The successful Disruptors were the 8-inch drive makers who were focused on *better before cheaper* in the 8-inch market!

Disruption's orthodoxy prescribes that incumbents avoid being Disrupted, not by attempting to move downmarket, but by creating new, independent business units focused on the foothold segment with the intent of riding the Disruptive wave upmarket. In other words, the three rules prescribe how to be successful within a product market. Disruption provides a way to identify which product markets, and which business models within them, are likeliest to have innovation-driven growth trajectories. Since success in one's foothold market is a sine qua non of Disruption, the three rules and Disruption are highly complementary.

Every era has its darling of the business community. In the 1980s, you could not write about business without talking about GE. In the 1990s, it was Microsoft or Southwest that commanded our attention. In the early 2000s, Google was an inescapable exemplar of everything good. And of late, it has been Apple. As it turns out, Apple is a wonderful example of adherence to, and departures from, both the three rules and Disruption.

Apple's Performance Profile reflects quite nicely the popular narrative of the company's fortunes as they have waxed and waned and waxed again over the decades. Through the mid-1980s the company's success with the Macintosh personal computer was legendary. As the so-called Wintel architecture came to dominate the personal computer industry, Apple found itself in the wilderness for a time. The launch of the iMac signaled a resurgence, and by the early 2000s the success of the iPod had Apple back in the game. The iPhone and iPad have secured Apple's position in business history.

By our lights, Apple is not a clearly exceptional performer over its full lifetime. It has a 98 percent probability of being a Miracle Worker, but thanks to the large number of companies with the same number of observations, it has too high a probability of being a false positive. One or two more years in the 9th decile of profitability—which certainly seems more than merely possible in light of the company's current performance—and it will have cleared even these benchmarks.

The company's defining products have been the Macintosh personal computer, the iPod digital music player, the iPhone smart phone, and iPad

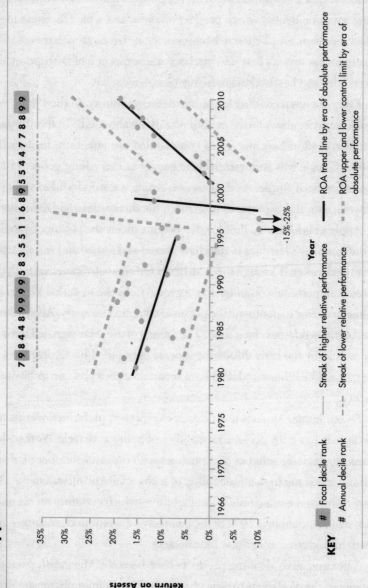

Figure 2 Apple

Return on Assets (y-axis): 35%, 30%, 25%, 20%, 15%, 10%, 5%, 0%, -5%, -10%

Year (x-axis): 1966, 1970, 1975, 1980, 1985, 1990, 1995, 2000, 2005, 2010

7 9 8 4 4 8 9 9 9 5 8 3 5 5 1 1 6 8 9 5 4 4 7 7 8 8 9 9

-15% -25%

KEY

Focal decile rank

Annual decile rank

— ROA trend line by era of absolute performance

--- ROA upper and lower control limit by era of absolute performance

— Streak of higher relative performance

--- Streak of lower relative performance

Source: Compustat; Deloitte analysis

Note: Portions of control limits omitted for convenience.

tablet. None of these products or their related services competed on price in their respective product markets; quite the contrary: each was materially more expensive than its closest substitutes at the time of introduction. Their success, then, is best attributed to being *better before cheaper*.

Only two of these four products were Disruptive, however. The Macintosh rode the personal computer wave, which was Disrupting the workstation and client-server architecture of distributed computing. The iPad has been riding a new wave of haptic (touch screen) interfaces and "app-based" software that promises to Disrupt the personal computer.

The iPod and iPhone, however, although both revolutionary in their respective markets, were sustaining innovations, for each sought to topple entrenched incumbents by targeting the same customer segments coveted by the incumbents of the day.[16] The iPod was attacking the mobile music market that had long been dominated by Sony, defeating not only the MP3 devices developed by relatively smaller rivals but also Sony's MiniDisc product.[17] The iPhone sought to displace the highly successful smart phones on offer from both global giants such as Nokia and agile, growing, relative start-ups such as Research in Motion.[18] Both products, however, were entirely consistent with *better before cheaper* and *revenue before cost*.

In short, the three rules apply to all of Apple's successes whether they were sustaining or Disruptive. Disruption accounts for some of Apple's successes but not others.

Now, during Apple's period of lower relative performance, as far as we can tell, the company was *also* pursuing product market strategies that were consistent with the three rules. The Newton, which might have Disrupted the personal computer, the Cube (sustaining in personal computers), and eWorld (sustaining in the online community market) were all attempts to earn pricing premiums from superior products and services, but attempts that were relatively less successful. Explanations for the company's performance during this period are abundant. Particularly popular are product proliferation, failing to manage the operating system platform and the related ecosystem, and poor execution.[19]

If this meant only that sometimes the rules are associated with success and sometimes with failure, we would not have much to go on. But the unit of analysis in our work is not the frequency of success or failure by product launch, it is the lifetime performance of the corporation. For Apple, the three rules are associated with a performance profile that is on the cusp of exceptional. Whether the company could or did pursue sustaining or Disruptive innovation was a function of the technologies available to it and the circumstances it found itself in at different points in time. The three rules, however, were consistently in evidence, and on balance have delivered a lifetime performance that most companies would envy.

This discussion of innovation speaks to the perspective that we believe *better before cheaper* and *revenue before cost* provide on many issues that matter to corporate performance. Innovation clearly matters, but in ways that, so far, defy the level of generalization available to our rules. In our sample, Linear, Medtronic, T&B, and A&F were all more innovative than their Long Runner counterparts. But Wrigley, Merck, Heartland, and Maytag were not. They were not demonstrably *less* innovative, but superior innovation was not a key determinant of their success. What mattered far more was its competitive position and how that enabled either a price premium or superior volume.

Similarly, leadership is undeniably an important determinant of any company's performance. As are organizational structure, human resources management, IT infrastructure, and any of a host of other considerations. But so far, we have been unable to identify underlying patterns in how specific, quantifiable differences in behavior contribute to differences in performance. It is for that reason that we invoke the third rule, that *there are no other rules*.

At least for now. Further research will, we hope, shed additional light on how these and many other determinants of corporate performance are connected. Our belief is that as we come to understand each of these drivers better, the first two rules will remain a constant backdrop and context for interpreting the influence of all the rest.

Defying Gravity

The eighteenth-century philosopher Immanuel Kant (a contemporary of David Hume's) formulated a "categorical imperative" that, he argued, should be the basis of all human action: Act only according to that maxim whereby you can, at the same time, will that it should become a universal law without contradiction.[20] Lying, for example, is immoral because if everyone lied, language would cease to have meaning and communication would become impossible—thereby making lies impossible as well.

There is a case to be made that success studies, as a class, founder on the shoals of Kant's principle. Success studies seek to provide advice on how to improve your relative performance, that is, on how to do better than the competition. This is very different from the sort of advice that seeks to help you improve compared with your own historical performance. A successful cost-cutting initiative will reduce your costs compared with what they were. That says nothing, however, about how your costs will compare with those of your competitors. If they are pursuing the same initiative equally successfully, and so reducing their costs at the same rate you are, you might improve compared with yourself but end up exactly where you started compared with them. It is this phenomenon that gives rise to the Red Queen effect, referred to in chapter 3, of having to run just to stand still.

Consequently, advice on how to compete successfully is subject to an irony that borders on paradox. If the advice is right, then it will be universally adopted; if it is universally adopted, it does not improve your relative performance; if it does not improve your relative performance, it is wrong. In other words, if the advice is right, then the advice is wrong.[21]

Although true, this criticism is overstated because it is based on the notion that success studies seek the secrets of eternal dominance. Certainly this one does not. Our objective is to make it possible to do better for longer than one otherwise would.

We think of it this way. Glider pilots, like all airplane pilots, know the expression "takeoffs are optional; landings are mandatory." It means that no matter how high, fast, or far you fly, you are going to come back down. Gravity always wins.

The same can be said of corporate performance. The only certainty for any company doing well is that eventually it will be doing worse. Every company that has ever soared has or will eventually become entirely average—or worse. Although you might not be able to predict precisely what will bring down any given high flier, it is a sure thing that something will.

Sometimes greatness erodes because of internal failings: inertia born of complacency might lead you to resist obvious and necessary changes; or entropy born of hubris might dilute your focus on key customers or markets. Sometimes external forces undermine performance: competitors, spurred on by your success, emulate your behaviors or even improve on your original insights, leaving you with no advantage at all; changes in customer preferences or regulatory or legislative constraints can render historical strengths irrelevant or even turn them into encumbrances. Whatever the proximate cause, just as no glider can stay aloft forever, no company can remain on top eternally.

This unfortunate fact of corporate life imposes an upper bound on the extent of the claims one can hope to make about the drivers of long-term, superior profitability. No advice can come with a credible promise of perpetual superiority. It might be theoretically possible for a corporation to deliver endlessly standout profitability, but as an empirical matter, we lack even an existence proof, never mind the sort of sample that might make possible the inference of general principles.

We have concluded, however, that even if defeating gravity is impossible, we can realistically hope to defy it. Despite the inevitability of a return to earth, some glider pilots do fly higher, faster, and farther than others. Using the same equipment in the same circumstances, some pilots—the *exceptional* ones—remain airborne far longer, soar far higher, and travel far greater distances than others. For these pilots, gliding is not a passive experience. They understand their aircraft, the conditions, and themselves and use that understanding to find lift where others find only the void, to achieve just the right angle of attack, or to exploit the paradox of diving earthward to generate lift and head skyward again. Even exceptional pilots must land— but not until long after the rest of us.

Similarly, some companies are exceptional. They are able, for a time— and occasionally for a long time—to overcome inertia, resist entropy, and adapt to competitive or environmental changes. They create better performance and sustain it for far longer than anyone has a right to expect. Nothing lasts forever, but then, that is not the goal. The objective is to deliver the best possible performance for as long as possible.

Every glider lands eventually. But how long it stays up, how far it flies, and the heights it reaches are all profoundly affected by the pilot's choices. It is our belief that by consciously adopting the three rules—*better before cheaper, revenue before cost,* and *there are no other rules*—you can reasonably hope to deny gravity its due for just that much longer.

ACKNOWLEDGMENTS

If the fool would persist in his folly, he would be wise.

William Blake (1757–1827), "Proverbs of Hell" (1793),

The Marriage of Heaven and Hell

We didn't know it at the time, but this project was conceived in late 2001. Mumtaz had been thinking about business model innovation, and that work culminated in a 2003 article, "Bottom Feeding for Blockbuster Businesses" in the *Harvard Business Review*. As we discussed whether that work had legs and could be the foundation for further research, we began questioning a fundamental premise of not only that effort but much business research: Why were the companies held up as exemplars and worthy of imitation so consistently the same, yet so consistently changing? Almost always, the claim is that a given company has done remarkably well because it has adopted this or that practice. But what, really, constituted remarkable performance? To state our concern in high-contrast terms, how could we know a company had really accomplished something worth understanding rather than simply having won a popularity contest thanks to a recent streak of what might have been nothing more than good luck?

The more insistently we asked this question, the more disillusioned we became with how most other investigators dealt with it. In particular, in the genre of research we came to call "success studies," we concluded that essentially no one had tackled with any rigor the issue of why a given company deserved attention. Their performance criteria were only ever justified with an appeal to our intuitions about what qualified as a noteworthy outcome. It seemed to us that there was no good reason to believe any of the success studies available at the time, or any that have come out since.

Thus began our efforts, christened "The Persistence Project" because we were after companies that had delivered persistent high performance. It was a project more in name than in substance, for as we noodled the problem from 2003 through 2006, our efforts were sporadic as we were distracted by other opportunities large and small. Any forward motion was thanks to unsuspecting colleagues we convinced to help us whitewash the fence: Jim Wappler was the first, succeeded by Paul Goydan and then Jim Guzcza and Jeff Schulz. We made some progress and were able to generate meaningful and maybe even useful insights, but our itch remained unscratched.

So we persisted.

It was in early 2007, when Mumtaz found Professor Andy Henderson at the University of Texas at Austin, that we began to get real traction on the problem. Andy's keen insight, creativity, technical expertise, good humor, and seemingly inexhaustible patience all proved invaluable. By late 2008 we had taken the first essential step: we had an "actuarial table" for corporate performance. Finally, we felt we could, if not know for sure that a company had delivered standout performance, at least quantify the likelihood that a company had achieved remarkable, special, exceptional performance. This work was published in the *Harvard Business Review* in 2009 and, with Andy as lead author, in the *Strategic Management Journal* in 2012. Our persistence had paid off.

The next step was to use this new tool to identify a sample of exceptional companies for closer examination. Lige Shao and Tamara Fossey were indispensable in keeping the project moving forward as we spent months poring over lists of companies and conducting preliminary research, trying to find comparisons that would allow us to identify the determinants of exceptional performance. Phil Rosenzweig of IMD made himself available for several very helpful conversations and offered welcome encouragement as we wrestled with the problem of sample selection. We considered several dozen research designs and many hundreds of companies in various combinations and permutations. It was painstaking and often frustrating work, but the promise of a case study sample that consisted of demonstrably exceptional companies was too alluring to abandon. So we persisted.

By 2008 we had settled on our trios—the case study companies featured in this book—and we began looking for relevant behavioral differences among them. Corralling colleagues in the United States and India, we had teams with rolling memberships working on each of the trios for up to a year.

Meaningful answers proved elusive. Our story in chapter 1 of dead ends and blind alleys and box canyons is no mere rhetorical device; that's really the way it happened. It fell to Margot Bellamy in the United States and Divakar Goswami in India to keep us on track. Margot and Divakar were indefatigable in coping with the constantly changing frameworks, organizing structures, needs for more or different data, bringing new team members on board quickly and effectively, and finding ways to condense masses of information into something digestible without losing nutritional value.

At different times, everyone in the table below found themselves making contributions of some kind to every other industry and trio study, but primary credit for what we know about each industry and trio belongs to the following:

Trio	Team
Semiconductors	Margot Bellamy, Florence Evina-Ze, Ally Ward
Medical Devices	Divakar Goswami, Sukanya Kannappan, Praveen Tanguturi
Electrical Wiring	Geetendra Wadekar, Susmit Datta, Divya Ravichandran, Ashish Gambhir, Anand Kalra
Clothing	Divakar Goswami, Selva Kandasamy, Siddharth Ramalingam
Confectionary	Ben Barclay, Andy Ho, Megana Gowda, Eric Chan
Groceries	Divakar Goswami, Selva Kandasamy, Geetendra Wadekar, Praveen Tanguturi, Ashish Gambhir
Pharmaceuticals	Divakar Goswami, Vinay Hukumchand, Divya Ravichandran, Anand Kalra, Lajja Modhiya
Trucking	Margot Bellamy, Kalyn Fink, Masha Rozen
Appliances	Margot Bellamy, Kalyn Fink

Mir Hyder Ali, Mitchell Evans, Zach Finlay, Aleen Khan, Vishwas Krishnamurty, and Ben Roberts also provided help with the monographs and a variety of other elements of the project. Thanks to their efforts, by 2011 for each of the trios examined in this book we had developed thirty-page monographs that reviewed the evolution of the industry, a wide range of relevant players beyond just the trio companies, and detailed explanations for the performance differences among the companies in each trio. For every fact on every company in this book, these teams unearthed a dozen more besides.

Our persistence had paid off.

In parallel with these efforts, we worked closely with Jeff Schulz to summarize our emerging findings and to build a quantitative connection between our case histories and the specifics of the performance differences we hoped to explain. We experimented with a variety of analytical techniques and conceptual framings that we felt would bring order to the chaos, several of which found expression in a series of *Deloitte Review* articles we coauthored with

Jeff, beginning in 2010. We have made presentations to our colleagues in the United States and around the world that talked about exceptional performance in terms of M&A, innovation, globalization, and execution. These efforts generated their own insights, but we always came up against vexing anomalies, recalcitrant data, and outright contradictions. So we persisted.

We reformulated all of it—all of it!—perhaps half a dozen times, abandoning months of work with each reboot. It was at times difficult not to be discouraged, and so we are enormously grateful for the unflagging support of Joe Echevarria, now Deloitte's CEO and during much of this project's gestation its COO. Joe ensured that the project was well funded and enlisted the endorsement of leadership across the firm in order that we could bring so many, so very capable people out of client service roles for months at a time. This was an act of faith on Joe's part that both inspired and humbled us. Our client service colleagues were unfailingly gracious and helpful in finding ways to give us welcome latitude in our discussion of companies we are proud to serve with distinction.

It wasn't until mid-2011 that the Performance Profile charts and the Elements of Advantage tables emerged as the key analytical tools that allowed us to see the three rules as the main drivers of exceptional performance. Selvarajan Kandasamy, Jeff Schulz, and Geetendra Wadekar suffered through innumerable iterations of these models, but tackled each request to see the data cut a new way with vigor and an attention to detail that belied what must have seemed at times to be unremitting drudgery. Andy Henderson, who thought he had escaped our clutches, graciously permitted himself to be pulled back in as we developed the statistical models that supported the general applicability of our core findings. Margot and Ben Barclay went the extra mile reviewing and synthesizing the models we used to estimate the materiality of behavioral differences to ROA differences. We finally had stable and, to us at least, compelling findings and a story that we felt was worth telling. Our persistence had paid off.

November 2011 marked the beginning of the writing process. Dwight Allen and Jeff Johnson now found themselves being punished for their help on previous projects as we inflicted on them one version after another. We experimented with different metaphors and levels of detail, tearing up and starting over almost monthly for the next eight months. Unlike much of the work that had gone before, the project had become an excruciatingly solitary effort. As before, however, our colleagues reassured us that the effort was worthwhile.

So we persisted.

By late summer 2012 we had the first chapter in place and the structure for the book you now hold. Then began a marathon sprint from Labor Day to Thanksgiving defined by 4:30 a.m. wake times and a production rate of a chapter a month. Thanksgiving to Christmas saw a complete revision and editing that cut the book's length by 30 percent. January and February were occupied with combing through the manuscript in order to get all the remaining details as close to completely right as we could, right down to the third decimal place in Appendix J. This fire drill tried everyone's patience, but no one showed it: Ben, Margot, Adam Brown, Divakar, Andy, Selva, and Geetendra were faced with seemingly endless "final" last-minute requests to double-check this, reformat that, rerun that analysis over there, you name it.

The result is this book, the most tangible output so far of our efforts and those of our colleagues. Realizing this dimension of the project has required its own supporting cast, which includes Wes Neff at the Leigh Bureau, who watched this project unfold almost from its beginning and offered well-timed and much-appreciated words of encouragement along the way, and Adrian Zackheim and Niki Papadopolous at Portfolio / Penguin, who have supported what we hope is a different but effective way to talk about strategy to a broad but demanding and discerning audience. In the final push to completion, Niki and Natalie Horbachevsky were unfailingly helpful in keeping us to our hurry-up offense so that we could hit our publication date.

Now we get to find out if our persistence has paid off.

We hope so, of course, and the impact this book has will be a measure of the merits of having embarked upon, and refusing to abandon, this unexpectedly lengthy and demanding journey. Whatever those results might be, we can't help but feel that this is merely the end of the beginning. From here, we hope to use not only the rules we have discovered but also the analytical methods we have developed to deepen and broaden our understanding of what drives exceptional performance in companies of all types from all over the world. We feel as though we have been laboring to build a watch that keeps time at sea, and having crafted a working prototype, we can now measure longitude accurately enough to explore the vast unknown before us. We are exhausted by our efforts, but exhilarated by what we feel they have made possible.

Finally, we end with a customary but still genuine and heartfelt personal expression of gratitude to those closest to us.

From Mumtaz

My mother, Jameela, for early lessons in persistence and excellence; my wife, Munira, for unflagging encouragement and support; and my daughters, Zohra and Zainab, for light entertainment throughout.

San Francisco, California

February 2013

From Michael

I shall always be astonished at, and grateful for, the persistence my wonderful wife, Annabel, has shown through all we have experienced. She never loses sight of what matters. Without her, I surely would.

Mississauga, Ontario

February 2013

Appendix A: Calculating the Elements of Advantage

By Margot Bellamy, Jeff Schulz, and Ben Barclay

A central analytical tool for our work is the decomposition of the ROA difference between two companies into differences in each of the elements of ROA. This provides a compass that points us in the directions to look when identifying the behaviors that contributed most to the observed ROA difference. Further, once the behaviors have been identified, decomposition analysis provides the quantitative evidence to support claims of causal relationships between management behaviors and performance outcomes.

The Arithmetic of Profitability

Let us begin our exposition of how ROA is decomposed into its constituent elements with a review of the fundamental arithmetic in question.

Return on assets is the ratio of income to assets. Since we are interested in individual years, the period in question is each company's fiscal year, which is a single, continuous twelvemonth.

At first blush, income is perhaps the most basic equation in financial economics:

$$\text{Income} = \text{Revenue} - \text{Cost}$$

Central to the usefulness of this calculation is the accurate allocation of revenue and cost to the time period of interest. The principles of revenue recognition address how much revenue to attribute to a given year while principles of cost allocation are used to determine which costs were incurred to generate that revenue.[1]

At its most fundamental, revenue is the product of unit volume and unit price. There are therefore two ways to increase revenue for a period: increase the number of units sold in that period or increase the price of each unit sold.

$$\text{Revenue} = \text{Unit Volume} \times \text{Unit Price}$$

Income is usefully thought of as derived in two steps. First, from the revenue for the period deduct the cost of goods sold (COGS), or the direct expenses incurred during the period, which consist typically of labor, materials, and allocated overhead (for example, heating and lighting expenses). If, for example, you operate a factory that makes plastic bags, the cost of goods sold consists of at least the wages of the machine operator and the cost of the plastic pellets that are extruded into bags. Revenue less COGS yields gross margin, which is therefore measured in dollars, and gross margin divided by revenue is a company's gross margin percentage for the period.

$$\text{Revenue} - \text{COGS} = \text{Gross Margin}$$

$$\textit{Gross Margin Percentage} = \frac{\textit{Gross Margin}}{\textit{Revenue}}$$

"Other costs" can be seen as a single category, but there are some high-level components worth breaking out. Sales, general, and administrative (SG&A), and research and development (R&D) are reasonably self-explanatory, if somewhat broad. Depreciation captures the noncash expense that reflects the level of reinvestment necessary to restore the company's fixed assets to the service potential it had at the beginning of the period. Nonoperating income is very often interest on financial assets (for example, cash balances) while extraordinary items pick up things like gains or losses on the disposal of assets.

Everything discussed so far shows up on the income statement, and we use these items to determine a company's return on sales (ROS), which captures the efficiency with which a company turns revenue into income.

$$Return\ on\ Sales = \frac{Income}{Revenue}$$

The balance sheet picks up the value of a company's assets, and for our purposes there are two types of assets: current and fixed. Current assets are typically financial assets, or real assets, such as inventory, that are easily converted to cash in less than one year. Inventory is often broken out as its own category of current asset. Fixed assets are tangible assets, such as buildings, not expected to be converted to cash in less than one year. Total assets is the sum of current and fixed assets. Total asset turnover captures the efficiency with which a company generates revenue from its assets.

$$Total\ Asset\ Turnover = \frac{Revenue}{Total\ Assets}$$

Return on assets connects the income statement to the balance sheet:

$$Return\ on\ Assets = Return\ on\ Sales \times Total\ Assets\ Turnover$$

. . . or:

$$Return\ on\ Assets = \frac{Income}{Revenue} \times \frac{Revenue}{Total\ Assets}$$

. . . or:

$$Return\ on\ Assets = \frac{Revenue - Cost}{Revenue} \times \frac{Revenue}{Total\ Assets}$$

. . . or:

$$Return\ on\ Assets = \frac{Unit\ price \times Unit\ volume - COGS - Other\ costs}{Revenue}$$
$$\times \frac{Revenue}{Total\ Assets}$$

ROA Decomposition

We begin by decomposing annual ROA performance for each year and then aggregate these annual values across a period of time (a streak or era). Analyzing the composition of performance over time narrows the range of possible explanations for a performance difference and provides a benchmark for assessing the consistency of behaviors with financial performance. In this way, decomposition analysis forces us to identify behaviors that contribute to differences in the structure of performance.

There are two steps to our decomposition. First, we separate the overall ROA advantage into its ROS and TAT elements; we call this Level I decomposition. In Level II decomposition we identify the Elements of Advantage within ROS (gross margin, SG&A, etc.) and TAT (current and fixed asset turnover).

Level I Decomposition

The mechanics of Level I decomposition vary depending on the sign of ROS for the two companies and the sign of the differences in ROS and TAT between two companies. Begin with a relatively straightforward case:

both companies have positive ROS and TAT, and the higher-performing company has lower ROS but higher TAT.

TABLE 38: **Case 1**

Company	ROA	ROS	TAT
A	13.2%	6.0%	2.2
B	12.0%	12.0%	1.0
A's Advantage	1.2 pp		

The percentage points of total ROA difference driven by differences in ROS and TAT is given by:

$$\text{B's pure ROS advantage} = [\text{Actual ROS advantage}]$$
$$\times [\text{Lower TAT value}]$$
$$= 6.0 \times 1.0 = 6.0\text{pp of ROA}$$

$$\text{A's pure TAT advantage} = [\text{Actual TAT advantage}]$$
$$\times [\text{Lower ROS value}]$$
$$= 1.2 \times 6\text{pp} = 7.2\text{pp of ROA}$$

Company A's total ROS advantage $= -6\text{pp}$

Company A's total TAT advantage $= 7.2\text{pp}$

A's overall ROA advantage $= -6.0\text{pp} + 7.2\text{pp} = 1.2\text{pp}$

This example is one of the five cases into which any given pair-wise comparison will fall.

Cases 2 and 3 follow Case 1 very closely.

TABLE 39: **Five ROA Decomposition Case Types**

Case	Description
1	At least one company has positive ROS; one company has ROS advantage, the other company has TAT advantage
2	One company has positive ROS, one has negative ROS; the company with positive ROS has both the ROS and TAT advantage
3	Both companies have negative ROS; one company has both the ROS and TAT advantage
4	Both companies have positive ROS; one company has both the ROS and TAT advantage
5	Both companies have negative ROS; one company has the ROS advantage, the other company has the TAT advantage

TABLE 40: **Case 2**

Company	ROA	ROS	TAT
A	16.0%	8.0%	2.0
B	−3.0%	−3.0%	1.0
A's Advantage	19.0 pp		

A's pure ROS advantage = [Actual ROS advantage]
$$\times \text{[Lower TAT value]}$$
$$= 11\text{pp} \times 1.0 = 11\text{pp of ROA}$$

A's pure TAT advantage = [Actual TAT advantage]
$$\times \text{[Higher ROS value]}$$
$$= 1.0 \times 8\text{pp} = 8\text{pp of ROA}$$

Company A's total ROS advantage = 11pp
Company A's total TAT advantage = 8pp
A's overall ROA advantage = 11pp + 8pp = 19pp

TABLE 41: **Case 3**

Company	ROA	ROS	TAT
A	−12.0%	−6.0%	2.0
B	−9.0%	−9.0%	1.0
A's Advantage	−3.0 pp		

A's pure ROS advantage = [Actual ROS advantage]
$$\times \text{[Lower TAT value]}$$
$$= 3\text{pp} \times 1 = 3 \text{ pp of ROA}$$

A's pure TAT advantage = [Actual TAT advantage]
$$\times \text{[Higher ROS value]}$$
$$= 1 \times -6\text{pp} = -6 \text{ pp of ROA}$$

Note: A has a TAT advantage when looking at TAT in isolation. However, since it was using its assets more effectively to sell products at a negative ROS, its TAT advantage results in an ROA disadvantage.

Company A's total ROS advantage = 3pp
Company A's total TAT advantage = −6pp
A's overall ROA advantage = 3pp + (−6pp) = −3pp

Cases 4 and 5 are more complex because they require the calculation and allocation of a "joint" component. This joint component allocation is necessary when one company has both a higher ROS and TAT value and both ROS values are positive *or* one company has either a higher ROS value or higher TAT value and both ROS values are negative. The table below shows the joint advantage for a company that has both an ROS and TAT advantage. When a joint advantage exists, it is allocated according to the ratio of the pure advantages.

TABLE 42: **Case 4**

Company	ROA	ROS	TAT
A	7.2%	6.0%	1.2
B	18.0%	9.0%	2.0
B's Advantage	10.8pp		

B's pure ROS advantage = [Actual ROS advantage]
$$\times \text{[Lower TAT value]}$$
$$= 3.0\text{pp} \times 1.2 = 3.6\text{pp of ROA}$$

B's pure TAT advantage = [Actual TAT advantage]
$$\times \text{[Lower ROS value]}$$
$$= 0.8 \times 6\text{pp} = 4.8\text{pp of ROA}$$

Pure advantage equals $3.6 + 4.8 = 8.4$pp of the total 10.8pp ROA advantage

Joint advantage equals $10.8 - 8.4 = 2.4$pp

Joint advantage allocated according to the ratio of the pure advantages:

   ROS attribution = $(3.6/8.4) \times 2.4\text{pp} = 1.0\text{pp}$

   Total ROS advantage: $3.6 + 1.0 = 4.6\text{pp}$

   TAT attribution = $(4.8/8.4) \times 2.4\text{pp} = 1.4\text{pp}$

   Total TAT advantage: $4.8 + 1.4 = 6.2\text{pp}$

Company B's total ROS advantage = 4.6pp

Company B's total TAT advantage = 6.2pp

Company B's overall ROA advantage = 4.6pp + 6.2pp = 10.8pp

TABLE 43: **Case 5**

Company	ROA	ROS	TAT
A	−6.0%	−6.0%	1.0
B	−18.0%	−9.0%	2.0
A's Advantage	12.0 pp		

A's pure ROS advantage = [Actual ROS advantage]
$$\times \text{[Lower TAT value]}$$
$$= 3\text{pp} \times 1 = 3\text{pp of ROA}$$

B's pure TAT advantage = [Actual TAT advantage]
$$\times \text{[Higher ROS value]}$$
$$= 1 \times -6\text{pp} = -6 \text{ pp of ROA}$$

(B has a TAT advantage when looking at TAT in isolation. However, since it was using its assets more effectively to sell products at a negative ROS, its TAT advantage results in an ROA disadvantage.)

The pure ROS + TAT advantage equals $3 + 6 = 9$pp of the total 12pp ROA advantage.

Joint advantage equals $12\text{pp} - 9\text{pp} = 3\text{pp}$

Attributed to ROS: $(3.0/9.0) \times 3.0\text{pp} = 1.0\text{pp}$

Total ROS advantage: $3.0 + 1.0 = 4\text{pp}$

Attributed to TAT: $(6.0/9.0) \times 3.0\text{pp} = 2.0\text{pp}$

Total TAT advantage: $6.0 + 2.0 = 8\text{pp}$

Company A's total ROS advantage = 4pp

Company A's total TAT advantage = 8pp

A's overall ROA advantage = 4pp + 8pp = 12pp

Level II Decomposition

Return on Sales

ROS can be further decomposed into gross margin (GM), and a number of expense categories: sales, general, and administrative expenses (SG&A), research and development (R&D), depreciation, discontinued operations, extraordinary items, minority interest, and income taxes, all expressed as a percentage of sales. TAT can be split into current asset turnover less inventory (CAT - Inv.), inventory asset turnover (Inv - AT), fixed asset turnover (FAT), and other asset turnover (Other - AT). In the Level II decomposition we attribute the ROS and TAT differences from the Level I decomposition to these elements.

These are the steps for allocating ROS differences to its constituent income statement elements:

1. Calculate each expense as a percentage of sales (columns A, B, and C in the table below).

2. For each expense category, calculate the pp advantage (column D) for the company with higher ROA.

3. Calculate the pure ROS advantage by multiplying the pp difference for each element by the lower TAT value.

4. If there is a joint advantage to allocate, calculate the relative proportion of the total pure ROS advantage that each element contributes. Take the pure advantage for each ROS element from column E and divide by the total pure ROS advantage, also in column E.

5. Calculate the pp element contribution to the joint advantage by multiplying the percentage of pure ROS advantage by the total ROS joint advantage (column G).

6. Sum the raw advantage and joint advantage for each element to get its total contribution.

Total Asset Turnover

Allocating TAT to its constituent elements is more nuanced. Asset turnover is a ratio, and in order to make the constituent elements additive we must work with the reciprocals. That is, although $CAT + FAT \neq TAT$, $1/CAT + 1/FAT = 1/TAT$.

1. Calculate the reciprocal for each TAT element (columns B & C).
2. For each component, calculate the pp difference (column D).
3. Calculate the relative proportion of the total TAT advantage that each element contributes (column E).
4. Calculate the pp pure TAT advantage by multiplying the relative proportion for each element by the total pure TAT advantage (column F).
5. If there is a joint advantage to allocate, multiply the relative portion of the total TAT advantage for each element by the total TAT joint advantage (column G).
6. Sum the raw advantage and joint advantage for each element to get its total contribution.

We will illustrate level II decomposition using Case 4, which has sufficient complexity to highlight the power of our method.

252   Appendix A: Calculating the Elements of Advantage

TABLE 44: Level II Decomposition

A	B Company A		C Company B		D Δ pp	E Pure ROS Advantage	F Percent of pure ROS Advantage	G Joint Advantage*	H Total Advantage
	in $	% of revenue	in $	% of revenue	[Company B− Company A]	(Δ pp* lower TAT)		(F *1.0)	(E + G)
Revenue	200	100%	300	100%	–	–	–	–	–
GM (1-COGS)	120	60%	195	65%	+5 pp	+6.00	167%	+1.67	+7.67
SG&A	30	15%	54	18%	−3 pp	−3.60	−100%	−1.00	−4.60
R&D	20	10%	24	8%	+2 pp	+2.40	67%	+0.67	+3.07
Depreciation	–	–	–	–	–	–	–	–	–
Income Taxes	58	29%	90	30%	−1 pp	−1.20	−33%	−0.33	−1.53
Disc. Ops	–	–	–	–	–	–	–	–	–
Extra. Items	–	–	–	–	–	–	–	–	–
Min. Interest	–	–	–	–	–	–	–	–	–
NonOp. Income	–	–	–	–	–	–	–	–	–
ROS (Net Income)	**12**	**6.0%**	**27**	**9.0%**	**3.0 pp**	**3.60 pp**	**100%**	**1.0 pp**	**4.60 pp**

*The ROS portion of the joint advantage (1.0) is allocated according to the ratio of the pure advantages. See Case 4 for additional detail.

A	B			C			D	E	F	G	H
	Company A			Company B							
	in $	ATR	1/ATR	in $	ATR	1/ATR	Δ 1/ATR (Company A – Company B)	Relative portion of TAT advantage (D/0.33)	Pure TAT advantage (E* 4.8)	Joint advantage (E *1.4)	Total advantage (F + G)
Revenue	120			300							
Current Assets Less Inventory											
Inventory	20	6	0.17	100	3	0.33	-0.17	-52%	-2.47	-0.72	-3.19pp
Fixed Assets	80	1.5	0.67	50	6	0.17	0.50	152%	7.27	2.12	9.39pp
Other Assets											
Total Assets	**100**	**1.2**	**0.84**	**150**	**2**	**0.5**	**0.33**	**100%**	**4.8**	**1.4**	**6.20pp**

*The TAT portion of the joint advantage (1.4) is allocated according to the ratio of the pure advantages. See Case 4 for additional detail. Figures may not total due to rounding.

Appendix B: Bibliography of Success Studies

We classified a book as belonging to the "success study" genre if its primary dependent variable was one or more of three corporate-level measures of performance: ROA, revenue growth or total shareholder returns (TSR). Efforts to understand specific behaviors, such as innovation or human resource management or operations efficiency, that used a comparative case study method were not considered success studies because a company can have great innovation but not have remarkable corporate-level performance due to other factors.

The genre is dominated these days by Jim Collins. Either in collaboration or on his own, his four best-selling books (*Built to Last, Good to Great, How the Mighty Fall,* and *Great by Choice*) command our deference. We would be negligent in attempting a similar study of our own without paying very close attention to his samples, methods, and findings. The others we included in our meta-analysis were chosen for any number of largely subjective reasons: we felt the authors were credible researchers, the books were commercially successful, or the findings have proven influential. Although it's not exhaustive, we feel our list is representative of the field.

It bears repeating: the analysis in chapter 2 looks only at questions of method, and sample selection in particular. We do not claim that the prescriptions made by other authors are wrong; we are questioning the foundations on which one might claim they are right. We feel we have some important points to make, but of course people of goodwill can disagree on matters of substance. For example, looking back at *In Search of Excellence*, Tom Peters observed that he and coauthor Waterman began with sixty-two companies chosen by canvassing McKinsey partners and "a bunch of other smart people" for their impressions of "who's cool" and "who's doing cool work." They then applied a set of quantitative measures that winnowed the list of sixty-two down to forty-three. Among those that did not make the cut back then was General Electric, which, according to Peters, "shows you how 'stupid' raw insight is and how 'smart' tough-minded metrics can be." [1]

What Peters says he took from the experience is that the right way to find those from whom you can learn the most is to trust your instincts first and then validate those intuitions empirically. That is certainly a defensible approach, but it rests on actually validating those intuitions. The success study method requires that the companies studied be exceptional according to the measure that matters for the study. The promise of *In Search of Excellence*, as with all the other success studies we reviewed, is that you can learn something useful that will make your company better according to a particular measure of corporate performance. The sample can be picked on any basis at all, provided that it is then tested. If it is not, then all one can claim is that one has learned something about how to improve one's performance against the criteria used to select the sample.

Since the companies in *In Search of Excellence* are not exceptional as a group as measured by ROA, revenue growth or TSR, the advice offered is demonstrably supportive only of the claim that it can improve a company's likelihood of being identified as a place where smart people do cool stuff. That is a worthwhile goal, but it is very different from the goal of achieving exceptional performance. The only way to develop sound arguments about how to deliver exceptional performance is to tether that advice to evidence gathered from companies that have actually delivered exceptional performance. In the case of *In Search of Excellence*, only one company had exceptional ROA, the median probability of having exceptional ROA for the sample is 29 percent, and the median growth and TSR ranks for the sample was 5. Peters and Waterman might have gone in search of excellence, but they found mediocrity. They just didn't know it.

Other studies on our list are only implicitly success studies. *Stall Points*, for example, looks at the phenomenon of reversals in growth trajectories, from increasing to decreasing. They compare a company's growth rates for t minus ten years (t_{-10}) and t plus ten years (t_{+10}) for every year t. The largest value x for $t_{-10} - t_{+10}$ is the year growth stalls. They then look for behavioral differences between the two periods.

A company need not be an exceptional grower to experience what they call a "stall." It could go from mediocre to horrible, or from horrible to catastrophic. Neither must the value of x be especially significant: it is only required to be the largest number in a set. In our discussion of the analysis of patterns of performance, we reviewed the notion that, as with lifetime performance, looking for inflection points also requires a reasonably statistically robust method. Since every set of numbers will have a largest element the method described in *Stall Points* does not meet this criterion.

In the table in chapter 2 we look only at the companies in *Stall Points* classified as "continuous growers"—companies that never experienced a stall. The explicit claim of *Stall Points* is that its advice can help a company avoid a stall in growth rates, and these claims are reasonable given their sample. At the same time, the implicit claim, to us at least, is that growing constantly at 0.1 percent per year, which would avoid a stall, is not the objective; exceptional growth is. Consequently, we believe it is worthwhile to assess whether or not the sample of continuous growers delivers notable lifetime growth; 17 percent of their sample does, with lifetime growth rates in the 9th decile. But 83 percent of their sample consists of companies below the 9th decile, and fully a quarter of their sample of continuous growers lies in the bottom 25 percent of all companies in our database.

We have attempted to be similarly generous in our assessments of the sample of the other studies we evaluated, including only those companies held up as exemplars and evaluating their sample using only data that would have been available at the time.

Success Study Citations

Tom Peters and Robert Waterman, *In Search of Excellence* (HarperBusiness, 2004; originally published 1982)

Jim Collins and Jerry I. Porras, *Built to Last* (HarperBusiness, 2004; originally published 1996)

Mehrdad Baghai, Stephen Coley, and David White, *The Alchemy of Growth* (Basic Books, 1999)

Jon Katzenbach, *Peak Performance* (Harvard Business Review Press, 2000)

Richard Foster and Sarah Kaplan, *Creative Destruction* (Crown Business, 2001)

Jim Collins, *Good to Great* (HarperCollins, 2005; originally published 2001)

Chris Zook and James Allen, *Profit from the Core* (Harvard Business Press, 2001)

William Joyce and Nitin Nohria, *What Really Works* (HarperBusiness, 2004)

Alfred Marcus, *Big Winners and Big Losers* (FT Press, 2005)

David G. Thomson, *Blueprint to a Billion* (John Wiley & Sons, 2006)

Matthew S. Olson and Derek Van Bever, *Stall Points* (Yale University Press, 2008)

Keith R. McFarland, *The Breakthrough Company* (Crown Business, 2008)

Patrick Viguerie, Sven Smit, and Mehrdad Baghai, *The Granularity of Growth* (John Wiley & Sons, 2008)

Jim Collins, *How the Mighty Fall* (HarperCollins, 2009)

Paul Leinwand and Cesare Mainardi, *Essential Advantage* (Harvard Business Review Press, 2010)

Jim Collins and Morten T. Hansen, *Great by Choice* (HarperBusiness, 2011)

Paul Nunes and Tim Breene, *Jumping the S-Curve* (Harvard Business Review Press, 2011)

Scott Keller and Colin Price, *Beyond Performance* (John Wiley & Sons, 2011)

Christian Stadler, *Enduring Success* (Stanford Business Books, 2011)

Appendix C: Identifying Exceptional Performance

Our primary measure of performance is lifetime ROA, but we also look at revenue growth and TSR. We use statistical methods to determine the relative performance of companies on each measure.

ROA

In our coin-flipping analogy it is easy to calculate the odds of achieving a given outcome because we know the probability of each of our two results for each flip: a 50 percent chance of getting heads and a 50 percent chance of getting tails on each toss. But what is the likelihood that a randomly chosen company with a 4th-decile rank in a given year will have a 7th-decile rank the following year? To figure that out we constructed a 10×10 matrix that captures the observed frequencies with which companies moved from any decile rank to any of the others in the next year.

Reading across row 1 in the table below, companies that were in decile 0 in year 1 ended up in the same decile the following year 52.8 percent of the time. They managed to get into the 1st decile 18.2 percent of the time, and so on, all the way up to landing in the 9th decile 4.4 percent of the time. Landing in the same decile the following year is by far the most frequent outcome, and this phenomenon is especially pronounced for companies with higher or lower decile ranks.

Using these frequencies, we could then run simulations to determine the likelihood of any given performance profile. Want to know the probability of turning in five 5th-decile ranks out of seven years of data starting from the 7th decile in year 1? Or eight 7th deciles out of ten years starting

TABLE 45: **The Decile Transition Matrix**

FROM \ TO	0	1	2	3	4	5	6	7	8	9
0	**52.8%**	18.2%	8.5%	4.9%	3.1%	2.4%	2.3%	1.9%	1.5%	4.4%
1	20.4%	**32.4%**	17.7%	9.1%	5.9%	3.9%	2.9%	2.3%	1.9%	3.5%
2	10.2%	19.2%	**24.8%**	17.3%	9.6%	5.9%	4.0%	3.1%	2.5%	3.2%
3	5.9%	11.1%	17.3%	**23.4%**	16.0%	9.8%	6.5%	4.2%	2.9%	3.0%
4	4.1%	6.7%	11.1%	17.0%	**22.0%**	16.6%	9.9%	5.9%	3.9%	2.9%
5	2.9%	4.7%	7.0%	11.0%	16.7%	**22.5%**	17.3%	9.6%	5.1%	3.3%
6	2.2%	3.4%	5.0%	7.2%	11.0%	17.1%	**23.4%**	18.0%	8.7%	4.2%
7	1.6%	2.6%	3.5%	4.7%	7.0%	10.4%	17.7%	**26.1%**	19.3%	7.2%
8	1.5%	1.8%	2.8%	3.3%	4.2%	6.4%	9.7%	18.8%	**33.9%**	17.7%
9	2.3%	2.5%	3.0%	3.1%	3.4%	3.8%	5.2%	8.5%	18.5%	**49.4%**

Source: Compustat; Deloitte analysis

from the 9th decile? Such calculations are of limited use, however. It is perfectly analogous to asking for the probability of any particular number of heads in a row when tossing a coin. Each specific outcome is rather unlikely, but *some* outcome is inevitable. A specific result matters only when it is intrinsically meaningful to us and statistically unexpected.

Think of it this way: A company might get a 9th-decile outcome in a given year because of a lucky break. Once it gets that 9th-decile outcome, there is a good chance it will get a 9th-decile outcome the next year simply because 9th-decile outcomes are sticky. Consequently, we cannot tell if a company got two 9th-decile years simply because of the echo of the lucky break that gave it the first one. But over time the impact of that lucky break fades, and so the likelihood of continuing to deliver 9th-decile outcomes simply by virtue of the residual impact of initial luck goes down. Delivering, say, nothing but 9th-decile years out of a lifetime of eleven observations becomes very unlikely indeed. This probability is what determines whether a company qualifies as a Miracle Worker.

However, it also matters how many other companies there were with eleven observations. If there were hundreds, or even thousands of them in our database, then it starts to become likely that one or more of those companies *would* get eleven 9th-decile years in a row as a result of repeated good luck coupled with the afterglow of each positive shock. For example, although tossing "heads" with a fair coin eleven times in a row is highly unlikely, you would need only about two thousand people in your coin-flipping contest to make it all but certain that at least one person would achieve such an outcome. Seemingly unlikely events become expected given enough trials, and attributing special cause variation in those circumstances is to fall victim to "false positives."

Using the decile transition matrix (table 45), we ran 1,000 simulations with as many companies as actually existed, starting from their actual decile ranks, and observed the frequency with which companies with different life spans delivered 9th-decile years. To illustrate, in our 1,000 simulations, there was only a 4.3 percent chance that a company with eleven years of data would have, due to randomness, five or more years in the 9th decile. Such an outcome is therefore sufficiently unlikely that if we see a company with five or more years out of eleven in the 9th decile we might feel justified in thinking that company has delivered exceptional performance.

However, it turns out that there are 856 companies in our population with eleven-year life spans. Even though the likelihood of any particular company getting five or more 9th-decile years is less than 5 percent, we still *expect* to see 37 companies with five or more years in the 9th decile simply by virtue of how many eleven-year companies there are.

In our population there are actually 45 companies with five or more years out of eleven in the 9th decile. So there are *more* companies than we would expect, and we can conclude with some confidence that at least some of them—most likely 8—are in fact exceptional. Unfortunately, we have no way of knowing *which* 8 those are. We can do no better than draw at random from that population of 45 companies, and live with the 82 percent chance (37 out of 45) that we have drawn a company that is no better than lucky—that is, we live with the 82 percent chance of a false positive.

To correct for the incidence of false positives we can raise our benchmark, insisting on more years in the 9th decile for a given life span until the likelihood of a false positive falls below a desired level. For a company to be a Miracle Worker, we have stipulated that it have enough 9th-decile years to have less than a 10 percent probability of having achieved that result due to luck alone *and* a less than 10 percent probability of being a false positive.

Because we are working with annual decile ranks, every company's performance is comparable to every other's in that year. And by using the

DTM to determine the likelihood of a given number of 9s (for Miracle Workers) or 6s, 7s, and 8s (for Long Runners) over the course of a given life span, we can compare every company's likelihood of being exceptional with every other company's, no matter what its lifetime or when it lived.

There is nothing magical about any of our benchmarks. Why a 10 percent cutoff? Why not 5 percent? Or 15 percent? Why define Miracle Workers in terms of years in only the 9th decile? We could have defined Miracle Workers as those companies that landed in the 8th or 9th deciles with unlikely frequency.

Any set of parameters is subject to little more than an intuitive assessment of its reasonableness. What matters is that our definition is used in the context of a rigorous statistical analysis: any company that meets any given criteria with sufficient frequency to be unlikely can lay claim to a form of exceptional performance. For our study to be at least potentially useful, all that is required is that the performance outcomes we have defined have adequate face validity. You must assess for yourself whether the performance criteria we have chosen capture your subjective notion of what constitutes a performance level worth aspiring to. After a certain point, the choice is based on convenience: make the standards too exigent, and we have no companies to study; make them too lax and the soundness of the findings is compromised.[1] The table below shows the number of years required in each focal decile or decile range required for different lifetimes in order to clear our 90 percent certainty thresholds.

There are some counterintuitive aspects to these calculations that warrant additional explanation. The number of years required in a focal decile or decile range does not increase monotonically as a function of a company's life span. Note, for example, that with a life span of twenty years a company requires twelve years in the 9th decile to qualify as a Miracle Worker while with a life span of thirty years the number drops to

TABLE 46: **Years Required in Focal Deciles to Achieve Exceptional Status**

Lifetime	Years in Focal Range	
	Miracle Workers (9th Decile)	**Long Runners (6th–8th Deciles)**
10	10	—
15	10	14
20	12	18
25	11	19
30	10	20
35	10	19
40	9	20
45	16	26

Source: Compustat; Deloitte analysis

ten, and at a life span of forty-five years it is back up to sixteen. This is a consequence of how we correct for the false positive problem, and it serves as another mechanism for coping with survivor bias.

Based on the DTM, Miracle Worker status requires more years in the 9th decile with thirty-five years of data than with twenty years of data. However, there are more companies with twenty years of data than there are with thirty-five years of data, so we must increase our benchmarks for the twenty-year companies in order to get our false positive probability below 10 percent.

The spike in the benchmark at forty-five years of data captures the relatively large population of long-lived companies—many of which were around prior to 1966 (when our database begins) and were still around in 2010 (when our database ends). Our quantile regressions capture at least some of the impact of survivorhood on ROA, but even so, if there is something special about these survivors, by compensating for the larger number of long-lived companies with higher benchmarks we reduce the likelihood that we are chasing survivor bias.

TSR and Revenue Growth

Identifying statistically exceptional growth and TSR performance requires a different approach because a company's performance over a period is a function of compounding: the compounded annual growth rate from year 0 to year 2 is dependent on that company's results in both year 1 and year 2. Consequently, a company can have superior relative growth in year 2 (for example, growth of 50 percent) if it had terrible growth the previous two years (years 0 and 1), which means its growth in year 2 is calculated on a small base. As a result, we felt that our annual decile ranking approach was inappropriate. To take an extreme example, a company that alternated years of 50 percent shrinkage followed by growth of 100 percent would have 50 percent of its observations with very high growth even though its overall growth for the period would be 0 percent.

Instead, we built a regression model for each of growth and TSR. (The two measures are treated effectively the same, conceptually.) This regression allows us to predict what each company's performance "should have been" in a given year in light of its size, year, industry, lifetime, and previous year's results. In each year, a company's actual performance will typically deviate from this predicted value, falling either above it (a positive residual) or below it (a negative residual). The sum of these residuals is a company's cumulative residual, or raw R-score.

We cannot, however, simply compare raw R-scores. Two companies that have the same annual raw scores will be scored differently in aggregate if they have different life spans: companies A and B will see their

R-scores grow by, say, 0.05 each year, but if company A survives for fifteen years and company B survives for twenty, company B will have the higher R-score by virtue of its longer life, not its superior growth. To correct for this, we use simulations to determine what the expected R-score is for companies with different numbers of observations. This yields a "corrected" R-score for every company that is comparable across all companies. We then order these corrected R-scores, leaving each company with a TSR and growth lifetime rank.

Appendix D: Category, Trajectory, and Era Analysis

When we began this project in early 2007 we had data through 2006. We developed our method and selected our sample by mid-2008. The case-study work took longer than anticipated, something we are sure has never happened to anyone else.

By the time we had developed our findings, it was early 2011. We could have pressed ahead with publication at that point, but felt that presenting our findings in late 2012 with a data set that ended in 2006 might have compromised the relevance of our findings, especially in light of the Great Recession. We wanted to know how our case-study companies had fared, and so we undertook to update all of our calculations with the additional four years of data (2007 to 2010 inclusive).

All of our Miracle Workers still qualified under the strict application of our decision rules of a 90 percent or better probability of belonging in the category and a less than 10 percent chance of being a false positive. Abercrombie & Fitch, Thomas & Betts, and Wrigley all saw their probability of being false positives go up slightly because at least some of the additional years were not in the 9th decile, but all of them remained well within our predefined parameters.

The Long Runners fared less well, but not poorly enough that we can say, definitively, we would have changed our minds about including them had we been working with 2010 data from the start. We made some exceptions to our decision rules when choosing our sample in 2006, most notably relaxing the "false positive" probability cutoff of 10 percent when finding Long Runners to match with our Miracle Workers: Finish Line,

Werner, HMI, and Hubbell—fully half of our sample—all miss that cutoff. We accepted this trade-off because of the importance of the qualitative similarities. The worst of them, Finish Line, was still better than a coin toss for being a true positive.

With the additional data, Finish Line is less than a coin toss, but only just. Werner, HMI, and Hubbell all saw their probabilities of being false positives rise, too, and by more, in absolute terms, but not in as qualitatively significant a way. It is possible that we would have sought out some new trios since, as a group, we likely would have wanted to have kept the probability of having false positives perhaps somewhat closer to our 10 percent cutoff. We do not believe these shifts materially undermine our conclusions, but we provide the data here so that you can assess this for yourself.

We also updated our streak analysis. The confidence intervals indicate how sure we are that a streak in relative performance is over. A higher confidence interval is therefore more "forgiving" of periods outside the focal decile range before declaring that a streak has ended.

In 2006, when we first selected our sample, we characterized the trajectories of our exceptional companies with a 90 percent confidence interval. When we updated our companies with 2010 data, some of them had changed trajectories at the 90 percent confidence level. No companies changed their overall trajectory at the 99 percent confidence interval, although the specifics of some change points shifted.

For example, A&F and Heartland both change from Kept It to Lost It trajectories at the 90 percent confidence interval from 2006 to 2010. At the 99 percent confidence interval, however, both companies remain Kept It Miracle Workers. (It is a curious feature of this sort of statistical analysis that the future can change the past: with additional years in the 9th decile, both of these companies might well reestablish a Kept It trajectory even at the 90 percent confidence interval.)

TABLE 47: **Category Analysis**

Category	Company	1966 to 2006		1966 to 2010	
		In category	False positive	In category	False positive
Miracle Workers	Abercrombie & Fitch	100%	2%	100%	4%
	Heartland Express	100%	0%	100%	0%
	Linear Technology	100%	2%	100%	0%
	Maytag	100%	3%	100%	2%
	Medtronic	100%	6%	100%	5%
	Merck & Co.	100%	1%	100%	0%
	Thomas & Betts	100%	2%	100%	7%
	Weis Markets	100%	0%	100%	0%
	Wm. Wrigley Jr. Co.	100%	5%	100%	3%
	AVERAGE	**100%**	**2%**	**100%**	**2%**
Long Runners	Finish Line	96%	49%	93%	51%
	Werner Enterprises	99%	26%	97%	39%
	Micropac Industries	100%	1%	100%	0%
	HMI Industries.	99%	14%	99%	25%
	Stryker Corp.	100%	6%	100%	4%
	Eli Lilly & Co.	100%	0%	100%	1%
	Hubbell	99%	13%	98%	18%
	Publix Super Markets	99%	7%	98%	13%
	Tootsie Roll Industries	100%	0%	100%	2%
	AVERAGE	**99%**	**12%**	**99%**	**16%**

Source: Compustat; Deloitte analysis

TABLE 48: Trajectory Analysis

	90% Confidence		99% Confidence	
	2006	**2010**	**2006**	**2010**
Miracle Workers				
Abercrombie & Fitch	Kept It	Lost It: 2008	Kept It	Kept It
Heartland Express	Kept It	Lost It: 2009	Kept It	Kept It
Linear Technology	Found It: 1991	Found It: 1992	Found It: 1992	Found It: 1992
Maytag	Lost It: 1990	Lost It: 1990	Lost It: 1991	Lost It: 1992
Medtronic	Found It: 1986	Found It: 1986	Found It: 1986	Found It: 1986
Merck & Co.	Other: 1976–1985	Other: 1977–1985, 2010	Other: 1976–1985	Other: 1978–1985
Thomas & Betts	Lost It: 1989	Lost It: 1985	Lost It: 1990	Lost It: 1986
Weis Markets	Lost It: 1998	Lost It: 1996	Lost It: 1998	Lost It: 1996
Wm. Wrigley Jr. Co.	Found It: 1986	Other: 1966–1985, 2007	Found It: 1986	Found It: 1986
Long Runners				
Finish Line	Lost It: 1999	Lost It: 2006	Kept It	Kept It
Werner Enterprises	Lost It: 2000	Lost It: 2002	Lost It: 2000	Lost It: 2002
Micropac Industries	Kept It	Kept It	Kept It	Kept It
HMI Industries	Lost It: 1989	Lost It: 1996	Lost It: 1991	Lost It: 1996
Stryker	Kept It	Kept It	Kept It	Kept It
Eli Lilly & Co.	Kept It	Kept It	Kept It	Kept It
Hubbell	Lost It: 2001	Lost It: 2002	Lost It: 2001	Lost It: 2005
Publix Super Markets	Kept It	Found It: 1982	Kept It	Found It: 1982
Tootsie Roll Industries	Kept It	Lost It: 2009	Kept It	Kept It

Source: Compustat; Deloitte analysis

TABLE 49: **Era Analysis**

	Last Year of Era 1	**Last Year of Era 2**
Miracle Workers		
Abercrombie & Fitch	1999 (63%)	–
Heartland Express	1994 (86%)	–
Linear Technology	–	–
Maytag	–	–
Medtronic	–	–
Merck & Co.	1985 (55%)	–
Thomas & Betts	1999 (86%)	–
Weis Markets	1990 (62%)	–
Wm. Wrigley Jr. Co.	–	–
Long Runners		
Eli Lilly & Co.	–	–
Finish Line	–	–
HMI Industries	1995 (61%)	–
Hubbell	1991 (58%)	–
Micropac Industries	–	–
Publix Super Markets	–	–
Stryker	1997 (95%)	–
Tootsie Roll Industries	1983 (88%)	1996 (62%)
Werner Enterprises	–	–
Average Joes		
Emrise	1999 (66%)	
International Rectifier	–	–
Invacare	2005 (84%)	
KV Pharmaceutical	1994 (77%)	2005 (79%)
P.A.M. Transportation Services	1991 (100%)	
Rocky Mountain Chocolate Factory	–	–
Syms	–	–
Whirlpool	1987 (76%)	
Whole Foods Market	–	–

Note: Companies with no entries have a single era of absolute performance consisting of the entire observation period. Companies with only one entry have two eras of absolute performance. Only Tootsie Roll and KVP have three eras in absolute performance, and so have two entries in this table.
Source: Deloitte analysis

Defining eras is similarly based on a probabilistic method, referred to in the notes in chapter 2.[1] Here are the probabilities associated with the years in which we identify eras. Because this is a Bayesian method, we declare an era to have begun in the year following any year with a probability of greater than 50 percent of being the last year of an era. Companies with no year meeting this criterion have one era in absolute performance.

Here is the breakdown of eras and trajectories for our full population of exceptional companies.

TABLE 50: **Trajectory-Era Counts**

Miracle Workers

| Eras | Trajectory | | | | Total |
	Kept It	Found It	Lost It	Other	
1	26	22	27	12	87
2	23	18	11	23	75
3+	1	1	2	8	12
Total	50	41	40	43	174

Long Runners

| Eras | Trajectory | | | | Total |
	Kept It	Found It	Lost It	Other	
1	77	7	9	8	101
2	32	8	10	8	58
3+	7	1	2	1	11
Total	116	16	21	17	170

Source: Deloitte analysis

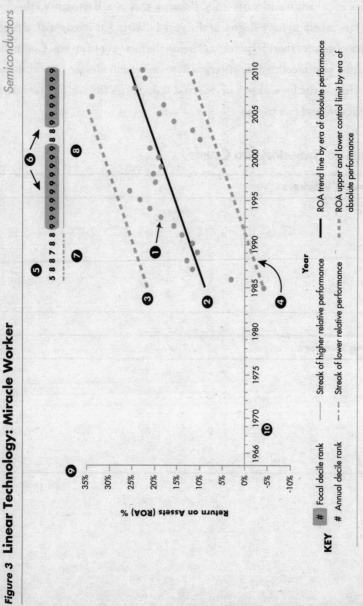

Appendix E: Performance Profile Charts

Figure 3 Linear Technology: Miracle Worker

Semiconductors

Return on Assets (ROA) %

KEY

Focal decile rank

Annual decile rank

—— Streak of higher relative performance

‑ ‑ ‑ Streak of lower relative performance

—— ROA trend line by era of absolute performance

‑ ‑ ‑ ROA upper and lower control limit by era of absolute performance

Source: Compustat; Deloitte analysis

1 Annual ROA values as reported by Compustat.

2 ROA trend line for each era in absolute performance. Eras are identified using the method referenced in Chapter 2. Trend lines are calculated using Ordinary Least Squares (OLS) regression.

3 Upper control limit (UCL) for each era in absolute performance. UCLs are set +1.5 standard deviations around the expected value for each year's ROA as determined by the OLS regression used to determine the trend line.

4 Lower control limit (LCL) for each era in absolute performance. LCLs are set at -1.5 standard deviations around the expected value for each year's ROA as determined by the OLS regression used to determine the trend line.

5 Annual decile ranks capture relative performance. Each year's absolute ROA is transformed into a decile rank using the method referenced in Chapter 2. Deciles are comparable across time, industry, and company.

6 Focal deciles for each company are highlighted. Miracle Workers have all 9s highlighted; Long Runners have all 6s, 7s, and 8s highlighted. Average Joes have no deciles highlighted.

7 A streak in relative performance that is below the focal deciles for the company. Streaks in relative performance are identifed using the method referenced in Chapter 2.

8 A streak in relative performance that is in focal deciles for the company. Streaks in relative performance are identifed using the method referenced in Chapter 2.

9 ROA values. The axes have been kept as consistent as possible across all charts to facilitate comparisons. Where the range has been shifted to accommodate more extreme values, the scale has been kept consistent so that the slope of the trend lines is still easily comparable.

10 Year. The axis has been kept consistent across all charts to facilitate comparisons.

KEY This summary key will be repeated on all charts as a mnemonic for this more detailed explanation.

Figure 4 Micropac Industries: Long Runner

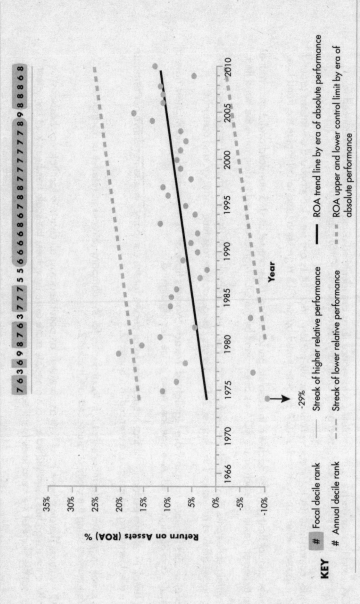

Semiconductors

Source: Compustat; Deloitte analysis

Figure 5 **International Rectifier: Average Joe**

Semiconductors

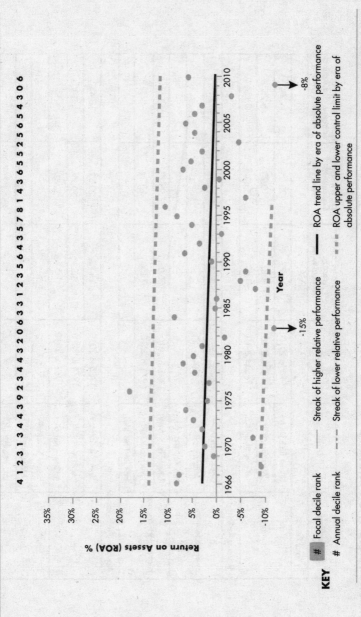

KEY

Source: Compustat; Deloitte analysis

Semiconductors Trio Summary

Appliances

Streaks/Eras	Trios	Years	Average Annual ROA	Compounded Annual TSR	Compounded Annual Revenue Growth
Total Period					
Summary	Linear Tech (MW)	1985 to 2010	16.9%	20.0%	18.4%
	Micropac (LR)	1975 to 2010	6.8%	10.2%	5.2%
	Int'l Rectifier (AJ)	1966 to 2010	1.5%	5.6%	8.1%
Relative Performance					
Lower performance period	Linear Tech (MW)	1986 to 1991	10.6%	31.0%	33.3%
	Micropac (LR)	–	–	–	–
	Int'l Rectifier (AJ)	–	–	–	–
Higher performance period	Linear Tech (MW)	1992 to 2010	20.0%	15.5%	13.5%
	Micropac (LR)	1975 to 2010	7.8%	10.2%	4.6%
	Int'l Rectifier (AJ)	–	–	–	–
Absolute Performance					
Era 1	Linear Tech (MW)	1985 to 2010	16.9%	20.0%	18.4%
	Micropac (LR)	1974 to 2010	6.8%	10.2%	5.2%
	Int'l Rectifier (AJ)	1966 to 2010	1.5%	5.6%	8.1%
Era 2	Linear Tech (MW)	–	–	–	–
	Micropac (LR)	–	–	–	–
	Int'l Rectifier (AJ)	–	–	–	–

Source: Compustat; Deloitte analysis

Medical Devices

Figure 6 Medtronic: Miracle Worker

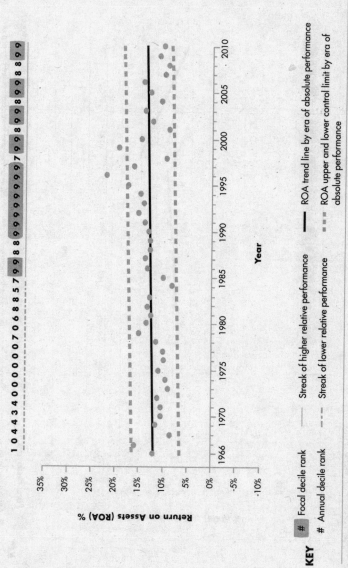

KEY

Focal decile rank

Annual decile rank

—— Streak of higher relative performance

--- Streak of lower relative performance

—— ROA trend line by era of absolute performance

--- ROA upper and lower control limit by era of absolute performance

Return on Assets (ROA) %

Year

Source: Compustat; Deloitte analysis

Medical Devices

Figure 7 Stryker: Long Runner

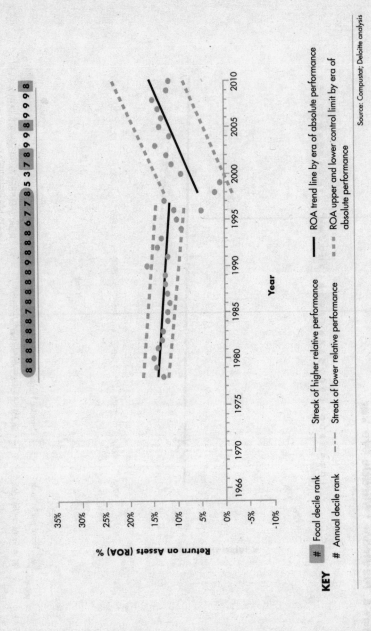

KEY

`#` Focal decile rank

`#` Annual decile rank

—— Streak of higher relative performance

- - - Streak of lower relative performance

—— ROA trend line by era of absolute performance

- - - ROA upper and lower control limit by era of absolute performance

Source: Compustat; Deloitte analysis

Figure 8 **Invacare: Average Joe**

Medical Devices

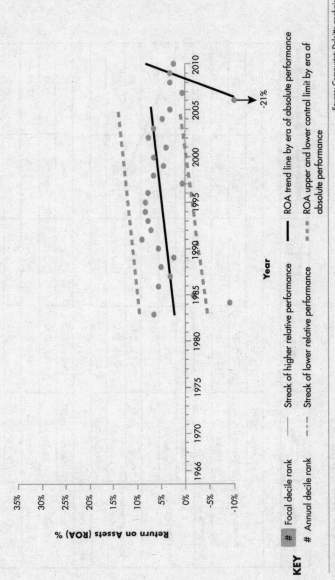

1 2 4 3 4 2 5 7 5 7 6 6 6 1 5 5 6 4 6 4 4 0 1 4 4 2

Return on Assets (ROA) %

Year

KEY

▢ Focal decile rank

\# Annual decile rank

—— Streak of higher relative performance

--- Streak of lower relative performance

—— ROA trend line by era of absolute performance

=== ROA upper and lower control limit by era of absolute performance

Source: Compustat; Deloitte analysis

Note: Portions of control limits omitted for convenience.

-21%

Medical Devices Trio Summary

Medical Devices

Streaks/Eras	Trios	Years	Average Annual ROA	Compounded Annual TSR	Compounded Annual Revenue Growth
Total Period					
Summary	Medtronic (MW)	1966 to 2010	12.6%	14.4%	20.1%
	Stryker (LR)	1978 to 2010	12.0%	23.0%	19.3%
	Invacare (AJ)	1983 to 2010	3.2%	13.9%	12.6%
Relative Performance					
Lower performance period	Medtronic (MW)	1966 to 1985	11.4%	8.8%	26.0%
	Stryker (LR)	–	–	–	–
	Invacare (AJ)	–	–	–	–
Higher performance period	Medtronic (MW)	1986 to 2010	13.5%	16.4%	15.5%
	Stryker (LR)	1979 to 2010	12.0%	23.0%	19.5%
	Invacare (AJ)	–	–	–	–
Absolute Performance					
Era 1	Medtronic (MW)	1966 to 2010	12.6%	14.4%	20.1%
	Stryker (LR)	1978 to 1997	12.0%	23.0%	19.3%
	Invacare (AJ)	1983 to 2005	3.29%	13.9%	12.6%
Era 2	Medtronic (MW)	–	–	–	–
	Stryker (LR)	1998 to 2010	10.8%	12.5%	17.1%
	Invacare (AJ)	2006 to 2010	-2.7%	5.5%	3.5%

Source: Compustat; Deloitte analysis

Figure 9 **Thomas & Betts: Miracle Worker**

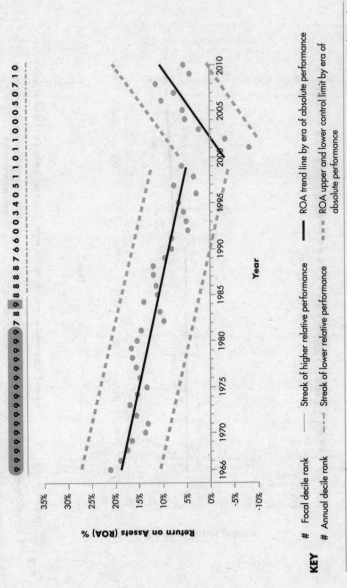

Electrical Wiring

9 9 9 9 9 9 9 9 9 9 9 9 9 9 8 9 8 8 8 8 7 6 6 0 0 3 4 0 5 1 1 0 1 1 0 0 0 5 0 5 0 7 1 0

Source: Compustat; Deloitte analysis

KEY

\# Focal decile rank   —— Streak of higher relative performance

\# Annual decile rank   - - - Streak of lower relative performance

—— ROA trend line by era of absolute performance

- - - ROA upper and lower control limit by era of absolute performance

Figure 10 Hubbell: Long Runner

Electrical Wiring

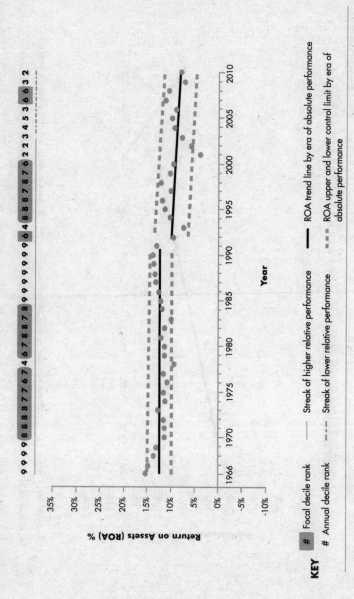

KEY
Focal decile rank
Annual decile rank

Streak of higher relative performance
Streak of lower relative performance

ROA trend line by era of absolute performance
ROA upper and lower control limit by era of absolute performance

Source: Compustat; Deloitte analysis

Figure 11 Emrise: Average Joe

Electrical Wiring

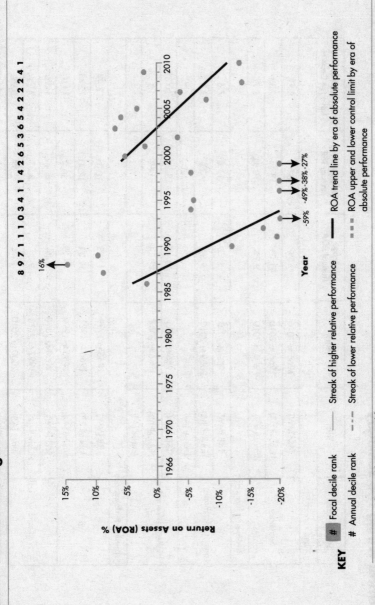

Source: Compustat; Deloitte analysis

Electrical Wiring Trio Summary

Electrical Wiring

Streaks/Eras	Trios	Years	Average Annual ROA	Compounded Annual TSR	Compounded Annual Revenue Growth
Total Period					
Summary	T&B (MW)	1966 to 2010	9.8%	8.9%	8.8%
	Hubbell (LR)	1966 to 2010	11.0%	13.3%	9.8%
	Emrise (AJ)	1986 to 2010	-8.9%	-19.9%	7.7%
Relative Performance					
Lower performance period	T&B (MW)	1986 to 2010	5.6%	5.7%	7.6%
	Hubbell (LR)	2005 to 2010	9.3%	9.3%	3.8%
	Emrise (AJ)	–	–	–	–
Higher performance period	T&B (MW)	1966 to 1985	15.1%	13.1%	10.3%
	Hubbell (LR)	1966 to 2004	11.3%	14.6%	10.8%
	Emrise (AJ)	–	–	–	–
Absolute Performance					
Era 1	T&B (MW)	1966 to 1999	11.9%	10.3%	12.7%
	Hubbell (LR)	1966 to 1991	12.3%	17.4%	12.4%
	Emrise (AJ)	1986 to 1999	-14.5%	-30.2%	14.0%
Era 2	T&B (MW)	2000 to 2010	3.4%	11.9%	1.3%
	Hubbell (LR)	1992 to 2010	9.3%	8.2%	6.7%
	Emrise (AJ)	2000 to 2010	-1.6%	-2.6%	0.9%

Source: Compustat; Deloitte analysis

Family Clothing

Figure 12 Abercrombie & Fitch: Miracle Worker

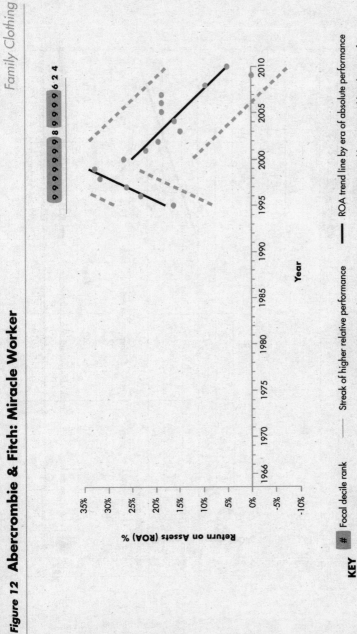

9 9 9 9 9 9 8 9 9 9 9 6 2 4

Year

Return on Assets (ROA) %

35%
30%
25%
20%
15%
10%
5%
0%
-5%
-10%

1966 1970 1975 1980 1985 1990 1995 2000 2005 2010

KEY

Focal decile rank

Annual decile rank

———— Streak of higher relative performance

–––– Streak of lower relative performance

———— ROA trend line by era of absolute performance

–––– ROA upper and lower control limit by era of absolute performance

Source: Compustat; Deloitte analysis

Figure 13 **Finish Line: Long Runner**

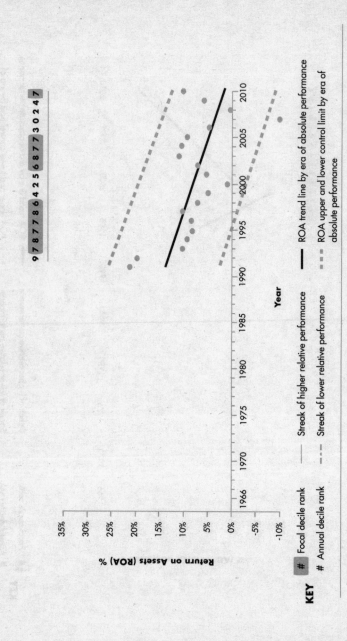

Family Clothing

Source: Compustat; Deloitte analysis

Family Clothing

Figure 14 Syms: Average Joe

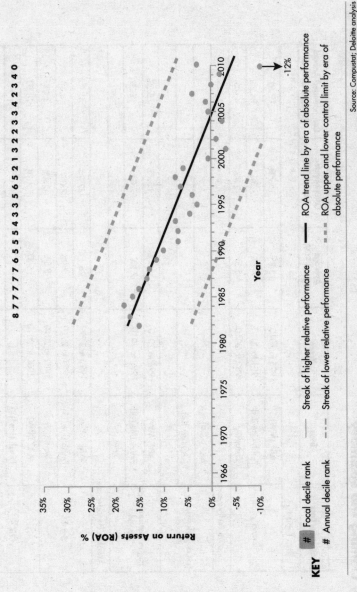

8 7 7 7 7 6 5 5 5 4 3 3 5 6 5 2 1 3 2 2 3 3 4 2 4 0

Return on Assets (ROA) %

Year

-12%

KEY

| # | Focal decile rank |
| # | Annual decile rank |

— Streak of higher relative performance
- - - Streak of lower relative performance

— ROA trend line by era of absolute performance
- - - ROA upper and lower control limit by era of absolute performance

Source: Compustat; Deloitte analysis
Note: Portions of control limits omitted for convenience.

Family Clothing Trio Summary

Family Clothing

Streaks/Eras	Trios	Years	Average Annual ROA	Compounded Annual TSR	Compounded Annual Revenue Growth
Total Period					
Summary	A&F (MW)	1995 to 2010	18.8%	15.7%	19.6%
	Finish Line (LR)	1991 to 2010	7.9%	7.0%	14.2%
	Syms (AJ)	1982 to 2010	5.5%	-2.4%	4.0%
Relative Performance					
Lower performance period	A&F (MW)	–	–	–	–
	Finish Line (LR)	–	–	–	–
	Syms (AJ)	–	–	–	–
Higher performance period	A&F (MW)	1996 to 2010	18.9%	15.7%	18.2%
	Finish Line (LR)	1992 to 2010	7.2%	7.0%	13.3%
	Syms (AJ)	–	–	–	–
Absolute Performance					
Era 1	A&F (MW)	1995 to 1999	26.1%	47.9%	45.0%
	Finish Line (LR)	1991 to 2010	7.9%	7.0%	14.2%
	Syms (AJ)	1982 to 2010	5.5%	-2.4%	4.0%
Era 2	A&F (MW)	2000 to 2010	15.4%	12.3%	10.9%
	Finish Line (LR)	–	–	–	–
	Syms (AJ)	–	–	–	–

Source: Compustat; Deloitte analysis

Figure 15 **Wm. Wrigley Jr. Company: Miracle Worker** *Confectionary*

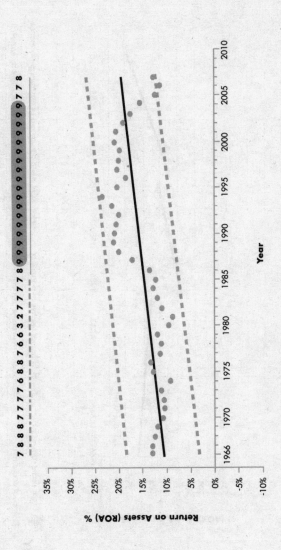

Source: Compustat; Deloitte analysis

Figure 16 Tootsie Roll Industries: Long Runner

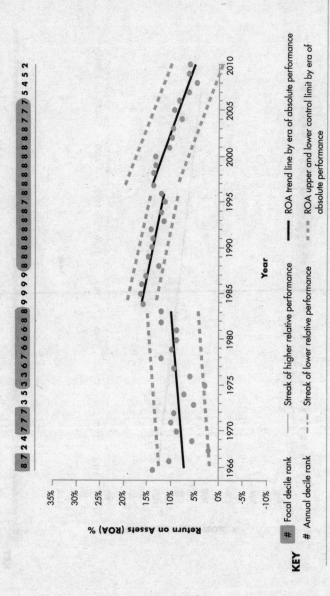

Confectionary

KEY `#` Focal decile rank

`#` Annual decile rank

—— Streak of higher relative performance

- - - Streak of lower relative performance

—— ROA trend line by era of absolute performance

- - - ROA upper and lower control limit by era of absolute performance

Source: Compustat; Deloitte analysis

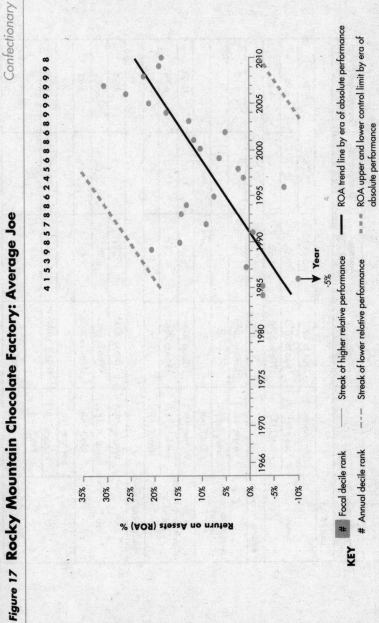

Figure 17 Rocky Mountain Chocolate Factory: Average Joe

Confectionary

4 1 5 3 9 8 5 7 8 8 6 2 4 5 6 8 8 6 9 9 9 9 9 9 8

Return on Assets (ROA) %

KEY

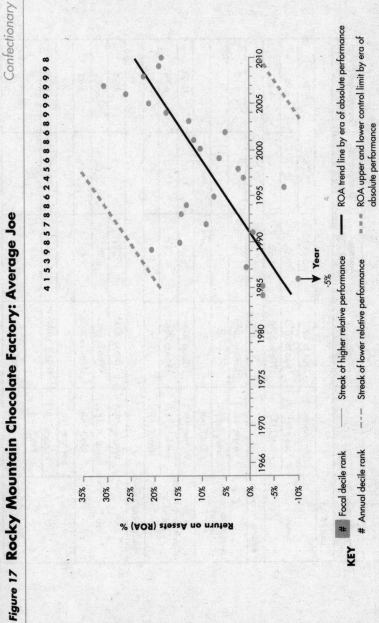

Focal decile rank

\# Annual decile rank

Streak of higher relative performance

Streak of lower relative performance

ROA trend line by era of absolute performance

ROA upper and lower control limit by era of absolute performance

Note: Portions of control limits omitted for convenience.

Source: Compustat; Deloitte analysis

Confectionary Trio Summary

Confectionary

Streaks/Eras	Trios	Years	Average Annual ROA	Compounded Annual TSR	Compounded Annual Revenue Growth
Total Period					
Summary	Wrigley (MW)	1966 to 2007	15.2%	15.7%	9.3%
	Tootsie Roll (LR)	1966 to 2010	10.5%	13.1%	6.9%
	RMCF (AJ)	1984 to 2010	7.6%	7.6%	8.6%
Relative Performance					
Lower performance period	Wrigley (MW)	1966 to 1985	11.6%	12.1%	8.1%
	Tootsie Roll (LR)	–	–	–	–
	RMCF (AJ)	–	–	–	–
Higher performance period	Wrigley (MW)	1986 to 2007	18.5%	17.4%	10.2%
	Tootsie Roll (LR)	1966 to 2010	10.5%	13.1%	6.9%
	RMCF (AJ)	–	–	–	–
Absolute Performance					
Era 1	Wrigley (MW)	1966 to 2007	15.2%	15.7%	9.3%
	Tootsie Roll (LR)	1966 to 1983	8.7%	8.8%	6.2%
	RMCF (AJ)	1984 to 2010	7.6%	7.6%	8.6%
Era 2	Wrigley (MW)	–	–	–	–
	Tootsie Roll (LR)	1984 to 1996	14.0%	22.9%	11.4%
	RMCF (AJ)	–	–	–	–
Era 3	Tootsie Roll (LR)	1997 to 2010	9.6%	3.4%	2.6%

Groceries

Figure 18 Weis Markets: Miracle Worker

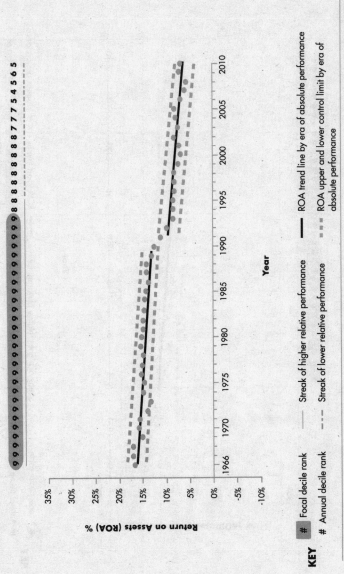

Figure 19 Publix Supermarkets: Long Runner

Groceries

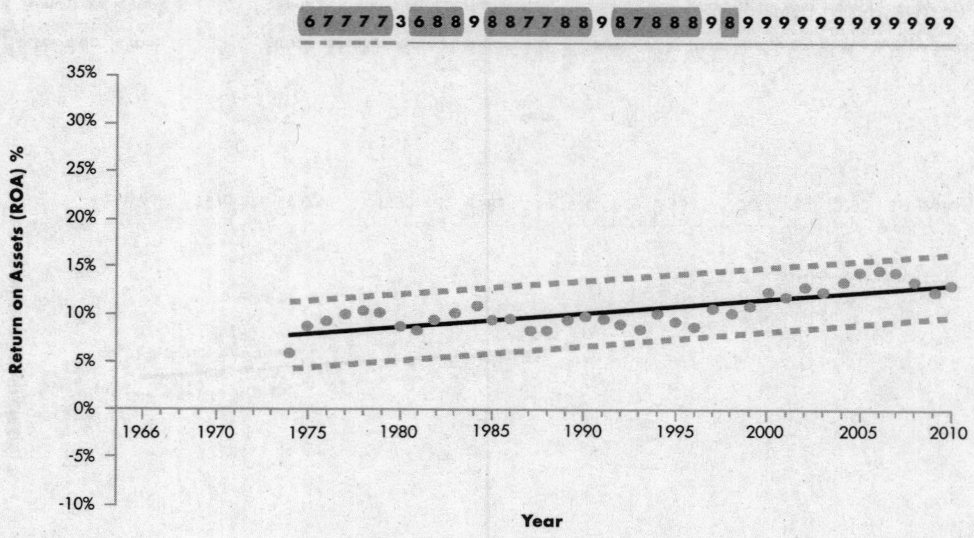

KEY

Focal decile rank

Annual decile rank

——— Streak of higher relative performance

－－－ Streak of lower relative performance

——— ROA trend line by era of absolute performance

－－－ ROA upper and lower control limit by era of absolute performance

Source: Compustat; Deloitte analysis

Figure 20 Whole Foods Markets: Average Joe

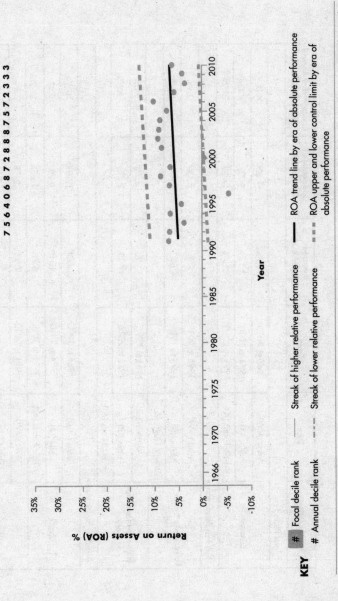

Groceries

7 5 6 4 0 6 8 7 2 8 8 8 7 5 7 2 3 3 3

Year

Return on Assets (ROA) %

35%
30%
25%
20%
15%
10%
5%
0%
-5%
-10%

1966 1970 1975 1980 1985 1990 1995 2000 2005 2010

KEY

    Focal decile rank

Annual decile rank

——— Streak of higher relative performance

- - - Streak of lower relative performance

——— ROA trend line by era of absolute performance

- - - ROA upper and lower control limit by era of absolute performance

Source: Compustat; Deloitte analysis

Groceries Trio Summary

Groceries

Streaks/Eras	Trios	Years	Average Annual ROA	Compounded Annual TSR	Compounded Annual Revenue Growth
Total Period					
Summary	Weis (MW)	1966 to 2010	11.7%	11.6%	7.1%
	Publix (LR)	1974 to 2010	10.8%	9.7%	9.4%
	Whole Foods (AJ)	1991 to 2010	5.7%	16.3%	27.2%
Relative Performance					
Lower performance period	Weis (MW)	1996 to 2010	7.3%	5.1%	2.9%
	Publix (LR)	1975 to 1981	9.8%	-	12.7%
	Whole Foods (AJ)	-	-	-	-
Higher performance period	Weis (MW)	1966 to 1995	13.9%	14.7%	9.3%
	Publix (LR)	1982 to 2010	11.2%	9.7%	8.6%
	Whole Foods (AJ)	-	-	-	-
Absolute Performance					
Era 1	Weis (MW)	1966 to 1990	14.8%	17.8%	10.1%
	Publix (LR)	1974 to 2010	10.8%	9.7%	9.4%
	Whole Foods (AJ)	1991 to 2010	5.7%	16.3%	27.2%
Era 2	Weis (MW)	1991 to 2010	7.8%	5.7%	3.8%
	Publix (LR)	-	-	-	-
	Whole Foods (AJ)	-	-	-	-

Source: Compustat; Deloitte analysis

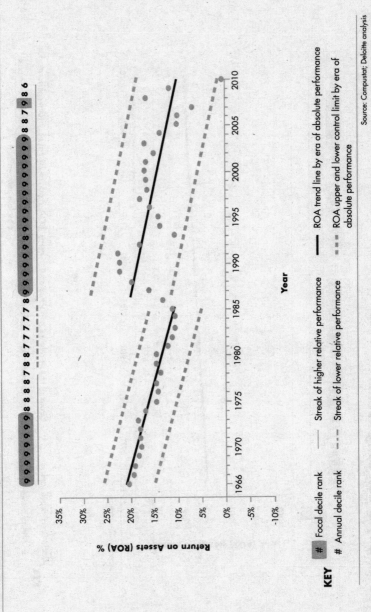

Pharmaceuticals

Figure 21 Merck & Co.: Miracle Worker

9 9 9 9 9 9 9 8 8 8 8 7 8 8 7 7 7 7 7 8 9 9 9 9 9 9 9 9 9 9 8 8 7 9 8 6

KEY

Focal decile rank — Streak of higher relative performance — ROA trend line by era of absolute performance

Annual decile rank --- Streak of lower relative performance --- ROA upper and lower control limit by era of absolute performance

Year

Return on Assets (ROA) %

Source: Compustat; Deloitte analysis

Figure 22 Eli Lilly & Co.: Long Runner

Pharmaceuticals

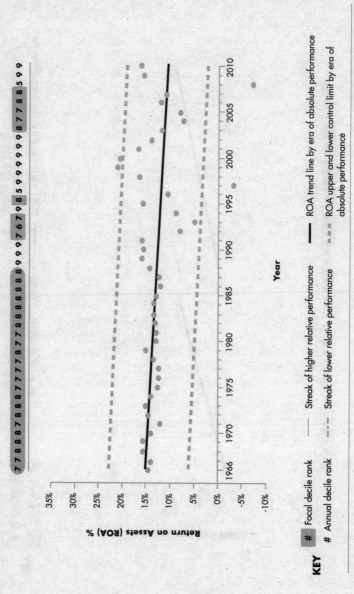

KEY

Focal decile rank — Streak of higher relative performance — ROA trend line by era of absolute performance

Annual decile rank --- Streak of lower relative performance ■■■ ROA upper and lower control limit by era of absolute performance

Source: Compustat; Deloitte analysis

Figure 23 **KV Pharmaceutical: Average Joe**

Pharmaceuticals

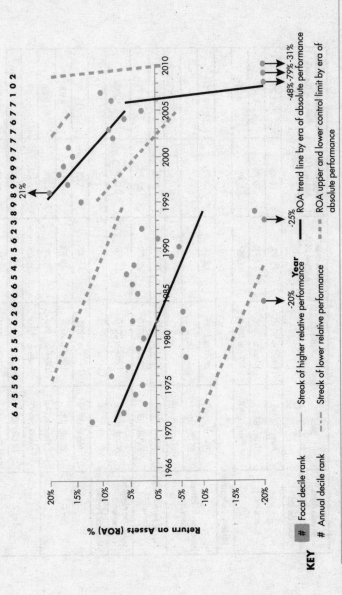

6 4 5 5 6 5 3 5 4 6 2 6 6 6 4 4 5 6 2 3 8 9 9 9 9 7 7 7 6 7 7 1 0 2

21%

-25%

-20%

-48% -79% -31%

KEY

[#] Focal decile rank

Annual decile rank

—— Streak of higher relative performance

– – – Streak of lower relative performance

—— ROA trend line by era of absolute performance

– – – ROA upper and lower control limit by era of absolute performance

Return on Assets (ROA) %

Year

Note: Portions of control limits omitted for convenience.

Source: Compustat; Deloitte analysis

Pharmaceuticals Trio Summary

Pharmaceuticals

Streaks/Eras	Trios	Years	Average Annual ROA	Compounded Annual TSR	Compounded Annual Revenue Growth
Total Period					
Summary	Merck (MW)	1966 to 2010	15.2%	11.4%	11.3%
	Eli Lilly (LR)	1966 to 2010	12.7%	10.7%	9.9%
	KV Pharma (AJ)	1971 to 2010	-0.3%	3.8%	4.6%
Relative Performance					
Lower performance period	Merck (MW)	1978 to 1985	12.3%	14.2%	8.7%
	Eli Lilly (LR)	–	–	–	–
	KV Pharma (AJ)	–	–	–	–
Higher performance period 1	Merck (MW)	1966 to 1977	17.5%	5.5%	13.7%
	Eli Lilly (LR)	1966 to 2010	12.7%	10.7%	9.9%
Higher performance period 2	Merck (MW)	1986 to 2010	15.0%	10.5%	10.6%
Absolute Performance					
Era 1	Merck (MW)	1966 to 1985	15.4%	9.6%	11.9%
	Eli Lilly (LR)	1966 to 2010	12.7%	10.7%	9.9%
	KV Pharma (AJ)	1971 to 1994	-0.7%	4.6%	9.7%
Era 2	Merck (MW)	1986 to 2010	15.0%	10.5%	10.6%
	Eli Lilly (LR)	–	–	–	–
	KV Pharma (AJ)	1995 to 2005	13.1%	17.9%	22.1%
Era 3	KV Pharma (AJ)	2006 to 2010	-27.8%	-42.8%	-50.2%

Trucking

Figure 24 Heartland Express: Miracle Worker

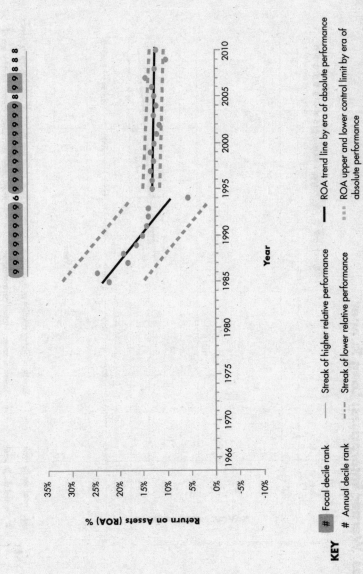

9 9 9 9 9 9 9 9 9 9 9 9 9 9 6 9 9 9 9 9 8 9 9 9 8 8 8

Return on Assets (ROA) %

35%
30%
25%
20%
15%
10%
5%
0%
-5%
-10%

1966 1970 1975 1980 1985 1990 1995 2000 2005 2010

Year

KEY

Focal decile rank

Annual decile rank

—— Streak of higher relative performance

--- Streak of lower relative performance

—— ROA trend line by era of absolute performance

···· ROA upper and lower control limit by era of absolute performance

Source: Compustat; Deloitte analysis

Trucking

Figure 25 Werner Enterprises: Long Runner

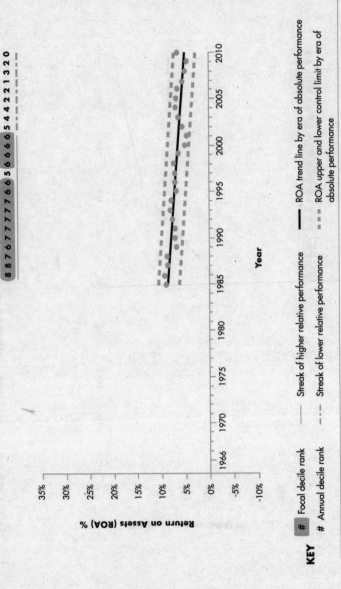

KEY

Focal decile rank

Annual decile rank

—— Streak of higher relative performance

– – Streak of lower relative performance

—— ROA trend line by era of absolute performance

– – – ROA upper and lower control limit by era of absolute performance

Source: Compustat; Deloitte analysis

Figure 26 **P.A.M. Transportation Services: Average Joe**

Trucking

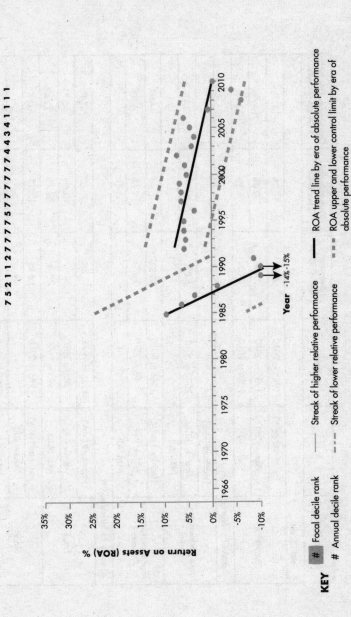

7 5 2 1 1 2 7 7 7 5 7 7 7 7 7 4 4 3 4 1 1 1 1

KEY   # Focal decile rank

Annual decile rank

—— Streak of higher relative performance

--- Streak of lower relative performance

—— ROA trend line by era of absolute performance

=== ROA upper and lower control limit by era of absolute performance

Source: Compustat; Deloitte analysis

Note: Portions of control limits omitted for convenience.

Trucking Trio Summary

Trucking

Streaks/Eras	Trios	Years	Average Annual ROA	Compounded Annual TSR	Compounded Annual Revenue Growth
Total Period					
Summary	Heartland (MW)	1985 to 2010	14.6%	17.3%	14.0%
	Werner (LR)	1985 to 2010	7.1%	10.6%	13.7%
	PAM (AJ)	1985 to 2010	2.0%	-1.2%	12.0%
Relative Performance					
Lower performance period	Heartland (MW)	–			–
	Werner (LR)	2002 to 2010	6.2%	7.7%	3.9%
	PAM (AJ)	–			–
Higher performance period	Heartland (MW)	1986 to 2010	14.3%	17.3%	14.0%
	Werner (LR)	1986 to 2001	7.4%	11.7%	18.9%
	PAM (AJ)	–			–
Absolute Performance					
Era 1	Heartland (MW)	1985 to 1994	17.8%	29.0%	31.5%
	Werner (LR)	1985 to 2010	7.1%	10.6%	13.7%
	PAM (AJ)	1985 to 1991	-2.8%	-50.7%	22.4%
Era 2	Heartland (MW)	1995 to 2010	12.6%	12.6%	6.6%
	Werner (LR)	–			–
	PAM (AJ)	1992 to 2010	3.8%	12.4%	9.3%

Source: Compustat; Deloitte analysis

Figure 27 Maytag: Miracle Worker

Appliances

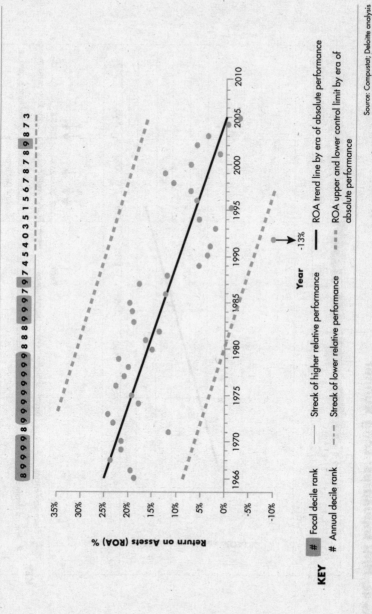

8 9 9 9 9 9 9 9 9 8 8 8 9 9 9 7 9 7 4 5 4 0 3 5 1 5 6 7 8 7 8 9 8 7 3

Return on Assets (ROA) %

-13%

Year

KEY

█ Focal decile rank

Annual decile rank

—— Streak of higher relative performance

- - - Streak of lower relative performance

—— ROA trend line by era of absolute performance

- - - ROA upper and lower control limit by era of absolute performance

Source: Compustat; Deloitte analysis

Note: Portions of control limits omitted for convenience.

Figure 28 **HMI Industries: Long Runner**

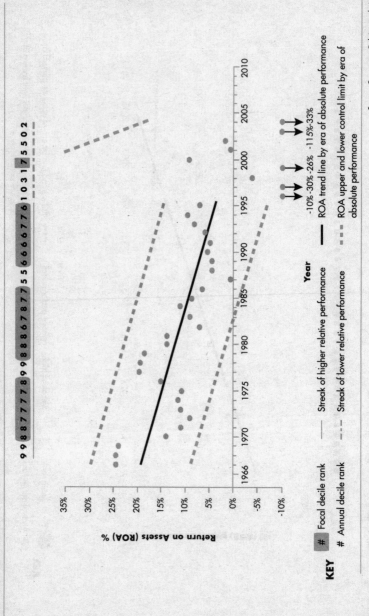

Source: Compustat; Deloitte analysis

Note: Portions of control limits omitted for convenience.

Appliances

Figure 29 Whirlpool: Average Joe

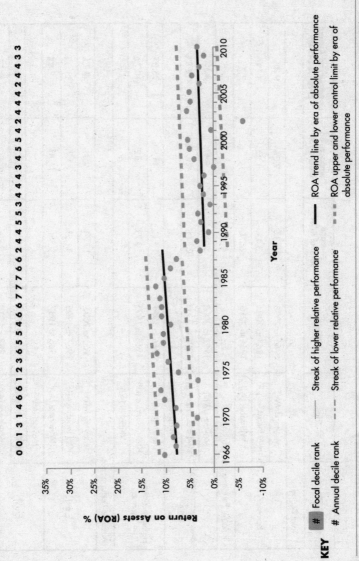

KEY

■ # Focal decile rank   —— Streak of higher relative performance   —— ROA trend line by era of absolute performance

   # Annual decile rank   - - - Streak of lower relative performance   - - - ROA upper and lower control limit by era of absolute performance

Source: Compustat; Deloitte analysis

Appliances Trio Summary

Appliances

Streaks/Eras	Trios	Years	Average Annual ROA	Compounded Annual TSR	Compounded Annual Revenue Growth
Total Period					
Summary	Maytag (MW)	1966 to 2005	12.3%	9.0%	9.7%
	HMI Industries (LR)	1967 to 2004	3.1%	-1.4%	4.1%
	Whirlpool (AJ)	1966 to 2010	6.0%	10.1%	7.7%
Relative Performance					
Lower performance period	Maytag (MW)	1992 to 2005	3.3%	4.4%	3.7%
	HMI Industries (LR)	1996 to 2004	-23.1%	-29.2%	-14.8%
	Whirlpool (AJ)	–	–	–	–
Higher performance period	Maytag (MW)	1966 to 1991	17.1%	11.9%	13.3%
	HMI Industries (LR)	1968 to 1995	10.7%	13.2%	10.7%
	Whirlpool (AJ)	–	–	–	–
Absolute Performance					
Era 1	Maytag (MW)	1966 to 2005	12.3%	9.0%	9.7%
	HMI Industries (LR)	1967 to 1995	11.2%	13.2%	11.1%
	Whirlpool (AJ)	1966 to 1987	9.4%	11.8%	8.8%
Era 2	Maytag (MW)	–	–	–	–
	HMI Industries (LR)	1996 to 2004	-23.1%	-29.2%	-14.8%
	Whirlpool (AJ)	1988 to 2010	2.7%	8.8%	6.7%

Appendix F: Consistency Analysis

Because we are using annual ROA as our "atom" of performance, treating any period of time longer than one year as a single undifferentiated block carries a risk that we are masking important annual variations. The streaks and eras that we use as our foundation for identifying relevant behavioral differences would be on especially shaky ground if there were wild swings in our independent variables (the ROS and TAT elements of ROA advantage over time) that we "accounted for" with relatively smooth or unchanging behavioral differences over those same periods of time.

To guard against this, we have examined each of our pair-wise comparisons for consistency in the composition of its Elements of Advantage over the relevant time periods. The tables below report the percentage of total observations for the entire sample for each case study pair that are consistent with the totals for the full period that we examine.

For example, if we look at the summary statistics for Miracle Workers versus Long Runners across all nine comparisons, we see that on average 87 percent of the time the annual gross margin advantage had the same sign as the gross margin advantage for the entire period over which Miracle Workers were compared to Long Runners. If we look only at periods of relative high performance, this rises to 90 percent while during periods of relative low performance this drops to 81 percent. The median value overall and during periods of relative high performance is 100 percent, and because this is the maximum value our consistency measure can take, it means that half the time or more there is perfect consistency between the sign of the annual values and the average value for the period.

Looking at a specific pair-wise comparison, we see in the case of Linear Technology versus Micropac Industries that the mean percentage points of ROA advantage attributable to a gross margin advantage is 25.7, the median is 25, the interquartile range (IQR) is 9.7, and that the consistency is 100 percent.

Below are the summary statistics for all three types of pair-wise comparisons and for all twenty-seven pair-wise comparisons so that you can judge for yourself whether the variation in the Elements of Advantage over the blocks of time identified by our statistical methods is sufficiently small to warrant our search for consistent behavioral differences over those same periods.

Summary Level: By Pair-Wise Comparisons for Case-Study Samples

Summary Statistics for the Sample

Miracle Workers Vs. Long Runners

	Consistency	Gross Margin	SG&A	R&D	Other	ROS	CAT	FAT	Other-AT	TAT	ROA
Overall	Mean (%)	87	87	95	85	85	82	82	77	88	87
	Median (%)	100	95	100	83	89	96	88	84	96	90
	IQR (pp)	22	28	9	24	27	20	32	38	17	20
Period of Relative High Performance	Mean (%)	91	82	93	87	90	93	83	76	90	89
	Median (%)	100	90	100	96	100	100	88	84	96	95
	IQR (pp)	0	36	16	23	18	5	28	32	17	18
Period of Relative Low Performance	Mean (%)	81	93	98	82	78	83	82	79	86	84
	Median (%)	89	100	100	78	77	81	91	82	93	83
	IQR (pp)	37	5	0	11	19	19	27	34	20	26

Miracle Workers Vs. Average Joes

	Consistency	Gross Margin	SG&A	R&D	Other	ROS	CAT	FAT	Other-AT	TAT	ROA
Overall	Mean (%)	92	89	95	83	90	74	76	76	75	89
	Median (%)	100	100	100	84	100	74	78	87	73	100
	IQR (pp)	6	19	0	29	12	32	21	46	34	17
Period of Relative High Performance	Mean (%)	97	86	89	85	94	76	82	80	78	93
	Median (%)	100	100	100	88	100	74	79	91	78	100
	IQR (pp)	2	29	11	28	10	31	14	27	27	13
Period of Relative Low Performance	Mean (%)	84	92	100	81	84	70	69	71	72	83
	Median (%)	100	100	100	72	100	73	69	68	70	87
	IQR (pp)	19	14	0	30	36	33	36	40	31	36

Long Runners Vs. Average Joes

	Consistency	Gross Margin	SG&A	R&D	Other	ROS	CAT	FAT	Other-AT	TAT	ROA
Overall	Mean (%)	92	94	100	74	88	67	73	71	75	86
	Median (%)	96	100	100	80	90	63	73	75	75	88
	IQR (pp)	13	0	0	25	17	31	24	24	37	20
Period of Relative High Performance	Mean (%)	92	93	100	77	88	64	73	69	74	86
	Median (%)	98	100	100	80	91	59	76	69	74	86
	IQR (pp)	11	8	0	14	15	28	32	24	37	16
Period of Relative Low Performance	Mean (%)	91	100	100	59	85	76	72	80	80	85
	Median (%)	89	100	100	56	89	83	67	78	83	89
	IQR (pp)	8	0	0	28	17	28	8	3	22	17

Summary Statistics for Each Pair-Wise Comparison
Semiconductors

Linear Technology Vs. Micropac Industries

	Gross Margin	SG&A	R&D	Other	ROS	CAT	FAT	Other-AT	TAT	ROA
Higher Relative Performance: 1992 to 2010										
Mean (pp)	25.7	2.8	–5.2	–7.1	16.2	–4.2	–0.9	–0.2	–5.3	11.0
Median (pp)	25.0	3.2	–4.3	–7.5	16.0	–4.3	–0.7	0.0	–5.1	11.2
IQR (pp)	9.7	1.6	1.7	3.5	5.0	3.2	0.6	0.3	3.2	7.9
Consistency	100%	95%	100%	100%	100%	100%	100%	85%	100%	100%
Lower Relative Performance: 1986 to 1991										
Mean (pp)	20.2	–9.0	n/a	–2.5	8.7	–2.3	–0.5	–.03	–2.8	5.8
Median (pp)	22.8	–8.5	n/a	–3.4	10.0	–2.1	–0.5	0.0	–2.5	8.0
IQR (pp)	3.8	3.3	n/a	2.9	3.0	1.4	0.2	0.0	1.5	3.7
Consistency	100%	100%	n/a	82%	100%	100%	100%	100%	100%	83%

Linear Technology Vs. International Rectifier

Higher Relative Performance: 1992 to 2010

	Gross Margin	SG&A	R&D	Other	ROS	CAT	FAT	Other-AT	TAT	ROA
Mean (pp)	19.9	3.8	−2.6	−3.3	17.7	−1.2	0.8	0.9	0.5	18.3
Median (pp)	20.0	3.5	−2.4	−3.3	16.9	−1.5	0.6	0.3	−0.6	16.4
IQR (pp)	5.6	2.1	1.5	4.1	5.1	2.7	0.9	1.1	2.4	6.3
Consistency	100%	100%	100%	84%	100%	74%	79%	79%	42%	100%

Lower Relative Performance: 1986 to 1991

	Gross Margin	SG&A	R&D	Other	ROS	CAT	FAT	Other-AT	TAT	ROA
Mean (pp)	17.0	−0.9	−4.3	0.7	12.5	0.9	−0.8	0.0	0.0	12.5
Median (pp)	18.3	−0.5	−4.0	1.4	13.2	1.2	−0.9	−0.1	0.1	13.6
IQR (pp)	1.5	2.4	2.2	3.1	7.8	3.2	2.0	0.2	0.7	9.4
Consistency	100%	67%	100%	67%	100%	67%	67%	50%	67%	100%

Micropac Industries Vs. International Rectifier

Higher Relative Performance: 1975 to 2010

	Gross Margin	SG&A	R&D	Other	ROS	CAT	FAT	Other-AT	TAT	ROA
Mean (pp)	−6.2	5.1	1.6	2.5	3.0	0.7	1.8	0.9	3.4	6.3
Median (pp)	−5.2	4.4	1.1	2.6	2.0	0.3	1.6	0.2	3.0	7.6
IQR (pp)	4.5	10.0	2.9	5.7	8.3	1.3	1.6	0.6	3.3	9.2
Consistency	92%	69%	100%	75%	67%	75%	94%	94%	94%	83%

Medtronic Vs. Stryker

Higher Relative Performance: 1986 to 2010

	Gross Margin	SG&A	R&D	Other	ROS	CAT	FAT	Other-AT	TAT	ROA
Mean (pp)	11.8	0.5	–3.1	–4.2	4.9	0.2	–0.4	–2.7	–2.9	2.0
Median (pp)	12.9	2.3	–2.8	–3.7	4.7	0.1	–0.3	–2.8	–3.7	1.1
IQR (pp)	8.4	9.2	1.6	4.4	2.2	2.9	1.0	1.5	2.8	4.5
Consistency	100%	64%	100%	96%	92%	52%	76%	88%	84%	64%

Lower Relative Performance: 1978 to 1985

	Gross Margin	SG&A	R&D	Other	ROS	CAT	FAT	Other-AT	TAT	ROA
Mean (pp)	15.1	–5.8	–4.7	–0.4	4.2	–3.1	–1.6	–0.8	–5.5	–1.4
Median (pp)	14.7	–5.4	–4.7	–0.5	4.5	–3.3	–1.6	–0.8	–5.6	–1.4
IQR (pp)	1.4	1.3	0.7	1.4	1.3	0.6	0.3	0.3	0.6	1.1
Consistency	100%	100%	100%	63%	100%	100%	100%	100%	100%	88%

Medical Devices

Medtronic Vs. Invacare

Higher Relative Performance: 1986 to 2010

	Gross Margin	SG&A	R&D	Other	ROS	CAT	FAT	Other-AT	TAT	ROA
Mean (pp)	34.4	−10.9	−6.5	−6.1	10.9	−0.6	−0.2	−0.4	−1.2	9.7
Median (pp)	35.5	−10.1	−6.9	−6.5	9.8	−0.7	−0.2	−0.5	−1.6	8.0
IQR (pp)	8.0	4.7	2.7	3.4	2.0	0.7	0.3	1.0	1.1	3.4
Consistency	100%	100%	100%	96%	100%	96%	96%	84%	96%	100%

Lower Relative Performance: 1983 to 1985

	Gross Margin	SG&A	R&D	Other	ROS	CAT	FAT	Other-AT	TAT	ROA
Mean (pp)	33.7	−11.8	−6.5	−4.1	11.3	0.6	0.2	0.1	0.9	12.2
Median (pp)	31.5	−13.5	−6.3	−4.0	11.0	0.6	0.2	0.2	1.1	12.0
IQR (pp)	3.4	3.1	0.5	2.3	2.2	1.7	1.4	0.3	3.4	5.7
Consistency	100%	100%	100%	100%	100%	67%	67%	67%	67%	100%

Stryker Vs. Invacare

Higher Relative Performance

Era 1: 1983 to 1997

	Gross Margin	SG&A	R&D	Other	ROS	CAT	FAT	Other-AT	TAT	ROA
Mean (pp)	29.8	−12.9	−5.2	−3.0	8.7	−0.9	−0.1	0.5	−0.5	8.2
Median (pp)	28.7	−14.2	−5.3	−3.4	7.5	−0.6	0.1	0.1	−0.4	7.3
IQR (pp)	5.3	3.5	2.9	4.0	5.7	1.8	0.7	1.3	1.3	6.0
Consistency	100%	100%	100%	80%	100%	80%	47%	53%	73%	100%

Era 2: 1998 to 2010

	Gross Margin	SG&A	R&D	Other	ROS	CAT	FAT	Other-AT	TAT	ROA
Mean (pp)	31.5	−16.5	−3.4	−2.5	9.1	−0.2	−0.1	−0.2	−0.5	8.6
Median (pp)	34.3	−16.2	−3.5	−3.5	7.8	−0.1	−0.2	0.0	−0.3	7.9
IQR (pp)	7.0	4.4	1.0	2.3	5.1	0.9	0.1	0.5	1.1	5.5
Consistency	100%	100%	100%	92%	85%	85%	92%	46%	69%	85%

Electrical Wiring

Thomas & Betts Vs. Hubbell

Higher Relative Performance: 1966 to 1985

	Gross Margin	SG&A	R&D	Other	ROS	CAT	FAT	Other-AT	TAT	ROA
Mean (pp)	18.1	−9.8	−0.3	−3.8	4.2	−1.5	−0.5	0.9	−1.1	3.1
Median (pp)	19.0	−8.0	n/a	−4.4	4.0	−1.8	−0.8	0.8	−1.6	3.9
IQR (pp)	8.8	11.6	0.1	2.0	3.1	1.1	1.0	0.5	2.2	2.4
Consistency	100%	90%	100%	100%	100%	100%	80%	100%	70%	90%

Lower Relative Performance

Era 1: 1986 to 1999

	Gross Margin	SG&A	R&D	Other	ROS	CAT	FAT	Other-AT	TAT	ROA
Mean (pp)	8.1	−7.5	−0.4	−3.6	−3.4	−0.6	−1.1	0.7	−1.0	−4.4
Median (pp)	5.0	−6.2	−0.2	−4.1	−3.8	−0.4	−0.7	0.4	−0.6	−4.7
IQR (pp)	12.2	7.6	0.6	2.7	2.2	1.1	1.4	1.4	1.0	2.6
Consistency	86%	100%	100%	93%	86%	86%	100%	71%	100%	100%

Era 2: 2000 to 2010

	Gross Margin	SG&A	R&D	Other	ROS	CAT	FAT	Other-AT	TAT	ROA
Mean (pp)	0.0	−1.7	−0.5	−0.8	−3.0	−0.7	−0.1	−1.2	−2.0	−5.0
Median (pp)	1.1	−0.1	−0.5	−1.0	−1.6	−0.7	−0.1	−1.1	−2.0	−4.0
IQR (pp)	2.6	3.2	0.9	2.4	5.1	0.5	0.2	0.8	1.0	4.5
Consistency	64%	55%	100%	73%	73%	91%	82%	100%	100%	82%

Thomas & Betts Vs. Emrise

Lower Relative Performance

Era 1: 1986 to 1999

	Gross Margin	SG&A	R&D	Other	ROS	CAT	FAT	Other-AT	TAT	ROA
Mean (pp)	1.0	9.5	6.9	−2.6	14.7	0.5	3.0	3.6	7.2	21.8
Median (pp)	−0.5	10.4	7.5	−2.6	12.8	0.0	2.3	1.5	4.1	16.3
IQR (pp)	4.5	10.3	4.6	6.9	16.6	1.5	5.7	4.7	8.8	23.1
Consistency	29%	86%	100%	71%	100%	50%	71%	79%	79%	86%

Era 2: 2000 to 2010

	Gross Margin	SG&A	R&D	Other	ROS	CAT	FAT	Other-AT	TAT	ROA
Mean (pp)	−9.4	12.5	3.2	−1.2	5.0	−0.5	0.0	0.4	0.0	5.0
Median (pp)	−7.7	12.1	3.0	−2.8	2.8	−0.2	−0.2	0.0	−0.2	2.3
IQR (pp)	6.0	2.7	1.2	5.2	13.4	0.5	1.2	1.5	2.2	16.9
Consistency	91%	100%	100%	73%	64%	82%	45%	45%	55%	64%

Hubbell Vs. Emrise

Higher Relative Performance

Era 1: 1986 to 1991

	Gross Margin	SG&A	R&D	Other	ROS	CAT	FAT	Other-AT	TAT	ROA
Mean (pp)	−15.1	23.0	n/a	3.8	11.7	−0.1	0.1	0.7	0.7	12.4
Median (pp)	−15.4	20.3	n/a	3.7	5.3	0.0	−0.4	0.2	−0.3	7.2
IQR (pp)	5.8	12.2	n/a	3.2	17.3	2.3	2.0	2.7	3.0	17.5
Consistency	100%	100%	n/a	83%	100%	50%	50%	50%	50%	83%

Era 2: 1992 to 2004

	Gross Margin	SG&A	R&D	Other	ROS	CAT	FAT	Other-AT	TAT	ROA
Mean (pp)	−6.8	19.6	6.9	−2.3	17.4	0.5	1.9	4.3	6.7	24.1
Median (pp)	−8.6	19.7	5.4	−4.2	15.4	0.2	0.9	1.5	2.3	17.4
IQR (pp)	14.1	5.3	5.8	1.7	21.3	1.3	3.1	6.4	10.7	33.7
Consistency	77%	100%	100%	85%	100%	54%	69%	77%	77%	100%

Lower Relative Performance: 2005 to 2010

	Gross Margin	SG&A	R&D	Other	ROS	CAT	FAT	Other-AT	TAT	ROA
Mean (pp)	−8.0	18.9	1.2	1.2	13.3	1.1	−0.3	0.9	1.7	15.0
Median (pp)	−9.0	18.8	0.0	−1.2	13.8	1.6	−0.6	0.7	1.9	16.1
IQR (pp)	4.6	1.6	0.0	5.3	10.3	1.5	0.6	0.6	1.0	11.6
Consistency	83%	100%	100%	33%	100%	83%	83%	83%	83%	100%

Clothing

Abercrombie & Fitch Vs. Finish Line

Higher Relative Performance

Era 1: 1996 to 1999

	Gross Margin	SG&A	R&D	Other	ROS	CAT	FAT	Other-AT	TAT	ROA
Mean (pp)	27.2	0.6	n/a	−13.4	14.4	5.1	0.1	1.0	6.2	20.6
Median (pp)	27.5	−0.1	n/a	−13.4	14.0	4.4	0.3	1.0	6.2	20.2
IQR (pp)	16.6	5.0	n/a	5.2	16.3	7.1	1.1	1.3	6.7	9.6
Consistency	100%	50%	n/a	100%	100%	100%	75%	75%	100%	100%

Era 2: 2000 to 2010

	Gross Margin	SG&A	R&D	Other	ROS	CAT	FAT	Other-AT	TAT	ROA
Mean (pp)	42.0	−20.7	n/a	−9.6	11.6	−0.3	−1.1	0.0	−1.4	10.2
Median (pp)	48.5	−29.6	n/a	−10.1	11.4	0.0	−1.4	0.0	−1.4	9.0
IQR (pp)	32.1	35.7	n/a	2.6	7.7	0.5	2.0	0.1	2.5	10.5
Consistency	100%	64%	n/a	100%	82%	55%	91%	36%	91%	82%

Abercrombie & Fitch Vs. Syms

Higher Relative Performance

Era 1: 1996 to 1999

	Gross Margin	SG&A	R&D	Other	ROS	CAT	FAT	Other-AT	TAT	ROA
Mean (pp)	9.1	13.0	n/a	–9.1	13.0	4.1	6.0	0.2	10.3	23.3
Median (pp)	6.4	10.0	n/a	–7.0	9.3	4.5	7.3	0.2	12.8	22.3
IQR (pp)	10.1	10.1	n/a	6.1	14.3	3.3	3.2	0.3	4.6	9.5
Consistency	100%	100%	n/a	100%	100%	100%	100%	100%	100%	100%

Era 2: 2000 to 2010

	Gross Margin	SG&A	R&D	Other	ROS	CAT	FAT	Other-AT	TAT	ROA
Mean (pp)	27.5	–1.5	n/a	–12.5	13.4	0.7	1.9	0.6	3.2	16.6
Median (pp)	35.5	–14.4	n/a	–10.5	14.8	0.1	0.4	0.6	1.3	17.2
IQR (pp)	36.2	31.6	n/a	4.5	3.0	1.5	2.9	0.7	4.5	5.5
Consistency	100%	55%	n/a	100%	91%	73%	91%	91%	91%	91%

Finish Line Vs. Syms

Higher Relative Performance: 1992 to 2010

	Gross Margin	SG&A	R&D	Other	ROS	CAT	FAT	Other-AT	TAT	ROA
Mean (pp)	–7.3	13.5	n/a	–2.3	3.8	–0.2	2.0	0.1	2.0	5.8
Median (pp)	–8.4	13.4	n/a	–0.9	3.2	0.1	2.3	0.0	2.1	4.7
IQR (pp)	4.0	11.5	n/a	5.2	5.9	1.0	2.2	0.4	1.8	6.6
Consistency	89%	100%	n/a	63%	79%	37%	95%	74%	95%	95%

Confectionary

Wm. Wrigley Jr. Company Vs. Tootsie Roll Industries

Higher Relative Performance: 1986 to 2007

	Gross Margin	SG&A	R&D	Other	ROS	CAT	FAT	Other-AT	TAT	ROA
Mean (pp)	8.2	−10.8	n/a	1.1	−1.5	2.1	0.5	5.3	7.9	6.4
Median (pp)	8.5	−10.2	n/a	1.3	−1.3	2.2	0.3	6.0	8.1	6.7
IQR (pp)	2.4	3.1	n/a	1.9	1.0	1.8	1.0	3.1	1.9	2.0
Consistency	100%	100%	n/a	77%	91%	95%	59%	91%	100%	95%

Lower Relative Performance: 1966 to 1985

	Gross Margin	SG&A	R&D	Other	ROS	CAT	FAT	Other-AT	TAT	ROA
Mean (pp)	15.1	−9.2	n/a	−2.6	3.4	−0.4	−0.7	−0.1	−1.2	2.1
Median (pp)	15.6	−7.9	n/a	−3.0	3.5	−0.7	−0.8	−0.1	−1.2	1.6
IQR (pp)	5.1	5.8	n/a	5.0	3.8	1.3	0.9	0.2	1.8	3.8
Consistency	100%	95%	n/a	75%	80%	70%	75%	100%	85%	70%

Wm. Wrigley Jr. Company Vs. Rocky Mountain Chocolate Factory

Higher Relative Performance: 1986 to 2007

	Gross Margin	SG&A	R&D	Other	ROS	CAT	FAT	Other-AT	TAT	ROA
Mean (pp)	37.8	−29.0	n/a	2.3	11.1	−0.4	1.0	−0.2	0.5	11.6
Median (pp)	34.8	−29.1	n/a	1.6	9.2	−0.2	0.6	0.4	1.3	10.7
IQR (pp)	19.4	10.9	n/a	6.4	14.2	1.3	1.7	2.2	4.2	12.3
Consistency	100%	100%	n/a	73%	77%	55%	73%	32%	68%	82%

Lower Relative Performance: 1984 to 1985

	Gross Margin	SG&A	R&D	Other	ROS	CAT	FAT	Other-AT	TAT	ROA
Mean (pp)	60.3	−40.8	n/a	−7.5	12.1	1.4	1.0	0.9	3.3	15.4
Median (pp)	60.3	−40.8	n/a	−7.5	12.1	1.4	1.0	0.9	3.3	15.4
IQR (pp)	22.8	15.9	n/a	3.7	3.2	3.0	0.4	0.5	3.2	0.0
Consistency	100%	100%	n/a	100%	100%	50%	100%	100%	100%	100%

Tootsie Roll Industries Vs. Rocky Mountain Chocolate Factory

Higher Relative Performance

Era 1: 1984 to 1996

	Gross Margin	SG&A	R&D	Other	ROS	CAT	FAT	Other-AT	TAT	ROA
Mean (pp)	28.9	−12.3	n/a	−2.7	14.0	−0.1	0.5	−0.5	−0.1	13.9
Median (pp)	25.6	−15.4	n/a	−2.9	11.6	−0.2	0.4	−0.1	0.1	14.6
IQR (pp)	15.8	17.1	n/a	5.4	13.2	2.7	1.5	4.2	3.2	19.8
Consistency	100%	83%	n/a	77%	92%	54%	62%	54%	46%	69%

Era 2: 1997 to 2010

	Gross Margin	SG&A	R&D	Other	ROS	CAT	FAT	Other-AT	TAT	ROA
Mean (pp)	7.1	−5.5	n/a	1.7	3.4	−0.9	−1.3	−6.1	−8.3	−5.0
Median (pp)	3.6	−4.9	n/a	1.4	2.1	−0.7	−1.1	−6.4	−8.3	−6.2
IQR (pp)	12.7	3.0	n/a	2.6	9.4	1.4	2.7	6.7	8.6	16.9
Consistency	86%	100%	n/a	93%	64%	93%	79%	100%	100%	64%

Groceries

Weis Markets Vs. Publix Super Markets

Higher Relative Performance

Era 1: 1974 to 1990

	Gross Margin	SG&A	R&D	Other	ROS	CAT	FAT	Other-AT	TAT	ROA
Mean (pp)	13.9	0.7	n/a	−5.4	9.2	−4.4	−0.1	0.1	−4.4	4.8
Median (pp)	14.1	0.0	n/a	−4.5	9.3	−4.6	−0.1	0.1	−4.5	4.7
IQR (pp)	10.0	4.5	n/a	4.1	0.9	1.0	0.2	0.2	0.8	1.2
Consistency	100%	64%	n/a	100%	100%	100%	59%	53%	100%	100%

Era 2: 1991 to 1995

	Gross Margin	SG&A	R&D	Other	ROS	CAT	FAT	Other-AT	TAT	ROA
Mean (pp)	5.9	−0.8	n/a	−0.4	4.8	−5.0	−0.2	0.1	−5.1	−0.3
Median (pp)	5.8	−1.5	n/a	−0.4	4.5	−5.0	−0.3	0.2	−5.1	−0.1
IQR (pp)	0.5	1.5	n/a	0.4	1.3	0.2	0.2	0.3	0.3	1.1
Consistency	100%	80%	n/a	80%	100%	100%	100%	60%	100%	60%

Lower Relative Performance: 1996 to 2010

	Gross Margin	SG&A	R&D	Other	ROS	CAT	FAT	Other-AT	TAT	ROA
Mean (pp)	−0.7	−4.4	n/a	1.9	−3.2	−2.0	−1.0	0.9	−2.1	−5.4
Median (pp)	−3.1	−5.1	n/a	2.5	−3.8	−1.2	−1.2	0.5	−1.7	−5.8
IQR (pp)	6.2	3.9	n/a	3.0	6.7	2.9	0.5	1.2	4.2	2.1
Consistency	60%	93%	n/a	80%	73%	100%	100%	93%	87%	100%

Weis Markets Vs. Whole Foods Market

Higher Relative Performance: 1991 to 1995

	Gross Margin	SG&A	R&D	Other	ROS	CAT	FAT	Other-AT	TAT	ROA
Mean (pp)	−10.2	14.0	n/a	2.3	6.1	−2.8	0.0	0.6	−2.3	3.8
Median (pp)	−11.1	14.0	n/a	2.4	5.6	−2.6	−0.1	0.6	−2.3	4.3
IQR (pp)	2.8	1.6	n/a	0.3	1.4	1.3	0.3	0.1	1.0	1.5
Consistency	100%	100%	n/a	100%	100%	100%	60%	100%	100%	100%

Lower Relative Performance: 1996 to 2010

	Gross Margin	SG&A	R&D	Other	ROS	CAT	FAT	Other-AT	TAT	ROA
Mean (pp)	−20.6	16.1	n/a	5.8	1.4	−0.7	0.3	0.7	0.2	1.6
Median (pp)	−21.3	15.6	n/a	5.5	−0.1	−0.5	0.3	0.6	0.3	0.7
IQR (pp)	7.1	3.0	n/a	2.5	3.6	1.2	0.4	0.6	1.0	2.6
Consistency	100%	100%	n/a	100%	47%	87%	80%	87%	73%	60%

Publix Super Markets Vs. Whole Foods Market

Higher Relative Performance: 1991 to 2010

	Gross Margin	SG&A	R&D	Other	ROS	CAT	FAT	Other-AT	TAT	ROA
Mean (pp)	−26.3	25.1	n/a	5.5	4.3	0.0	1.4	0.5	1.9	6.2
Median (pp)	−26.0	24.0	n/a	4.7	3.1	−0.2	1.6	0.5	2.0	5.1
IQR (pp)	5.6	4.7	n/a	4.7	3.9	1.0	1.3	0.8	1.2	3.8
Consistency	100%	100%	n/a	100%	90%	45%	90%	80%	95%	100%

Pharmaceuticals

Merck & Co. Vs. Eli Lilly & Co.

Higher Relative Performance

Era 1: 1966 to 1977

	Gross Margin	SG&A	R&D	Other	ROS	CAT	FAT	Other-AT	TAT	ROA
Mean (pp)	2.0	2.2	0.5	–3.4	1.3	1.6	0.9	–0.3	2.2	3.5
Median (pp)	1.9	1.7	0.6	–3.5	0.5	2.1	1.4	–0.1	2.5	3.3
IQR (pp)	1.1	2.1	0.7	2.2	2.1	1.5	2.6	0.4	2.1	1.6
Consistency	100%	100%	83%	100%	75%	83%	67%	92%	83%	100%

Era 2: 1986 to 2010

	Gross Margin	SG&A	R&D	Other	ROS	CAT	FAT	Other-AT	TAT	ROA
Mean (pp)	–5.9	2.2	3.3	1.5	1.1	1.2	1.1	–0.3	2.0	3.1
Median (pp)	0.6	1.0	1.9	0.1	1.1	0.6	1.4	0.1	2.6	3.7
IQR (pp)	14.6	5.2	3.1	4.4	7.9	1.6	2.3	3.2	5.8	8.0
Consistency	44%	60%	84%	52%	60%	80%	68%	48%	64%	64%

Lower Relative Performance: 1978 to 1985

	Gross Margin	SG&A	R&D	Other	ROS	CAT	FAT	Other-AT	TAT	ROA
Mean (pp)	0.1	1.3	–0.6	–0.8	0.0	0.4	–1.4	–0.1	–1.1	–1.1
Median (pp)	0.0	1.3	–0.6	–0.8	–0.1	0.4	–1.3	0.0	–1.3	–1.3
IQR (pp)	3.2	0.9	0.7	1.3	1.2	0.6	0.2	0.3	0.7	1.9
Consistency	50%	100%	88%	75%	50%	75%	100%	63%	100%	75%

Merck & Co. Vs. KV Pharmaceutical

Higher Relative Performance

Era 1: 1971 to 1977

	Gross Margin	SG&A	R&D	Other	ROS	CAT	FAT	Other-AT	TAT	ROA
Mean (pp)	45.7	−16.9	−6.9	−9.4	12.6	−1.1	−1.5	0.6	−2.0	10.5
Median (pp)	46.4	−17.8	−7.3	−8.7	12.6	−0.8	−1.1	0.5	−1.7	11.7
IQR (pp)	13.5	6.5	2.4	3.8	2.4	0.8	1.1	0.2	1.5	4.7
Consistency	100%	100%	100%	100%	100%	100%	100%	100%	100%	100%

Era 2: 1986 to 2010

	Gross Margin	SG&A	R&D	Other	ROS	CAT	FAT	Other-AT	TAT	ROA
Mean (pp)	14.9	1.8	−0.9	−0.4	15.5	1.8	−0.8	0.4	1.4	16.9
Median (pp)	10.1	2.2	−0.1	−2.4	8.3	1.2	−0.9	−0.2	0.1	8.2
IQR (pp)	27.9	12.4	2.0	7.3	18.7	2.8	1.4	2.1	2.6	23.6
Consistency	84%	71%	54%	72%	88%	76%	76%	36%	56%	84%

Lower Relative Performance: 1978 to 1985

	Gross Margin	SG&A	R&D	Other	ROS	CAT	FAT	Other-AT	TAT	ROA
Mean (pp)	37.2	−12.2	−4.6	−6.4	14.0	0.4	0.7	0.1	1.1	15.1
Median (pp)	36.9	−11.8	−4.7	−6.2	13.3	−0.1	0.2	0.0	0.3	13.8
IQR (pp)	7.1	2.8	0.9	3.4	3.8	1.6	2.2	0.5	4.0	7.3
Consistency	100%	100%	100%	100%	100%	50%	50%	50%	50%	100%

Eli Lilly & Co. Vs. KV Pharmaceutical

Higher Relative Performance: 1971 to 2010

	Gross Margin	SG&A	R&D	Other	ROS	CAT	FAT	Other-AT	TAT	ROA
Mean (pp)	26.9	–5.8	–4.7	–2.8	13.7	0.0	–0.5	0.1	–0.5	13.2
Median (pp)	29.5	–5.8	–4.8	–5.2	10.9	–0.2	–0.8	0.1	–1.0	8.5
IQR (pp)	18.8	13.3	4.8	5.3	9.8	1.7	1.5	0.9	3.3	14.2
Consistency	100%	74%	97%	80%	98%	55%	73%	55%	60%	93%

Trucking

Heartland Express Vs. Werner Enterprises

Higher Relative Performance

Era 1: 1986 to 1994

	Gross Margin	SG&A	R&D	Other	ROS	CAT	FAT	Other-AT	TAT	ROA
Mean (pp)	2.6	n/a	n/a	3.6	6.2	–1.2	4.1	0.0	2.9	9.1
Median (pp)	3.7	n/a	n/a	3.3	7.2	–1.3	2.7	0.0	2.3	9.3
IQR (pp)	2.7	n/a	n/a	2.9	1.4	1.0	3.3	0.0	2.8	3.4
Consistency	78%	n/a	n/a	89%	89%	100%	100%	63%	100%	89%

Era 2: 1995 to 2010

	Gross Margin	SG&A	R&D	Other	ROS	CAT	FAT	Other-AT	TAT	ROA
Mean (pp)	7.4	n/a	n/a	0.3	7.6	–2.5	1.4	–0.3	–1.4	6.2
Median (pp)	8.0	n/a	n/a	0.2	7.7	–2.5	0.9	–0.1	–1.6	6.0
IQR (pp)	5.1	n/a	n/a	3.3	1.6	0.9	2.3	0.1	1.5	1.3
Consistency	100%	n/a	n/a	56%	100%	100%	94%	100%	81%	100%

Trucking

Heartland Express Vs. P.A.M. Transportation Services

Higher Relative Performance

Era 1: 1986 to 1994

	Gross Margin	SG&A	R&D	Other	ROS	CAT	FAT	Other-AT	TAT	ROA
Mean (pp)	16.1	n/a	n/a	0.5	16.6	0.1	1.7	0.1	1.9	18.5
Median (pp)	16.1	n/a	n/a	1.4	13.6	0.4	1.6	0.1	2.2	19.8
IQR (pp)	10.1	n/a	n/a	6.2	9.0	1.7	1.8	0.4	2.9	14.8
Consistency	89%	n/a	n/a	56%	89%	56%	78%	67%	78%	100%

Era 2: 1995 to 2010

	Gross Margin	SG&A	R&D	Other	ROS	CAT	FAT	Other-AT	TAT	ROA
Mean (pp)	8.0	n/a	n/a	1.7	9.7	−1.6	0.9	0.3	−0.4	9.2
Median (pp)	6.7	n/a	n/a	2.5	9.2	−1.7	0.7	0.1	−0.7	7.8
IQR (pp)	8.4	n/a	n/a	5.7	2.6	1.5	1.2	0.1	1.0	3.3
Consistency	100%	n/a	n/a	63%	100%	88%	81%	100%	69%	100%

Werner Enterprises Vs. P.A.M. Transportation Services

Higher Relative Performance

Era 1: 1986 to 2001

	Gross Margin	SG&A	R&D	Other	ROS	CAT	FAT	Other-AT	TAT	ROA
Mean (pp)	5.6	n/a	n/a	−0.4	5.2	0.2	0.2	0.1	0.5	5.7
Median (pp)	3.0	n/a	n/a	1.1	3.2	0.2	−0.5	0.2	0.0	2.5
IQR (pp)	13.3	n/a	n/a	4.7	5.3	0.5	1.1	0.2	0.5	5.4
Consistency	63%	n/a	n/a	38%	88%	63%	38%	75%	50%	88%

Lower Relative Performance

Era 2: 2002 to 2010

	Gross Margin	SG&A	R&D	Other	ROS	CAT	FAT	Other-AT	TAT	ROA
Mean (pp)	3.1	n/a	n/a	0.6	3.7	0.5	0.2	0.1	0.8	4.5
Median (pp)	2.1	n/a	n/a	0.4	2.6	0.5	0.1	0.2	0.8	3.4
IQR (pp)	5.2	n/a	n/a	0.4	4.4	0.4	0.5	0.3	0.3	5.0
Consistency	89%	n/a	n/a	89%	89%	100%	67%	78%	100%	89%

Appliances

Maytag Vs. HMI Industries

Higher Relative Performance: 1967 to 1991

	Gross Margin	SG&A	R&D	Other	ROS	CAT	FAT	Other-AT	TAT	ROA
Mean (pp)	−1.4	7.0	n/a	−3.2	2.5	3.4	−2.2	1.6	2.7	5.2
Median (pp)	−1.1	5.6	n/a	−3.0	1.1	3.4	−1.8	1.4	1.7	6.1
IQR (pp)	5.8	6.6	n/a	4.0	4.7	4.1	3.8	1.5	4.9	7.1
Consistency	60%	100%	n/a	76%	72%	100%	88%	100%	88%	80%

Lower Relative Performance: 1992 to 2004

	Gross Margin	SG&A	R&D	Other	ROS	CAT	FAT	Other-AT	TAT	ROA
Mean (pp)	−14.1	34.7	−1.1	−6.2	13.4	0.7	2.1	1.4	4.2	17.5
Median (pp)	−8.0	35.9	0.0	−5.7	4.7	0.2	−0.7	−0.2	0.0	4.5
IQR (pp)	16.7	28.9	1.2	12.1	33.8	0.7	1.3	0.6	1.3	36.3
Consistency	92%	100%	100%	77%	62%	77%	31%	38%	46%	62%

Maytag Vs. Whirlpool

Higher Relative Performance: 1966 to 1991

	Gross Margin	SG&A	R&D	Other	ROS	CAT	FAT	Other-AT	TAT	ROA
Mean (pp)	24.3	−7.4	n/a	−7.2	9.7	−0.7	−0.9	0.7	−0.9	8.8
Median (pp)	27.1	−8.6	n/a	−8.3	10.3	−0.6	−0.8	0.7	−1.0	9.2
IQR (pp)	12.5	4.5	n/a	4.2	6.3	1.5	1.3	0.6	1.7	7.1
Consistency	96%	81%	n/a	88%	100%	69%	88%	92%	73%	100%

Lower Relative Performance: 1992 to 2005

	Gross Margin	SG&A	R&D	Other	ROS	CAT	FAT	Other-AT	TAT	ROA
Mean (pp)	−1.4	2.6	0.6	−1.2	0.5	0.3	0.0	−0.1	0.3	0.8
Median (pp)	−0.2	1.3	0.7	−0.4	1.6	0.2	0.0	0.0	0.1	1.7
IQR (pp)	7.7	3.1	0.4	3.1	8.1	0.5	0.2	0.4	0.6	9.2
Consistency	50%	86%	100%	71%	64%	79%	36%	57%	50%	64%

HMI Industries Vs. Whirlpool

	Gross Margin	SG&A	R&D	Other	ROS	CAT	FAT	Other-AT	TAT	ROA
Higher Relative Performance: 1968 to 1995										
Mean (pp)	17.7	−11.8	1.1	−1.5	5.5	−2.0	0.3	−0.3	−2.0	3.4
Median (pp)	17.9	−11.7	1.3	−0.5	4.3	−2.2	0.1	−0.3	−2.0	2.6
IQR (pp)	13.6	7.1	2.1	6.2	5.5	2.9	0.4	0.7	3.2	7.7
Consistency	96%	100%	100%	61%	96%	82%	86%	64%	75%	71%
Lower Relative Performance: 1996 to 2004										
Mean (pp)	15.7	−38.5	1.7	3.7	−17.4	−1.8	−4.4	−1.8	−8.0	−25.4
Median (pp)	13.5	−39.7	1.8	5.7	−10.8	0.0	−0.6	−0.4	−0.7	−12.1
IQR (pp)	16.5	8.6	3.0	17.3	24.2	3.7	7.4	1.3	7.4	31.6
Consistency	100%	100%	100%	56%	67%	44%	67%	78%	56%	67%

Appendix G: The Statistical Analysis of Small Samples

Many of us learn what is affectionately referred to as "cookbook" statistics: normal distribution, mean and standard deviation, t-tests of significance. These methods were rarely of use to us in our analysis. For our large-scale work, we used a number of nonparametric methods, such as quantile and LOESS regressions, to account for the idiosyncrasies of ROA and the nature of the phenomena we were attempting to quantify.

Thanks to the much smaller size of the data set defined by our case study companies, we had to use different methods, which has implications for the strength of the conclusions we draw from that analysis.

To give you a sense of how we approached this problem, below is a condensed version of table 6 from chapter 3, which looks at the likelihood of a relationship between relative competitive position and relative performance in our case study samples by pair-wise comparison. (In table 6, we look at the trios as a whole, and so there is an "in the middle" competitive position. When looking at pair-wise comparisons, only price and non-price positions are possible.)

When looking at the Miracle Worker versus Average Joe comparison we observe that seven Miracle Workers have a non-price position and two have a price position. In every case there was a difference between the Miracle Worker and the Average Joe.

This sample of 9 pair-wise comparisons is 5.2 percent of our total population of 174 Miracle Workers, ignoring the problem of false negatives. If

TABLE 51: **Relative Competitive Position by Pair-Wise Comparison**

Relative competitive position	Miracle Worker Vs. Average Joe	Miracle Worker Vs. Long Runner	Long Runner Vs. Average Joe	TOTAL
Non-price	7	6	6	19
Price	2	1	2	5
No difference	0	2	1	3
Likelihood of a relationship	97.5%	87.3%	87.3%	99.9%

Source: Authors' analysis
In referring to our "population" of Miracle Workers and Long Runners we are ignoring the problem of false negatives.

our sample were perfectly representative of our population, we would be justified in concluding that Miracle Workers have non-price positions relative to Average Joes 78 percent of the time. This is an overwhelming majority and argues persuasively for a strong association between exceptional performance and non-price positions.

However, our sample is likely not perfectly representative, largely due to its small size. Small samples can generate extreme outcomes much more easily than large samples. Typically, one would calculate the confidence interval around our estimate of 78 percent but this becomes unworkable with small samples. Instead, we test the likelihood that our sample could have come from a distribution that was evenly split among the three possible outcomes. So, if we assume that a Miracle Worker is equally likely to have a non-price, price, or the same relative competitive position as an Average Joe, we can estimate the likelihood of getting the sample we actually got.

By way of analogy, it is rather like estimating the likelihood that a coin is fair based on the result of a specified number of tosses. If you assume the coin is fair and observe six heads in ten tosses, the likelihood that the coin is biased toward heads is the probability of getting six heads or more out of ten, which is 38 percent. At this point, evaluation becomes subjective: Does that mean there is *only* a 38 percent chance the coin is fair? Or does it mean the coin probably is? If you could, you would gather more data. If you cannot gather more data, you must draw a conclusion based on what you have or withhold judgment altogether.

When testing for patterns with multiple cells, as in the table above, one would typically look for significant clustering in contingency tables using chi-squared statistics. However, those are not valid for small samples (for example, where $N < 30$) or instances where expected cell counts are below 5 for more than 20 percent of the cells. Here, for example, if we have 9 companies in a column or row, then the expected count in each cell is 9/3, which is less than 5.

Given this, we proceed instead by simulation. In effect, we toss an equally weighted three-sided coin k times, where k is the number of companies in a row or column. Then we assess whether m or more simulated companies landed in the same cell. We repeat that process ten million times, calculating the percentage of times that m or more simulated companies out of k landed in a single cell.

Thus, the precise test we're applying is whether m or more companies out of k could be expected to cluster in any of three cells in a row (or column) due to chance. Thus, the percentages above are the probabilities that the observed clusters are not due to randomness (defined as each firm's having an equal probability [$p = 1/3$] of landing in each cell). In turn, we are not claiming that the population looks like our sample. Rather, we are claiming that, given our sample, the smart money is on the idea that there are systematic relationships between relative competitive position and pairwise comparison type.

So, when Miracle Workers compared with Long Runners are six times more likely to have non-price than price-based relative competitive positions, we do not claim that this is representative of the larger population. Rather, we claim that that 6:1 split is very unlikely to have come from a population with a uniform distribution across the alternatives, and therefore Miracle Workers are likelier to have non-price positions than price-based positions. It is as though we tested a coin on the assumption it was fair and then flipped six heads out of seven tries. That coin has a 1.6 percent chance of not being biased toward "non-price positions." We cannot say for certain that it is not biased in this way, but we wouldn't bet on it.

Appendix H: Changes in Position and Changes in Performance

The regression reported in chapter 3 uses standard ordinary least squares (OLS) techniques. Typically, since our independent and dependent variables are three-category discrete variables, one would use an ordered probit model, since we are trying to estimate the probabilities of landing in one of three ordered categories of the dependent variable (performance: negative, no change, positive).

However, such analyses require that each predictor has variance in each state of the dependent variable. Here, unfortunately, Change in Position = 0 in each of the five instances in which Change in Performance = 0. When that occurs, one can get highly inaccurate estimates of regression coefficients and standard errors.

In comparison, OLS handles such data. We lose efficiency in going to OLS, since the dependent variable (Change in Performance) is categorical rather than continuous. However, that is preferable, because it is more conservative, to obtaining biased estimates via ordered probit.

For each of our eighteen exceptional companies we can characterize the relationship between change, or its absence, in each of performance and strategic position. There are three relationships at work here. First, Long Runners are more likely to suffer declines regardless of changes in position. Second, companies with a non-price position are more likely to enjoy an increase in performance, regardless of category.

It is the third observation that is the most important and the most statistically significant, however: a change in position *toward* a *non-price* position is associated with a subsequent *increase* in performance while a change in position *toward* a *price* position is associated with a subsequent *decrease* in performance.

Here are the specifics of the regression analysis reported in chapter 3.

TABLE 52: **Data Table**

	Performance Category	Initial Position	Change in Position	Change in Performance
HMI	0	1	−1	−1
Maytag	1	1	−1	−1
T&B	1	1	−1	−1
FL	0	0	0	0
Hubbell	0	0	0	−1
Tootsie	0	−1	0	0
Weis	1	−1	0	−1
Werner	0	−1	0	−1
A&F	1	1	0	0
Heartland	1	1	0	0
Eli Lilly	0	1	0	0
Merck	1	1	0	0
Micropac	0	0	0	0
Medtronic	1	1	0	1
Wrigley	1	0	0	1
Linear	1	0	1	1
Publix	0	0	1	0
Stryker	0	0	1	0

Category		Change in Position	
LR	0	−1	toward price
MW	1	0	no change
		1	toward non-price

Position		Change in Performance	
non-price	1	−1	negative
itm	0	0	no change
price	−1	1	positive

REGRESSION 1: **Stryker and Publix Treated as Changing Their Performance**

Summary Output

Regression Statistics

Multiple R	0.83
R Square	0.68
Adjusted R Square	0.61
Standard Error	0.50
Observations	18.00

Anova

	df	SS	MS	F	Significance F
Regression	3.00	7.45	2.48	9.95	0.00
Residual	14.00	3.50	0.25		
Total	17.00	10.94			

	Coefficients	Standard Error	t Stat	P-value	Lower 95%
Intercept	−0.25	0.17	−1.46	0.17	−0.61
Category	0.18	0.25	0.71	0.49	−0.37
Position	0.36	0.19	1.93	0.07	−0.04
Change in Position	1.21	0.22	5.44	0.00	0.73

REGRESSION 2: **Stryker and Publix Treated as Not Having Changed Their Performance**

Summary Output

Regression Statistics

Multiple R	0.82
R Square	0.67
Adjusted R Square	0.63
Standard Error	0.49
Observations	18.00

Anova

	df	SS	MS	F	Significance F
Regression	2.00	7.32	3.66	15.18	0.00
Residual	15.00	3.62	0.24		
Total	17.00	10.94			

	Coefficients	Standard Error	t Stat	P-value	Lower 95%
Intercept	−0.17	0.13	−1.34	0.20	−0.43
Position	0.40	0.17	2.34	0.03	0.04
Change in Position	1.20	0.22	5.51	0.00	0.74

Appendix I: The Structure of Profitability Advantages

By constructing regressions for differences in each of gross margin, other costs and asset turnover against differences in ROA for each company-year observation compared to industry median values we are able to test the relationship between ROA advantage and its drivers independently of the algebraic identities among them.

The quantile regression results reported below are summarized in the main text in chapter 4. The parameters for the main effects of gross margin, other costs and asset turnover capture the rate at which Average Joes translate an additional point in gross margin advantage over the industry median into additional percentage points of ROA advantage. The coefficient of 0.32 for gross margin means that for each additional percentage point of gross margin advantage an Average Joe can expect 0.32 percentage points in ROA advantage.

The main effects for Miracle Workers and Long Runners mean that those companies can expect ROA advantages over the industry medians that are 4.82pp and 1.92pp more, respectively, than Average Joes enjoy. (Recall, however, that Average Joes on average have an ROA advantage over the industry median of essentially 0pp, so the main effects for Miracle Workers and Long Runners effectively capture their edge over Average Joes as well.) Similarly, when Average Joes enjoy an asset turnover advantage of a full additional turn they see a decline in their ROA advantage of 1.56pp while an increase in their other costs advantage of one percentage point translates into an additional 0.27 percentage points of ROA advantage. (The sign is negative because of how the model is constructed, but should be interpreted as described above.) These parameters capture the "efficiency" with which each type of advantage in a given driver becomes a profitability advantage.

The parameters for the interaction effects capture incremental efficiency with which Miracle Workers and Long Runners convert advantages in gross margin, other costs, and asset turnover into ROA advantage. Adding the parameters for the interaction effect to the main effect give the total effect for each performance category.

The descriptive statistics reported below show the range over which each of these drivers varies, which indicates the opportunity to realize meaningful ROA advantage from changes in that driver. The distributions are somewhat thick tailed, and so the interquartile range (Q3-Q1 in the table below) is perhaps the best point estimate of the variability of each driver.

These distributions also reveal that Miracle Workers enjoy gross margin advantages more frequently than Long Runners, and that Miracle Workers endure cost disadvantages more frequently than Long Runners. This is consistent with observations from our case studies, where we see Miracle Workers, such as Heartland and A&F, achieving their superior gross margin as a consequence of higher other costs.

The consonance between this large-scale statistical analysis and the fine-grained detail revealed in our case studies gives us a high degree of confidence that the Miracle Workers in general rely on gross margin for their performance advantages, and they achieve their gross margin lead because of their higher other costs. In other words, the three rules are supported not merely by our case study results but also by the structure of the profitability advantages observed in our full population of exceptional companies.

TABLE 53: **Quantile Regression on the Structure of Profitability Advantages**

	Parameter	DF	Estimate	Standard Error	95% Confidence Limits		t Value	Pr > |t|
	Intercept	1	0.0012	0.0002	0.0007	0.0016	4.8500	<.0001
Main Effects								
	Gross Margin	1	0.3165	0.0064	0.3040	0.3289	49.7700	<.0001
	Asset Turnover	1	−0.0156	0.0006	−0.0167	−0.0145	−27.0500	<.0001
	Other Costs	1	−0.2709	0.0056	−0.2819	−0.2599	−48.3400	<.0001
	Miracle Worker	1	0.0482	0.0014	0.0454	0.0510	33.6100	<.0001
	Long Runner	1	0.0192	0.0008	0.0175	0.0208	22.7700	<.0001
Interaction Effects								
Miracle Worker								
	Gross Margin	1	0.1929	0.0133	0.1668	0.2189	14.5200	<.0001
	Asset Turnover	1	−0.0149	0.0022	−0.0193	−0.0106	−6.7300	<.0001
	Other Costs	1	−0.2010	0.0121	−0.2247	−0.1773	−16.6200	<.0001
Long Runner								
	Gross Margin	1	0.0973	0.0124	0.0730	0.1216	7.8500	<.0001
	Asset Turnover	1	0.0021	0.0016	−0.0010	0.0051	1.3400	0.1812
	Other Costs	1	−0.1293	0.0111	−0.1511	−0.1075	−11.6300	<.0001

Source: Authors' analysis

TABLE 54: Descriptive Statistics

	Miracle Workers			Long Runners			Average Joes		
Unique Companies	174			170			1208		
Company-year Observations	4333			4776			24376		

Distribution of Advantage Vs. Industry Median

Quantiles	Gross Margin (pp)	Other Costs (pp)	Asset Turnover	Gross Margin (pp)	Other Costs (pp)	Asset Turnover	Gross Margin (pp)	Other Costs (pp)	Asset Turnover
100% Max	82.7	74.0	4.93	78.2	74.3	4.94	80.9	73.4	4.98
99%	53.1	38.2	2.68	51.0	38.5	2.58	35.0	33.6	3.01
95%	37.1	26.0	0.84	33.3	22.4	1.15	18.3	15.7	1.20
90%	30.3	19.2	0.47	23.2	16.0	0.63	12.4	9.9	0.59
75% Q3	19.9	9.9	0.17	12.3	6.8	0.16	4.9	3.0	0.18
50% Median	9.8	1.9	0.00	3.0	0.0	-0.04	0.0	-0.6	0.00
25% Q1	1.4	-4.7	-0.17	-3.5	-8.0	-0.27	-5.1	-6.0	-0.13
10%	-5.3	-21.0	-0.59	-12.7	-21.7	-0.70	-11.5	-13.0	-0.33
5%	-12.8	-34.7	-1.02	-18.5	-33.8	-1.23	-16.7	-19.2	-0.56
1%	-27.0	-64.6	-2.33	-33.3	-61.9	-2.22	-30.3	-35.8	-1.69
0% Min	-60.0	-84.9	-4.99	-51.1	-84.4	-4.89	-92.8	-82.9	-4.95

Note: Due to the structure of the regressions, a positive value in Other Costs indicates a cost disadvantage.

Appendix J: Behavioral Differences by Pair-Wise Comparison

To facilitate our analysis of behavioral differences within and among pair-wise comparisons we constructed a series of tables that coded each behavior as 0 if two companies evinced the behavior to the same degree, 1 if the first company named in a pair did more of that behavior, and -1 if it did less of that behavior.

These behaviors are subject to a great many different and equally valid characterizations. For example, we coded mergers and acquisitions (M&A) based solely on the number of deals done during a comparison period. This overlooks that deals can be of very different sizes: five deals that account for 10 percent of a company's revenue would show up as "more M&A" than two deals that accounted for 50 percent of a company's revenue. One could attempt different weightings, but in the end, every choice proved merely different rather than any one emerging as clearly better.

As a result, we make relatively little of this analysis, relying on it instead to provide a more complete yet readily accessible format for the data that led us to formulate our third rule, *there are no other rules*. (Where no coding is entered in a cell we were unable to reach a conclusion about meaningful similarities or differences.)

TABLE 55: Differences in Behavior

Miracle Worker	Long Runner	M&A	Product	Diversification — Geographic Region	Diversification — Line of Business	Diversification — Market Segment	Average
Linear Technology	Micropac Industries	0	1	1	1	1	0.75
Medtronic	Stryker	1	1	1	1	1	0.6
Thomas & Betts	Hubbell	-1	-1	-1	0	-1	0
Abercrombie & Fitch	Finish Line	-1	-1	0	-1	0	-0.4
Wm. Wrigley Jr. Company	Tootsie Roll Industries	-1	-1	0	0		-0.2
Weis Markets	Publix Super Markets	-1	0	-1	0	0	-0.5
Merck & Company	Eli Lilly & Company	-1	0	0	0	0	0
Heartland Express	Werner Enterprises	-1	-1	0	-1	-1	0
Maytag	HMI Industries	-1	1	1	-1	-1	-0.2
	Behavior average	-0.22	0	0.22	-0.25	0.25	0.0056

Miracle Worker	Average Joe	M&A	Product	Geographic Region	Line of Business	Market Segment	Average
Linear Technology	International Rectifier	-1	1	-1	0	0	0.2
Medtronic	Invacare	-1	1	-1	1	1	0.2
Thomas & Betts	Emrise	-1	1	-1	0	-1	0
Abercrombie & Fitch	Syms	0	1	0	0	-1	0.4
Wm. Wrigley Jr. Company	Rocky Mountain Chocolate Factory	1	1	-1	-1	-1	1

Weis Markets	-1	0	0	0	-1	-0.25
Merck & Company	1	1	1	-1	-1	0.5
Heartland Express	0	-1	0	-1	0	-0.4
Maytag	-1	-1	-1	-1	-1	-1
Behavior average	-0.33	0.63	-0.13	-0.14	0.25	0.055
						0.072

Long Runner / **Average Joe**						
International Rectifier	-1	1	-1	1	-1	-0.5
Invacare	-1	-1	-1	0	-1	-0.4
Emrise	-1	1	-1	0	-1	0.4
Finish Line	-1	1	0	-1	-1	0.4
Syms						
Rocky Mountain Chocolate Factory	-1	1	-1	1	1	1
Whole Foods Markets	-1	1	0	0	-1	0
KV Pharmaceutical	-1	1	-1	-1	-1	-0.2
PAM Transportation Services	1	-1	1	0	1	0
Whirlpool	-1	-1	-1	0	1	-0.25
HMI Industries	-1	-1	0	0	1	-0.25
Behavior average	-0.25	0.71	-0.71	0.29	0.14	0.036
						0.05

Source: Authors' analysis

Chapter 1: More Than a Fortune Cookie

1. Malcolm Gladwell, *Outliers: The Story of Success* (New York: Little, Brown & Co., 2008).

2. Michael Raynor, "Theory to Practice: Management by Imitation," *The Conference Board Review*, July 2012.

3. Precisely how many exceptional companies one identifies is a function of the assumptions one makes. We will argue that some assumptions are indefensible, others debatable, and still others boil down to matters of taste. Different iterations of this research have reported different numbers of exceptional companies based on different assumptions that fall into this third category. The figures reported here are based on the specific assumptions detailed in Chapter 2 and Appendix C.

4. The number of carriers almost tripled, from approximately 16,100 in 1977 to about 47,800 in 1991. Thanks to all the new supply, prices fell: the price per ton-mile shipped had been rising at 3.5% p.a. between 1960 and 1980, but grew at only 0.9% p.a. from 1980 to 2005. Growth in tons shipped increased from 3% p.a. before 1980 to 3.5% p.a. after 1980, and trucking's share of total shipments in the United States, which had been growing at 1% p.a. prior to deregulation, jumped to 1.5% p.a.

5. Mark Sirower, *The Synergy Trap: How Companies Lose the Acquisition Game* (New York: Free Press, 1997).

6. Our characterization of PAM is based on annual reports and other SEC filings.

7. At the most trivial level this categorization is necessarily true since any mutually exclusive system of the form "x or ~x" must be collectively exhaustive. One could just as correctly say that all value is either blue or non-blue. Such a system would be of limited use, however. Dividing customer value into price and non-price dimensions seems both logically correct and consistent with how customers actually think about product or service value.

8. Pricing data are notoriously difficult to compare, especially over a period of years. Our sources are interviews with industry experts who consistently and independently estimated Heartland's price premium at 10% to 12%.

9. The notion that good advice must be falsifiable is an important principle for us, but not everyone is similarly adamant about this. In *In Search of Excellence*, Tom Peters and Robert Waterman report that some of their findings were greeted by MBA students with an "of course" sort of shrug: pay attention to customers, treat employees like adults, and so on. Practicing executives responded enthusiastically, they say, because they had an intuitive sense or an explicit

understanding of just how hard it is to do these things well enough to make a difference. The importance of falsifiability is a function of the nature of what one seeks to discover. If one seeks the "what," then falsifiability is essential, and "give customers what they want" fails as substantive advice. If the aim is to provide guidance on how to achieve this necessarily desirable outcome, then "give customers what they want" is merely the starting point. The success study genre seems to us focused squarely on the "what," although we admit that the what/how distinction is often blurry. See Michael E. Raynor, "What's Wrong with *What* Is That It's Not *How*," *The Conference Board Review*, Winter 2010.

10. The details can get complicated, and it often varies on a product-by-product basis. On some high-profile products that customers pay careful and consistent attention to (e.g., milk), Family Dollar is very careful to be consistently highly price competitive. In some instances, it plays out as described in the main text, and Family Dollar is simply more expensive per unit on highly comparable items. In other cases Family Dollar might appear less expensive per unit, but when assessed on a per-unit-of-quality basis, Family Dollar has higher prices. Offering lower-quality products with lower absolute prices is, ceteris paribus, price-based competition. However, it is the other non-price value dimensions of the model (convenient locations, smaller basket sizes), both of which serve to drive up Family Dollar's costs, that make these lower-quality items acceptable to customers who choose to shop elsewhere when they can.

11. A tour through the leading discount stores and Family Dollar—indeed, any of the "extreme value" retailers—reveals an increasing convergence of the two models. Our analysis speaks to the central tendencies that have defined the differences between the two approaches over more than thirty years. The convergence over the last five years or so seems to be driven in part by the success of the extreme value retailers at the expense of the traditional megastore discounters, which has triggered a copycat response, and in part by the desire of the extreme value retailers to grow by encroaching on the discounters' traditional turf.

12. It is tempting to view Merck's advantage as a simple case of economies of scale. But economies of scale show up as lower unit cost as a consequence of greater total volume. That is not the case here: Merck's unit cost of production does not appear to have been any lower, relative to unit price, than Eli Lilly's. Given Eli Lilly's superior gross margin, it appears to be just the opposite. It is only when we factor in all the other costs associated with producing and selling pharmaceuticals that Merck's advantage becomes apparent. A fuller discussion of the variable and fixed cost elements of this case will feature in chapter 5.

13. Once again, there is no necessary trade-off here. One can perfectly well imagine a company having higher prices, higher margin, and lower cost. In fact, such companies appear to exist: in some consumer electronics markets, such as tablets, Apple seems to have both the lowest cost—volume production lowers input cost, while retail efficiency lowers selling cost—and the highest prices thanks to its highly differentiated position. Our claim, which will be substantiated at greater length in chapter 4, is that it turns out that companies with exceptional performance actually experience such a trade-off, stumping for higher revenue over lower cost.

14. Sean Gregory, "Abercrombie & Fitch: Worst Recession Brand?," *Time*, August 25, 2009.

15. These prescriptions for action are taken from, respectively, Jim Collins, *Good to Great* (HarperCollins, 2001), Paul Nunes and Tim Breene, *Jumping the S-Curve* (Harvard Business Review Press, 2011), William Joyce and Nitin Nohria, *What Really Works* (HarperBusiness, 2004), and Alfred Marcus, *Big Winners and Big Losers* (FT Press, 2005).

16. See Jim Collins and Morten T. Hansen, *Great by Choice* (HarperBusiness, 2011), Collins's *Good to Great* (op. cit.), and Matthew S. Olson and Derek van Bever, *Stall Points* (Yale University Press, 2009).

Chapter 2: Finding Signal in the Noise

1. We are not the first to cast a critical eye on the genre, or these works in particular. See especially Phil Rosenzweig, *The Halo Effect ... and the Eight Other Business Delusions That Deceive Managers* (New York: Free Press, 2007), and Jeffrey Pfeffer and Robert I. Sutton, *Hard Facts, Dangerous Half-Truths & Total Nonsense: Profiting from Evidence-Based Management* (Boston: Harvard Business School Press, 2006).

2. See Michael J. Mauboussin, *The Success Equation: Untangling Skill and Luck in Business, Sports, and Investing* (Boston: Harvard Business Review Press, 2012).

3. Jerker Denrell, "Random Walks and Sustained Competitive Advantage," *Management Science* 50(7) (July 2004): 922–934.

4. There have been isolated attempts in the academic literature to take this on. The citations in our papers (see note 12) cite much of this work. Of efforts by consulting firms, only *Creative Destruction* tackles this problem head-on. Also from McKinsey, see Janamitra Devan, Matthew B. Klusas, and Timothy W. Ruefli, "The Elusive Goal of Corporate Outperformance," *McKinsey Quarterly*, 2007, a three-page, Web-only research brief that applies some of the methods developed by Ruefli in his academic work. (Ruefli is a professor at the University of Texas at Austin, which, coincidentally, is where Andy Henderson, our statistical consultant, also teaches.)

5. W. Edwards Deming, *Out of the Crisis* (The MIT Press, 2000), originally published 1986.

6. See Michael E. Raynor, Mumtaz Ahmed, and Andrew D. Henderson, "Are 'Great' Companies Just Lucky?," *Harvard Business Review* (April 2009); Andrew D. Henderson, Mumtaz Ahmed, and Michael E. Raynor, "Where Have You Gone, Joe DiMaggio: Just what is really great business performance?" *Ivey Business Journal* (May/June 2009); Michael E. Raynor, Mumtaz Ahmed, and Andrew D. Henderson, "A Random Search for Excellence: Why 'great company' research delivers fables and not facts," Deloitte (2008) (www.deloitte.com/us/persistence); Andrew D. Henderson, Michael E. Raynor, and Mumtaz Ahmed, "How Long Must a Firm Be Great to Rule Out Luck? Benchmarking superior performance," Best Paper winner, Academy of Management Proceedings (2009); Andrew D. Henderson, Michael E. Raynor, and Mumtaz Ahmed, "How Long Must a Firm Be Great to Rule Out Luck?

Benchmarking sustained superior performance without being fooled by random walks," *Strategic Management Journal* (April 2012).

7. In *Great by Choice,* Jim Collins and Morten Hansen discuss the impact of unexpected events—luck—on corporate performance and conclude that higher-performing companies react more effectively, taking better advantage of lucky breaks and blunting the impact of unlucky breaks. The problem, however, is that the companies being held up as higher performers do not have demonstrably higher performance. We cannot know if the companies in question have delivered performance beyond what lucky breaks would have led us to expect. Finding a post hoc explanation for what actually happened is not merely always possible, it is essentially inevitable given the human animal's proclivity for retrospective sense making. Consequently, finding an explanation only matters when you first have a good reason to believe that there is something worth explaining.

8. One could define any combination of deciles as a focal performance outcome and use our method to identify companies that are "exceptional" by virtue of having achieved that outcome more frequently than expected. If you felt that the 2nd, 6th, and 8th deciles were special in some way, you could look for companies that landed in that noncontiguous range more often than they should have.

9. There is the potential for a gap in our performance bands: companies that deliver enough 9s to *reduce* the number of years in the 6th–8th band to below the threshold required for Long Runner status, but not *enough* 9s to qualify as Miracle Workers. We did not study these companies, because we wanted a more distinct separation between our categories of exceptional performers so that we would have a better chance of seeing distinct differences in behavior. In analyzing the incidence of statistically exceptional performance in other success studies, however, we have included what we will call "Super Long Runners" as exceptional companies.

10. See Michael Raynor, Ragu Gurumurthy, and Mumtaz Ahmed, with Jeff Schulz and Rajiv Vaidyanathan, "Growth's Triple Crown," *Deloitte Review* (2012).

11. In our quantile regressions we include a dummy variable for companies that existed prior to 1966, the first year of our observation window, in order to account for the possibility that this characteristic introduces bias.

12. For our analysis of streaks in decile ranks we used LOESS regression; see T. Hastie, R. Tibshirani, and J. Friedman, *The Elements of Statistical Learning: Data Mining, Inference, and Prediction* (New York: Springer, 2001). Our analysis of absolute performance involved the development of a novel application of existing methods by one of our statistical consultants; see James G. Scott, "Nonparametric Bayesian Multiple Hypothesis Testing of Autoregressive Time Series," *Annals of Applied Statistics* (September 2008).

13. Note that due to the way we control for the autoregressive nature of ROA, for some companies we have one fewer observation of relative performance than for absolute performance.

14. Rosenzweig, *Halo Effect.*

15. Clayton M. Christensen, *The Innovator's Dilemma* (Boston: Harvard Business School Press, 1997).

16. Rosenzweig, *Halo Effect*.

17. Collins, *Good to Great*.

18. This is a common and much-studied and commented-upon problem. For a discussion of how it can lead one astray when analyzing case histories, see David Hackett Fischer, *Historians' Fallacies* (New York: Harper & Row, 1970).

19. Stryker is featured in Jim Collins's most recent book, *Great by Choice,* as a "great" company. We would concur that Stryker's performance has been remarkable, although not as remarkable as Medtronic's. Stryker delivered superior shareholder returns thanks to the company's transformation from a manufacturer of lower-tech medical devices such as cast cutters to more sophisticated medical implants. The dramatic improvement in ROA and growth that Stryker enjoyed relative to its own historical performance drove significant share price appreciation. Medtronic delivered superior profitability on twice the revenue—but because the firm was a more consistent performer, its stock price performance, although impressive, lagged Stryker's. This is a textbook example of the inappropriateness of equity value as a measure of company performance when seeking insight into company behavior.

20. Beyond prescription lies prediction, which requires yet another very different research design. The predictive power of frameworks in this space remains untested, our work included. Taking on predictive tests, however, is extraordinarily rare. For an example of such an attempt, see Michael E. Raynor, *The Innovator's Manifesto: Deliberate Disruption for Breakthrough Growth* (Crown Business, 2011).

21. That is not to say that our sample is *numerically* large enough to be a representative sample; it is, frankly, difficult to imagine how one might reasonably make such a claim with any sample size short of a complete census. To determine the size required for a statistically representative sample we would need a plausible estimate of the variance of the population with respect to key measures. This puts us in a rather uncomfortable Catch-22, for we don't know what those measures are until after we've done the case study work, which requires having chosen the sample.

22. These specifics are as of 2010, when the performance categorizations for these companies were made.

Chapter 3: Better Before Cheaper

1. See Craig Galbraith and Dan Schendel, "An Empirical Analysis of Strategy Types," *Strategic Management Journal* 4 (1983): 153–73, and C. Campbell-Hunt, "What Have We Learned About Generic Competitive Strategy? A meta-analysis," *Strategic Management Journal* 21 (2000): 127–54, for reviews of various typologies of strategy.

2. See, for example, Berend Wierenga, *Handbook of Marketing Decision Models* (New York: Springer Science+Business Media, 2008), especially Part II.

3. It can sometimes be slightly more complicated. In the case of a durable good like a car, "total cost of ownership" might well feature prominently in the form of not only purchase price but also financing terms, operating costs, maintenance costs, disposal costs, or resale value. Price value might therefore have multiple dimensions as well. We are also setting to one side the rather rarefied air in which high price is a signal of other valuable attributes, such as quality, or creates other valuable attributes such as scarcity, as with some types of wine or fashion items.

4. Breakthrough success awaits those who manage to break trade-offs, something that can be seen as innovation. See Michael E. Raynor, *The Innovator's Manifesto* (New York: Crown Business, 2011). Innovation plays out over time, but at any given point in time, there are necessarily binding constraints of some sort that mandate making trade-offs.

5. Michael E. Porter, "What Is Strategy?," *Harvard Business Review* (November–December 1996).

6. Campbell-Hunt, "What Have We Learned About Generic Competitive Strategy?"

7. In the unlikely case of two identical companies, we would then not know where to put them in competitive space, since we would have nothing to compare them with.

8. The more typical term of art is "stuck in the middle" (SITM), but "stuck" has a negative connotation we wish to avoid, since we wish to be open to the possibility that "in-the-middle" positions might not be as harmful to one's profitability as others have suggested.

9. It is a deep philosophical question precisely what causality is, never mind what constitutes evidence of it. We will rely on more commonsense notions of what it means for one thing to cause another rather than presuming to resolve a centuries-long debate.

10. There are 203 companies in SIC 3674 (semiconductors) on which we had enough data to evaluate their performance using our method. Linear Technology was the only Miracle Worker and Micropac the only Long Runner. International Rectifier was one of 27 Average Joes.

11. We recount these case studies in the past tense because our study period ended in 2010. "Micropac appears to have been well run" is no basis for inferring that it is no longer well run.

12. In most trios the Average Joe is not remarkable in this way, but IR was the best fit we could find for Linear.

13. There are 274 companies in SICs 3845 and 3842 on which we had enough data to evaluate their performance using our method. The decile ranks of each company are based on their respective SIC control variables, but these two four-digit codes are considered together due to the suitability of the comparisons across SIC boundaries. Medtronic is one of four Miracle Workers, Stryker is one of six Long Runners, and Invacare is one of twenty-eight Average Joes.

14. See each company's annual reports, cross-checked with equity analysts' reports published over that time period. Such assessments are inevitably somewhat subjective, but very little turns on the specifics of our findings, because our claim is only that the two were comparable in the pace and magnitude of their new product introductions.

15. The careful reader will observe that the changes in decile rank between the 1960s and the 1980s appear disproportionate to, and sometimes even negatively correlated with, the changes in absolute ROA for those periods. The seemingly extremely low deciles in the early years of our observation period are in part an artifact of controlling for industry effect. During this time there were very few publicly traded companies in Medtronic's SIC code, and therefore much of the company's ROA is attributed to industry effects. As competition in the space "heats up," the same absolute ROA gets attributed less to industry effects and more to firm effects. By the early 1980s, when we are comparing Medtronic with Stryker, this confounding effect has largely disappeared.

16. William P. Barnett, *The Red Queen Among Organizations: How Competitiveness Evolves* (Princeton, N.J.: Princeton University Press, 2008).

17. Thomas & Betts and Emrise overlap only during T&B's period of low relative performance from 1985 to 2010. During this period Hubbell outperforms T&B, and so is the more revealing comparison. The structure of the Elements of Advantage for T&B and Hubbell over Emrise are essentially identical, however: a gross margin disadvantage but an overall ROS and TAT advantage due to superior performance in essentially all other elements.

Chapter 4: Revenue Before Cost

1. There is an additional level of detail here that we are ignoring, but including it would merely complicate the exposition of our argument, not change its fundamental message. Specifically, the value a corporation creates must be divided among many stakeholders, of which the four most obvious are shareholders (in the form of dividends), employees (in the form of wages and benefits), society (practically speaking, government, typically in the form of taxes, but there are often other discretionary elements such as charitable giving), and customers (in the form of products or services provided). The priority a company gives to each of these stakeholders is a philosophical question, not an economic one; see Michael E. Raynor, "End Shareholder Value Tyranny: Put the corporation first," *Strategy & Leadership* (January 2009). However a corporation decides that question, the first step for a corporation that seeks exceptional performance is to create value, and that demands securing revenue from customers. The second step is to capture value for itself in the form of profits. Then comes the thorny issue of how to divide that value among employees, shareholders, and society.

2. Other constituencies capture value via other mechanisms, for example, dividends, wages, etc.

3. See Appendix I, table 56. The 25th percentile Miracle Worker still enjoys a gross margin percentage advantage but the analogous Long Runner has a lower gross margin percentage than industry median performers. With other costs, it's a different story: the median Miracle Worker has an other cost disadvantage while the median Long Runner has lower other costs.

4. For what it's worth, we did not cotton on to the importance of ROA decomposition until more than a year after we had selected our trios and were deeply invested in understanding the case histories of each. Consequently, we did not have to "ignore" these data when choosing our trios; we simply did not have them available to us.

5. For those reading closely, recall that we tested for a relationship between changes in position and changes in performance in the previous chapter, while we have not tested for a relationship between changes in profit formula and changes in performance. There are a number of reasons for this. First, a change in performance by an exceptional company often results in a drop in profitability to the point that there is no profitability advantage to explain. For Lost It exceptional companies, the period of lower relative performance often means an ROA that is lower than its relevant comparison company. Consequently, it is impossible to say what the company's "profitability formula" is. We might have looked for a relationship between the profitability formula for Kept It and Lost It exceptional companies during their period of higher performance, but our sample sizes do not allow us to see any relationship that might exist. Recall that we have nine Miracle Workers with three of each in the Lost It and Found It, two Kept Its, and one Other. Both Kept It Miracle Workers have revenue-driven profitability formulas, while two of the three Lost It Miracle Workers have revenue-driven profitability formulas. A 2:0 vs. 2:1 split is barely even suggestive of a difference in the "durability" of a given profitability formula. With Long Runners we have a slightly different story. The five Kept It Long Runners are split 3:2 between revenue and cost profitability formulas, while the four Lost It Long Runners are split 2:2 between revenue and cost profitability formulas. Nothing short of a unanimous outcome would have provided statistical evidence with even the slightest credibility to support a relationship between profitability formula and the durability of exceptional performance. Our view is that the primary observable determinant of the durability of exceptionalism is maintaining a non-price competitive position.

6. One commentator wryly observed the irony that A&F sells, of all things, *clothing*.

7. That is not as absurd as it might sound. Recall, Miracle Worker status is a function of enough 9th-decile performances, and a company's decile rank is a function of its standing relative to the entire economy, not relative only to its industry. Consequently, although not every company in an industry can be at the top of its industry, every company in an industry could, in theory, be a Miracle Worker in the context of the larger population of companies that makes up the entire economy, even after controlling for the impact of industry on profitability. (This footnote is for you, Phil.)

8. Ellen Schlossberg, William Blair & Company, July 28, 1999. Schlossberg is citing the U.S. Bureau of the Census (1990).

9. Michael T. Glover, Raymond James & Associates, Inc. (August 3, 1999).

10. John A. Quelch and David Harding, "Brands Versus Private Labels: Fighting to win," *Harvard Business Review* (January–February 1996).

11. Kevin Lane Keller, *Strategic Brand Management: Building, Measuring, and Managing Brand Equity* (Englewood Cliffs, N.J.: Prentice Hall, 1997).

12. Valerie Seckler, "Private Labels Win Market Share," *Women's Wear Daily*, July 23, 2003.

13. Janet Rovenpor, "Abercrombie & Fitch: An upscale sporting goods retailer becomes a leader in trendy apparel," in Michael A. Hitt, R. Duane Ireland, and Robert E. Hoskisson, *Strategic Management: Competitiveness and Globalization* (South-Western College Pub., 2008).

14. "Magalog" is a portmanteau of "magazine" and "catalog" that blurred (further?) the line between journalism and advertising. It included stories, recipes, and travel essays, but featured the company's clothing and new product introductions.

15. According to the company's annual reports for 2003 and 2004, A&F found itself settling class action lawsuits in 2003 and 2004 related to uncompensated requirements that sales staff wear A&F clothing and to racial discrimination in its hiring practices. New policies were implemented that sought to increase the ethnic and racial diversity of the sales force without compromising the company's strategic priorities. See also Emine Saner, "Abercrombie & Fitch: For beautiful people only," *The Guardian*, April 27, 2012.

16. Yingjiao Xu, "Impact of Store Environment on Adult Generation Y Consumers' Impulse Buying," *Journal of Shopping Center Research* 14(1) (2007).

17. Ellen Schlossberg, William Blair & Company, July 28, 1999.

18. Stacy C. Pak and Bret Cicinelli, *Abercrombie & Fitch* (Credit Suisse First Boston Corporation, January 13, 1999).

19. Xu, "Impact of Store Environment."

20. Ellen Schlossberg, William Blair & Company, July 28, 1999.

21. This is a well-documented phenomenon. See, for example, Kathleen Rees and Jan Hathcote, "The U.S. Textile and Apparel Industry in the Age of Globalization," *Global Economy Journal* 4(1) (2004); Gary Gereffi and Olga Memedovic, *The Global Apparel Value Chain: What Prospects for Upgrading by Developing Countries?* (Vienna: United Nations Industrial Development Organization, 2003); Frederick Abernathy, "The Future of the Apparel and Textile Industries: Prospects and choices for public and private actors," Harvard Center for Textile and Apparel Research (December 2005).

22. Kelly Armstrong, *Abercrombie & Fitch* (Wheat First Butcher Singer, January 1998).

23. Rovenpor, "Abercrombie & Fitch."

24. Abercrombie & Fitch's sourcing strategy was much discussed in analyst reports, and admiration for the company's choices remained strong over time. Here is a selection of reports from 1997 through 2010: Dorothy S. Lakner and D. Tiffany Tamplin, "Abercrombie & Fitch (Specialty Retailing)," Oppenheimer & Co., Inc., August 12, 1997; Kelly Armstrong, "Company Report (Abercrombie & Fitch)," Wheat First Butcher Singer, January 23, 1998; Eliot S. Laurence, "Abercrombie & Fitch (Apparel Retail)," Jefferies & Company, Inc. Equity Research, November 9, 2000; Robin S. Murchison, "Abercrombie & Fitch (Specialty

Retail)," Jefferies & Company, Inc. Equity Research, September 10, 2003; Michelle L. Clark and Chi H. Lee, "Abercrombie & Fitch, Initiation of Coverage: No more room to run," Morgan Stanley Research, North America, July 9, 2007; "Abercrombie & Fitch Co.— SWOT Analysis," GlobalData Company Profiles, July 12, 2010.

25. Laurence, "Abercrombie & Fitch."

26. Erin M. Loewe, "Feminine Energy: The Finish Line's Paiva concept is taking women's fitness apparel to a new level," *Display & Design Ideas* (October 2006).

27. "Finish Line Launches New Branding Campaign," *PR Newswire*, March 13, 1998.

28. Katie Maurer, "Retailer Feeling Blue," *Indianapolis Business Journal*, August 12, 2002.

29. Susan Lisovicz, "Abercrombie & Fitch Rolling Out Store for Teens, Hollister," CNN*fn*: The Biz (August 30, 2001).

30. David Moin, "A&F Finds a New Life by Aiming its Weapons at a Younger Shopper," *Women's Wear Daily*, February 25, 1997.

31. Erin White, "Rival Clothing Retailers in U.S. Tussle over the Same Teens: Prices at A&F and American Eagle hit new lows," The *Wall Street Journal*, December 21, 2001.

32. Bruce Watson, "Abercrombie and Fitch: The biggest brand loser of the recession," *DailyFinance*, August 26, 2009.

33. Sapna Maheshwari, "At Abercrombie & Fitch, Sex No Longer Sells," *BusinessWeek*, August 30, 2012.

34. "Refashioning Perks Up Abercrombie—CEO Credits Slimmer Inventories and Faster Reaction to Trends for Stronger-Than-Expected Results," *The Wall Street Journal*, November 15, 2012; "Hong Kong's Million-Dollar Retail Rent Challenge," *The Wall Street Journal*, October 10, 2012.

35. Associated Press, *The New York Times*, November 2, 2011.

36. The corporation emerged from bankruptcy protection in 2012, but as Trinity Place Holdings, Inc. The new entity has declared its sole purpose as being to sell off remaining assets for the benefit of shareholders. Syms, as a going concern in any form, is no more. See company press releases, September 17, 2012.

37. Michael Redclift, *Chewing Gum: The Fortunes of Taste* (Routledge, 2004).

38. "Food Fundamentalism," *The Economist*, December 4, 1993.

39. "The Top 100 Brands," *BusinessWeek*, August 6, 2001.

40. Interview with Jim and Lisbeth Echeandias of the American Consulting Corporation, December 17, 2008.

41. "Wm. Wrigley Jr. Co.: All gummed up," Bear Stearns Equity Research, January 11, 2007.

42. Interview with Jim and Lisbeth Echeandias of the American Consulting Corporation, December 17, 2008.

43. "Tootsie Roll Industries, Inc.," *Great Lakes Review*, May 4, 1995.

44. In the confectionary trio, Wrigley is "in the middle," which means it has a "price position" versus RMCF and a "non-price position" versus Tootsie.

45. Harvard Business School, "Wrigley in China: Capturing Confectionary (D)," Case study publication (2009).

46. "A Billion Jaws Chewing," *Asia Times*, August 13, 2005.

47. Revenue growth rates "net of acquisitions" are calculated by subtracting the total revenue in the year of acquisition of all the deals done over a particular time period from reported total revenue for the last year in the period.

48. Interview with Jim and Lisbeth Echeandias of the American Consulting Corporation, December 17, 2008.

49. Collins, in *Great by Choice*, notes that his higher-performing companies often have higher cash balances.

50. "Whole paycheck" is identified as a synonym for Whole Foods in The Urban Dictionary (http://www.urbandictionary.com/define.php?term=whole%20paycheck; accessed October 4, 2012). While we do not outsource the determination of competitive position to the site, this entry is indicative of the company's public image.

51. John Letzing, "CEO Bemoans 'Whole Paycheck' Nickname," *Wall Street Journal Market-Watch* (March 3, 2011). http://articles.marketwatch.com/2011-03-03/industries/30736343_1_foods-market-executive-john-mackey-unhealthy-items. Accessed October 4, 2012.

52. Robert L. Steiner, "The Nature and Benefits of National Brand/Private Label Competition," *Review of International Organizations* 24 (2004): 105–27.

53. Business Wire, "Abercrombie & Fitch selects Celarix to improve supply chain efficiency," November 27, 2000.

54. Neither company provides a detailed breakdown of its reliance on private-label products. Figures in this table are estimates only. The most salient and relevant fact is that as far as we can tell it took close to twenty years for our estimates of the percentage of sales from private labels to converge. Whether that convergence happened two or three years earlier or later than we have estimated does not affect our argument, and we believe it is unlikely that we are materially mistaken by a decade.

55. Todd Sharkey and Kyle Stiegert, "Impacts of Non-Traditional Food Retailing Supercenters on Food Price Changes," *Food Service Research Group Monograph Series* (February 20, 2006).

56. U.S. Department of Agriculture, Economic Research Service Web site. http://www.ers.usda.gov/data-products/food-expenditures.aspx. Accessed October 7, 2012.

57. Stephen Martinez, "Competition Alters the U.S. Food Marketing Landscape," *Amber Waves*, November 2005.

58. According to the Thomson M&A database, deal activity peaked in 2000 with more than sixty transactions, while an analysis of the U.S. Census Bureau's "Monthly Retail Trade Survey" reveals that the share of total grocery retail controlled by the four largest grocery retailers grew from under 20% in 1987 to over 30% by 2005.

59. "Private Label Trends in the Supermarket Channel," *Information Resources, Inc.* (IRI) (October 2002).

60. Based on Deloitte analysis, this figure is the asset-weighted average of all publicly traded grocery retailers covered by Compustat on which there are reliable data from 1966 through 2010.

61. Robert Simons and Antonio Davila, "How High Is Your Return on Management?," *Harvard Business Review* (January 1998).

Chapter 5: There Are No Other Rules

1. The most comprehensive review of the M&A literature we are familiar with is Robert F. Bruner, *Applied Mergers & Acquisitions* (Hoboken, N.J.: John Wiley & Sons, Inc., 2004).

2. The literature here is vast. Cornerstone findings include Richard P. Rumelt, "Diversification Strategy and Profitability," *Strategic Management Journal* 3 (1982): 359–69; L.H.P. Lang and R. M. Stulz, "Tobin's Q, Corporate Diversification, and Firm Performance," *Journal of Political Economy* 102(6) (1994): 1248–80; P. G. Berger and E. Ofek, "Diversification's Effect on Firm Value," *Journal of Financial Economics* 37 (1995): 39–65. Recent investigations, however, suggest that we've been wasting our time and that the so-called diversification discount is little more than an artifact of segment-based reporting. See Xi He, "Corporate Diversification and Firm Value: Evidence from post-1997 data," *International Review of Finance* 9(4) (2009): 359–85.

3. Cynthia A. Montgomery and Birger Wernerfelt, "Diversification, Ricardian Rents, and Tobin's q," *The RAND Journal of Economics* 19(4) (1988): 623–32.

4. A. D. Chandler, *The Visible Hand: The Managerial Revolution in American Business* (Cambridge, Mass.: Harvard University Press, 1997).

5. Tarun Khanna, and Krishna G. Palepu, "Is Group Affiliation Profitable in Emerging Markets? An analysis of diversified Indian business groups," *Journal of Finance* 55(2) (2000): 867–91.

6. Robert C. Schmidt, "On the Robustness of the High-Quality Advantage under Vertical Differentiation," *Journal of Industry, Competition and Trade* 6 (2006): 183–93.

7. See, respectively, Robert D. Buzzell, "Is Vertical Integration Profitable?" *Harvard Business Review* (January–February 1983); Richard A. D'Aveni and D. J. Ravenscraft, "Economies of Integration Versus Bureaucracy Costs: Does vertical integration improve performance," *Academy of Management Journal* 37(8) (1994): 1167–1206; Richard T. Mpoyi and K. E. Bullington, "Performance Implications of Changing Vertical Integration Strategies," *American Business Review* (January 2004).

8. Kathryn Rudie Harrigan, "Matching Vertical Integration Strategies to Competitive Conditions," *Strategic Management Journal* 7 (1986): 535–55.

9. Cf. Hau L. Lee, "Aligning Supply Chain Strategies with Product Uncertainties," *California Management Review* 44(3) (2002); and Srinivasan Balakrishnan and B. Wernerfelt, "Technical Change, Competition and Vertical Integration," *Strategic Management Journal* 7 (1986): 347–59.

10. J. M. Campa and S. Kedia, "Explaining the Diversification Discount," *The Journal of Finance* 57 (2002): 1731–62; Belen Villalonga, "Does Diversification Cause the 'Diversification Discount'?" *Financial Management* 33(2) (2004).

11. J. D. Daniels and J. Bracker, "Profit Performance: Do foreign operations make a difference?" *Management International Review* 29(1) (1987): 46–56; Michael A. Hitt, R. E. Hoskisson, and Hicheon Kim, "International Diversification: Effects on Innovation and Firm Performance in Product Diversified Firms," *Academy of Management Journal* 40(4) (1997): 767–98; Stephen Tallman and L. Jaitao, "Effects of International Diversity and Product Diversity on the Performance of Multinational Firms," *Academy of Management Journal* 39(1) (1996): 179–96.

12. There is an argument to place KVP "in the middle" based on a comparison of KVP with other generic drug manufacturers; that is, companies that exclusively manufacture off-patent medications with no attempt to create some form of differentiation. There are at least two reasons not to do this. First, our analysis is based on the direct comparison of the companies in each trio, as described in chapter 3. Second, it does not appear that "pure manufacturers" of off-patent medications are as common as one might at first think. Many, perhaps most, generic drugmakers seek to differentiate themselves with respect to at least some of their products or technologies. Since that part of KVP's portfolio that was not pure generic drug synthesis was not a differentiator, KVP's position through the mid-1990s is pretty clearly one of price-based competition, compared not only with Merck and Eli Lilly, but also with the bulk of other generic drugmakers. It was only in the 1990s, when KVP shifted strongly to drug discovery, that one can say it was moving toward a non-price position, ending up, compared with Merck and Eli Lilly, in the middle.

13. Melody Peterson, *Our Daily Meds: How the Pharmaceutical Companies Transformed Themselves into Slick Marketing Machines and Hooked the Nation on Prescription Drugs* (New York: Farrar, Straus and Giroux, 2008).

14. Although thalidomide has a number of clinical applications, it was most infamously prescribed to pregnant women as a treatment for morning sickness in the early 1960s. The children of these women experienced a dramatically higher incidence of phocomelia, or "seal limb" syndrome. See Trent Stephens and Rock Brynner, *Dark Remedy: The Impact of Thalidomide and Its Revival as a Vital Medicine* (New York: Basic Books, 2001).

15. Peter B. Hutt, "The Importance of Patent Term Restoration to Pharmaceutical Innovation," *Health Affairs* 1(2) (Spring 1982).

16. Lacy G. Thomas, "Regulation and Firm Size: FDA impacts on innovation," *The RAND Journal of Economics* 21(4) (Winter 1990).

17. Peter Temin, "Technology, Regulation, and Market Structure in the Modern Pharmaceutical Industry," *The Bell Journal of Economics* 10(2) (Autumn 1979).

18. William Bogner and Howard Thomas, *Drugs to Market: Creating Value and Advantage in the Pharmaceutical Industry* (Oxford: Pergamon Press, 1996).

19. B. Achilladelis and N. Antonakis, "The Dynamics of Technological Innovation: The case of the pharmaceutical industry," *Research Policy* 30 (2001): 535–88.

20. Company documents; Deloitte estimates.

21. Company documents; Deloitte estimates.

22. Company documents; Deloitte estimates.

23. Roy P. Vagelos and Louis Galambos, *Medicine, Science and Merck* (Cambridge: Cambridge University Press, 2004). Although this source is written by Vagelos, it provides data on publications and other measures of productivity that are objective and support the claim that the Washington University labs improved dramatically under Vagelos's leadership and became among the best in the world. The evidence that this improvement was a consequence of Vagelos's guidance is strong.

24. Alfonso Gambardella, *Science and Innovation: The U.S. Pharmaceutical Industry During the 1980s* (Cambridge: Cambridge University Press, 1995); Patents: Patent board; Products: Deloitte analysis based on announcements in company annual reports.

25. The question of R&D productivity versus simply R&D output is a thorny one thanks to a general inability to connect specific R&D inputs with specific outputs over the relevant time periods. We have chosen simply to look at the overall ROA of the companies over time as our aggregate measure of the appropriateness of the trade-offs each has made with respect to R&D and all the other elements of the business (such as international diversification). Our claim here is merely that Merck's output was greater, and we see this as a major contributing factor to the company's higher ROA. It might well have had less productive R&D than Eli Lilly; we do not have an opinion on that. What we can say, however, is that the seemingly higher R&D output leads to greater therapeutic area and product diversity. This seems a major contributing factor to revenue growth, while the company's greater geographic diversification also drives growth and superior ROA. It is the combination of all these factors on which our case rests.

26. There is a valid and important debate in the health care community about the ultimate benefit of drug proliferation within therapeutic areas. The rise of the "comparative effectiveness" school seeks to impose objective criteria on the value of what some commentators have derided as merely commercially motivated "tweaks" to underlying compounds designed to secure patent protection with little benefit to patients. See, for example, Marcia Angell, *The Truth About the Drug Companies: How They Deceive Us and What to Do About It* (New York: Random House, 2004).

27. Congressional Budget Office, "Research and Development in the Pharmaceutical Industry" (October 2006).

28. Henry Grabowski and Margaret Kyle, "Mergers and Alliances in Pharmaceuticals: Effects on innovation and R&D productivity," in Klaus Gugler and Burcin Yurtoglu, eds., *The Economics of Corporate Governance and Mergers* (Northampton, MA: Edward Elgar Pub., 2008), 262–87.

29. "FDA Advisory Committee Recommends Aldendronate [Fosamax] for Osteoporosis," *Medical Science Bulletin* (Pharmaceutical Information Associates, Ltd., August 1995). Accessed February 10, 2010, at http://www.oralchelation.com/calcium/foxamax6.htm.

30. Gardiner Harris, "Back to the Lab: Merck to shed Medco, its drug-benefits unit, in bid to boost stock—Company is under pressure as five major products go off patent—resisting calls for a merger," *The Wall Street Journal*, January 29, 2002; "Merck Announces Plans to Divest its PBM Subsidiary," *Drug Marketing*, February 6, 2002.

31. We have simply added back to net income the gain or loss each company experienced upon disposal of its PBM division and recalculated the differences in ROA under that scenario. The range in our estimate is driven by attempts to account for the timing of the realization of the gains or losses, but the differences are minor: we estimate that between 62.6% and 66.8% of Merck's actual ROA advantage from 1993 to 2003 is accounted for by the different results realized by each company from its PBM deal.

32. J. E. Flynn, "KV Pharmaceutical: Company report," Kidder, Peabody & Company (November 29, 1991).

33. Company documents: 10-K filing for fiscal year ended March 31, 1993.

34. Merck's Vioxx anti-inflammatory was approved in 1999 and withdrawn in 2004 over safety concerns relating to adverse cardiovascular events. In 2009 Eli Lilly pleaded guilty to the off-label marketing of Zyprexa, an antipsychotic. Beyond whatever human suffering was involved, both events incurred litigation and material legal costs, heavy fines, or settlement payments.

35. Charles Perrow, *Normal Accidents: Living with High Risk Technologies* (New Haven, CT: Princeton University Press, 1999).

36. The greater a performance advantage in absolute terms, the likelier it is that there will be more than one driver of that advantage: as a practical matter, gross margin or asset turnover advantages can only be so high.

37. These higher cash balances show up as a drag on current asset turnover with an offsetting advantage in interest income, which is reflected in the nonoperating income line and contributes to ROS.

38. Company documents and Chaodong Han, T. M. Corsi, and C. M. Grimm, "Why Do Carriers Use Owner Operators in the U.S. For-Hire Trucking Industry?" *Transportation Journal* 47(3) (2008): 22–35.

39. John R. Wells and Nassan S. Dossabhoy, "The Major Home Appliances Industry in 1984: Revised," Harvard Business School Publishing case 9-386-115 (1994); Jonathan C. Roche, U. Srinivasa Rangan, and Stephen A. Allen, "U.S. Major Home Appliances Industry in 2002," Babson College case BAB049 (2003); Stephen A. Allen, "Maytag Corporation 2002," Babson College case BAB047 (2003); Michael Rehaut and Jonathan F. Barlow, "Appliance Industry," JPMorgan North American Equity Research (New York) (January 8, 2004).

40. Maytag Corporation 1982 annual report.

41. Maytag Corporation 1986 annual report.

42. Babson College, "U.S. Major Home Appliance Industry in 2002."

43. Rehaut and Barlow, "Appliance Industry."

44. Citigroup Smith Barney, "Maytag Corporation: Stuck in the spin cycle" (January 19, 2005).

45. Conversation with Jeff Fettig, CEO of Whirlpool.

46. Taken from Leonard Mlodinow, *The Drunkard's Walk: How Randomness Rules Our Lives* (New York: Pantheon Books, 2008).

Chapter 6: Why You Should Use the Three Rules

1. Jim Collins, *How the Mighty Fall* (Collins, 2009), 17.

2. Karl E. Weick, "Sources of Order in Underorganized Systems: Themes in recent organizational theory," in Karl E. Weick (Hrsg.), *Making Sense of the Organization* (Malden, Mass.: University of Michigan/ Blackwell Publishing, 2001), 32–57.

3. Warren Thorngate, "'In General' vs. 'It Depends': Some comments on the Gergen-Schlenker Debate," *Personality and Social Psychology Bulletin* 2 (1976): 404–10.

4. A common interpretation of Weick's model is that no theory can be all of simple, accurate, and general. We see it differently: that Weick is pointing out that a given theory must give up at least one dimension in order to improve on the other two. So for our "three rules" theory to be more accurate we will have to add more detail, which reduces its simplicity. When comparing two different theories, however, there seems to us no reason why one theory cannot be all of more accurate, simple, and general than another. By way of an existence proof, consider Lamarckian and Darwinian evolution. The former is more complex, less accurate, and less general than the latter. Similarly, our hope is that the three rules theory is simpler, more accurate, and more general than competing theories of persistent, superior corporate performance.

5. Barry Schartz, *Paradox of Choice* (New York: HarperPerennial, 2004).

6. Herbert A. Simon, *Administrative Behavior: A Study of Decision-Making Processes in Administrative Organization*, 1st ed. (New York: Macmillan, 1947); and H. A. Simon, "Rational Choice and the Structure of the Environment," *Psychological Review* 63(2) (1956): 129–38. (Page 129: "Evidently, organisms adapt well enough to 'satisfice'; they do not, in general, 'optimize.'" Page 136: "A 'satisficing' path, a path that will permit satisfaction at some specified level of all its needs.") For a discussion of the origin of Simon's concept, see Reva Brown, "Consideration of the Origin of Herbert Simon's Theory of 'Satisficing' (1933–1947)," *Management Decision* 42(10) (2004): 1240–56.

7. Gerd Gigerenzer and Wolfgang Gaissmaier, "Heuristic Decision Making," *Annual Review of Psychology* 62 (2011): 451–82.

8. Donald Sull and Kathleen M. Eisenhardt, "Simple Rules for a Complex World," *Harvard Business Review* 90(9) (2012).

9. David Hume, *An Enquiry Concerning Human Understanding* (1748).

10. Phil Rosenzweig, *The Halo Effect . . . and the Eight Other Business Delusions That Deceive Managers* (New York: Free Press, 2007).

11. *Good to Great* vs. *How the Mighty Fall*.

12. Laurie Burkitt, "China Retailer CRE Adopts Rivals' Western Ways," *The Wall Street Journal*, October 23, 2012.

13. Jeff Bennett, "Goodyear Rides Again," *The Wall Street Journal*, September 15, 2011.

14. Clayton M. Christensen, *The Innovator's Dilemma* (Cambridge: Harvard Business School Press, 1997).

15. Michael E. Raynor, *The Innovator's Manifesto* (New York: Crown Business, 2011).

16. The characterization of the iPod and iPhone as sustaining might surprise some people. Certainly it is not a characterization that is universally endorsed by everyone who subscribes to Disruption theory. An innovation is sustaining or not according to whether it is targeted at the customer segments within a product market that dominant incumbents value and whether it is intended to be substitutable for the solutions provided by the incumbents. In the portable music market, few customers would own a Samsung Yepp *and* an iPod or a Sony MiniDisc *and* an iPod. These products were substitutes. Each was therefore sustaining in the portable digital music market. There are any number of explanations for why the iPod came out on top, but for present purposes, those are not relevant: we are not explaining its success, we are describing the nature of the innovation it represented.

The characterization of the iPhone is similarly contentious. There has been an ongoing discussion of whether or not the iPhone was *really* disruptive; see, for example, http://b.qr.ae/IVr4GF, a discussion forum on Quora.com. The commentators there focus on the notion that the iPhone did "different jobs"—but consistently miss that it *also* did the *same* jobs as the other smart phones available at the time and was targeted at the same customer segments. That the iPhone had a different combination of attributes (for example, allegedly a worse phone, not as good at e-mail, but better at other things) that were ultimately preferred by more customers is simply another way of saying that the iPhone was better. The iPhone would have been a form of new market disruption if most of its early adopters purchased the iPhone for one purpose and kept their old phone for another, and then as the iPhone improved they dropped their previous phone. There are existence proofs that this was indeed the case for some customers, but there are no data we have seen showing that this is what drove the iPhone's success.

In other words, because the iPhone was targeted at and purchased by people already using mobile phones, and they typically abandoned their existing smart phone for the iPhone, and the iPhone was more expensive, the iPhone was neither a low-end nor a new-market disruption. No less an authority on Disruption than Clayton Christensen characterized the iPhone as a sustaining innovation. See Jane McGregor, "Clayton Christensen's Innovation Brain," *Bloomberg Businessweek*, June 15, 2007.

17. Michael E. Raynor, *The Strategy Paradox* (New York: Crown Business, 2007).

18. Raynor, *Innovator's Manifesto*.

19. Richard P. Rumelt, *Good Strategy, Bad Strategy* (New York: Crown Business, 2011); Walter Isaacson, *Steve Jobs* (New York: Simon & Schuster, 2011).

20. Immanuel Kant, *Grounding for the Metaphysics of Morals*, 3rd ed. (1785), transl. James W. Ellington (Hackett, 1996), 30. As philosophical principles go, this one has had a pretty good run. As you might expect, it is not without its critics, but it has resisted any credible reformulations until only very recently; and even here the conversations are just beginning: you cannot expect a principle that has held its ground for more than two hundred years to topple over in a relative instant. See Derek Parfit, *On What Matters* (New York: Oxford University Press, 2011).

21. See Phil Rosenzweig, *The Halo Effect* (New York: Free Press, 2007).

Appendix A: Calculating the Elements of Advantage

1. The principles of revenue recognition and cost allocation that give meaning to the concept of income for a period have changed over time and evolved to cope with the evolution of economic activity. Since our analysis is based primarily on a company's relative annual performance within its industry, what matters most to us is that these principles are applied consistently within industries at a point in time. Differences across industries and changes over time likely have little impact on our findings.

Appendix B: Bibliography of Success Studies

1. As an aside, we note that General Electric qualifies as an exceptional company in our analysis, which covers the period 1966 to 2010. However, in the early 1980s, when Peters and Waterman were selecting their sample, it would not have qualified as an exceptional performer: its run of 9th-decile years coincided with Jack Welch's period as CEO, which began in 1981. It is possible that the sources Peters and Waterman tapped to identify their sample were looking forward, and saw in what Welch was doing the seeds of dramatically improved performance, and so picked the company as a place where cool people were doing cool work. But one can only look at relationships between past performance and past behaviors. Consequently, we do not concede Peters's point, that raw insight is clearly better than hard-minded metrics, simply because General Electric fell off their list. In our view, that was the right outcome at that time.

Appendix C: Identifying Exceptional Performance

1. One might be tempted to dismiss a definition of "exceptional" that had a company landing in the 2nd-to-8th-decile range, since it is a band so broad as to be of little interest.

Appendix D: Category, Trajectory, and Era Analysis

1. James Scott, "Nonparametric Bayesian Multiple Testing for Longitudinal Performance Stratification," *The Annals of Applied Statistics* (2009).